Charlemagne, Genghis Khan, and Scipio Africanus: History's Ultimate Trilogy (3 manuscripts)

By Michael Klien

The Warrior King Charlemagne

The Man Who Created
the Second Roman Empire

By
Michael Klein

Table of Contents

Dedication

To the scholars, priests, bishops, and countrymen who took the time to document events as they were happening, making it plausible for my colleagues and I to study it as history, I personally give you my thanks.

Introduction
Breaking the Barbarian Stigma

Think about everything that's ever been shown on television and movies, or written in fiction books regarding the story and description of barbarians. In those works, how often were barbarians shown in a positive light, In most instances, most of these barbarians are portrayed as ugly, messy, unruly grunts who marauder across the countryside, wielding large axes and murdering any and all they came across. These brutes have no respect for property, destroying buildings and homes while parading the corpses of their conquered foes. Typically, barbarians are associated with wolf like tendencies and at the very least, a pack mentality. The alpha brute; the biggest, strongest, and most tenacious man rules the camp, ordering his brothers and colleagues around in quests of pillaging and plundering.

Barbarians have often been compared to Vikings, pirates, and other ruthless, aggressive men throughout history. In multiple pieces of literature, the three are depicted as drunks, criminals, and godless heathens whose only purpose is to gather as many riches as possible while still craving only the treasures of the flesh. Stories of the three are told raping and pillaging along the coast and countryside, raising all sorts of a ruckus while only padding their own reputation and coffers. However, the comparisons with the three of these ends with the stigma related to them. Historically, the three warriors were incredibly different.

Pirates were merchants, sailors, and other nautical crewmen who turned to a life of crime, opting to live on the open sea and pillage from the large, freight bearing vessels and incredibly large ports. Their purpose in life wasn't to conquer or capture, but to simply get rich and eventually retire, though that rarely was the case. The captain would inherit the ship, either from a previous captain or commandeered from some random port. Many were religious, belonging to the Catholic Church though not actively practicing because of their constant life at sea. They were loyal with a clear, definitive structure of power.

Vikings were similar to pirates in that they preferred to attack seafaring vessels and port cities while operating from a very small vessel. Unlike pirates, however, they were linked by more than just a single ship, but linked as a tribe, belonging to a much larger entity. These Vikings would pillage and destroy, taking what they came for, but would eventually settle in various places to make pillaging easier. By actively settling new villages, Vikings were able to raid easier, heading back from time to time to continue raiding.

Barbarians are a much different entity than the previous two. The first is that they're primarily land dwelling, not operating with much of a navy. They settled near rivers, waged wars with each other, and worshiped their respective Gods. They began as small tribes, eventually assimilating with other tribes, either through marriage, military alliance, or conquering. These barbarians were organized and strategic, benefiting from the fall of the Roman Empire when they were graced to exist. With Greek and Roman technology at their disposal, either through stealing it or acquiring it by another means, the barbarians were fortunate enough to have the means to expand their empires. Though there was somewhat of an alpha mentality amongst the leaders, the leadership was passed down heretically or through other similar means.

Many leaders have come and gone, whether elected, ascended via birthright, or simply took over via some form of coup. No matter the period of history, political unrest and uncertainty always seem to follow the government changing hands. People will always mourn their former leaders at their passing and wish the best for their current magistrate, but in reality, what they're wanting is stability. A stable nation is one that can grow, prosper, and become better. A stable nation can conquer its enemies and defend its walls. Even at war, a nation can be stable.

This is the aspect that sets decent rulers from good ones. To put your nation into a complete sense of turmoil and upheaval just to conquer your enemies is not stable; eventually your empire will crumble from within. Infrastructure is important, and building a solid, attainable foundation is even more critical. Many examples in history can attest to how this is an incredibly true statement. Leaders who have built empires from either the remnants of a fallen enemy to the ashes of their own previous demise have fallen by the sword from an aggressive expansion. One mention of one of these empires that will be brought up in this work is the Avar Khaganate. Though their history is shrouded in the shadows and their origins aren't easily known, it is possible to loosely trace their origins to the Huns of Mongolia. Following their settling around the Danube River, the Avars continued to be a dominant, aggressive entity. They conquered their neighbors and invoked a state of fear around the area, but at the end of the day, they could not get past the Byzantine Empire based out of Constantinople.

Another instance, and a more central one in popular history, is that of Napoleon Bonaparte. While a tremendous leader and one of the greatest tacticians to ever live, Napoleon's invasion of Russia led to his demise. By stretching his army too thin and crippling his supply lines, Napoleon authored his own demise. Adolf Hitler and the Nazi Party in Germany felt the same fate as Napoleon. By stretching yourself too thin and being too aggressive, you open yourself up to a cruel fate. Had both of these leaders slowed down their invasion, curtailing their aggression for a few months and laid down the foundation for success where they were at, their wars could have ended much differently.

Barbarians have always been associated with ruthless aggression and tyrannical practices. The stigma associated with them is that of someone who is barely clothed with long, tattered hair and a giant beard, wielding a weapon that's as tall as a small tree. They've been depicted as people who are heathens, having no thought or concern toward a conscience or religion. Barbarians have been associated with only thinking in the here and now, versus thinking on an afterlife and spiritual world. Though we cannot fully go into what religion each and every barbarian tribe was, it is important to note that these men and women did have a sense of spirit. Many were deeply religious, holding onto their various beliefs even while being conquered by other tribes. Forced conversions were the norm, with those not believing as they did to be put to the sword and executed, often times being burned in effigy. The spiritual world was incredibly important to any barbarians, whether Vikings, Germans, Frankish, Celtic, Saxon, or any other barbarian in history. Godlessness is not the norm when it comes to the barbarian world. These men were prideful in their conviction, which was devoted and unshakable.

As for the appearance, many barbarians adopted their own cultural garb, wearing their hair in a certain way that was deemed acceptable to the standards of their society. Their clothes were traditional, usually based off of what materials were around. The Egyptians wore cotton while the Germans wore wool. The materials were available to them to wear these clothes. Fashion didn't matter, unless you were in a major metropolitan area. Clothes were designed to be functional before anything else.

However, when it came to battle, innovation came at great lengths. While the Romans, Greeks, Egyptians, and other large civilizations came up with engineering feats to capitalize on battle, barbarians were a bit more direct. Armor became the norm, whether leather and tied together in knots to provide a great deal of support and protection, or the eventual wearing iron and plate, encapsulating the soldier's body in metal to protect them from the harms of the battlefield. Weapons were revolutionized over time, whether becoming sharper or lighter, or in the case of ranged combat, to be able to fire faster and farther while also being able to reload quicker. These weapons and bits of armor were not meant to be fashionable either, though often they would have tribal symbols or other bits painted on them for ceremonial reasons.

Barbarians did not lack intelligence. Many were smart and strove to learn more about the world and the universe, while others were simply uninformed. Languages were spoken in different dialects and tongues as they were able to communicate with another. Some languages died out while others thrived and survived. But, the point that barbarians were able to create a language out of sounds and other vocal cues is a sign to intelligence. Many of them wrote, creating their own alphabets and taking note of their history and other things. They had currency, allowing them to exchange a coin that had a perceived value for a good. The things that we as an advanced civilization take for granted, these barbarians were still able to do them. They lacked technology, especially after the fall of Rome, but they were able to thrive.

The period where the barbarian enjoyed their most success is referred to as the "Dark Ages," or, when the lights went out in Europe. The Roman Empire was a great civilization, uniting much of the Europe creating a massive infrastructure of roads, buildings, magistrates, and other entities that allowed the realm to survive. The army conquered the various loose tribes of barbarians individually, submitting them to Roman rule and starting to, as they put it, civilize them. The barbarian, at first, did not want to be civilized, but as generations changed, acceptance, followed by dependency set in. To be a part of the Roman Empire was a great thing for the barbarians who were conquered. They gained access to schools, religion, roads, and other technological advances that they would not have had without being conquered and subjugated. By becoming a loyal subject in the Roman Empire, the barbarians gained access to things that would, essentially, turn them away from being considered to be barbarians. They were becoming civilized.

However, when Rome finally fell and the Western Roman Empire descended into darkness, the barbarian tribes rose up, conquering the remnants of the Empire and reforming themselves into kingdoms. The barbarians in this time created the feudal system as a way to hold lords accountable but to maintain their loyalty. The lords would do the same, by having vassals work the land and allowing them to eat what was produced. Barbarians in Europe created a system that worked for them and allowed them to thrive once the Roman Empire was gone.

Barbarian leaders were smart, charismatic, and many were tactically brilliant, leading sieges and revolutionizing strategies that are still in use to this day. Whether we're talking about Attila the Hun, who ravaged the Roman Empire and put the first nail into the coffin of the Western Half, or

Genghis Khan, the man who struck fear into the Chinese and conquered nearly twelve million square miles, these men were strategically brilliant. Whether Hannibal of Carthage, Boudica of the Celts, or Arminius of the Germanic Cherusci tribe, these barbarians have gone down in history as some of the greatest to every step food on a battlefield.

In conclusion, Barbarians were not as fiction writers have depicted. Though some ruthless grunts existed, the bulk of the barbarian tribes all possessed traits that are remarkably similar to how modern civilizations act. They had religion, a defined power structure, and a vibrant culture that we still treasure and value today.

Prologue

Charles the 1st of France, or Charlemagne, is still today regarded as one of the greatest rulers to ever hold court and one of the greatest military leaders to ever step foot on a battlefield. While his tactics were not revered as innovative or overtly strategic, like say, Shaka Zula of the Zulus in Southern Africa with the use of the horned techniques or Hannibal's use of flanking against the Romans at the Battle of Cannae, his methods and tactics were reflective of the time and sufficient for what he was accomplishing. He is regarded as a phenomenal leader and a charismatic individual with an incredible acumen at details.

He achieved a great deal of things in his lifetime. With his devout faith in Christianity, specifically Roman Catholicism with an immense dedication to the papacy, Charlemagne recreated the Roman Empire from the ashes of the countries that had from its wreckage. While fighting wars all across Europe, Charlemagne embraced the feudal tendencies, establishing Lords in the lands that he conquered while slowly spreading his rule, expanding his territories past Germany and into Italy and parts of Spain. However, arguably his greatest achievement was the beginning of the reconquista in Spain. Though Charlemagne took a major defeat when he went there personally, his son was able to eventually secure victory for his father and bring northern Spain into Charlemagne's empire.

Charlemagne was a barbarian king and one of the greatest to ever live. He was ruthless, killing many on the battlefield, as well as killing many pagans who refused to convert and pay homage to the church. He is credited for becoming the first emperor of the West after the fall of the

Roman Empire, having the Byzantine emperor recognize him as such, though after a long struggle. He is also credited as being the first Emperor of the Holy Roman Empire, being recognized by papal authority and uniting all of the conquered territory under one banner, though this coronation was not the same territory that was declared under Papal rule in 962 CE under Otto.

Throughout this work, we will tell the tale of Charlemagne and how his rule created the new Roman Empire. His rise to power, coupled with the history of the Merovingian Empire in France, will be a focal point in this work, creating the setting for how Charlemagne was able to be successful. We will discuss how each different battle and campaign shaped his rule, allowing him to be effective and efficient. We will also go over his tactics, while not incredibly brilliant, were effective and his use of the technologies of the time were astute and conquered his enemies with a great skill. His charisma, his stature, and his reputation all lead to him being successful on the battlefield, in the throne room, and make him still revered throughout history as one of the greatest barbarian rulers to ever live.

Chapter 1
Europe after the Fall of Rome

The Roman Empire is still regarded as one of the greatest entities to ever rule. From the founding of the Roman Republic in 509 BC to the creation of the Roman Empire in 27 BC, and finally to the division of the Roman Empire in 285 CE, the land possessed by the Romans was quite expansive. Their territory spanned from the tip of the Iberian Peninsula in Spain to Babylonia from east to west, while ranging as far north as Hadrian's Wall, the dividing point between England and Scotland, and several hundred miles down the Nile River to the south. The incredible expansion, however, led to problems with governing and maintaining the areas. While the Romans were incredible at creating infrastructure in their conquered areas, due to their large mass, they were unable to maintain a consistent form of rule in the outlying areas. In 285 CE, the Roman Empire split into two halves. The Eastern Roman Empire would rule from Macedonia, in Greece, all the way to the eastern tip in Babylonia and setting their capital city in Byzantium, which would later be renamed Constantinople after the Byzantine Emperor, Constanine V. This partition would eventually become the Byzantine Empire, lasting until the 1453 CE when the Ottoman Turks captured Constantinople. The Western Roman Empire would remain seated in Rome, and would rule all of the territory from Italy to Spain. This partition would ultimately fall to various tribal warriors, as each section of land would slowly succumb to the rule of different invading barbarians. In 476, Rome was sacked by the Vandals and the Western Roman Empire was no more.[1]

---

[1] Gregory of Tours, Historia Froncorum Book 2 Chapter 27

From this sacking, however, the papal authority survived. The Catholic Church survived the various attacks on Rome, continuing to unite the cardinals, bishops, and priests while offering guidance to the many leaders who accepted their help. Though the Catholic Church kept their eyes firmly on the Eastern side of their religion, they watched them divide and change the papal law, creating the Eastern Orthodox Church. This is regarded as one of the first great schisms in Christianity and will sow the seeds for years of turmoil between the two sects. The Byzantine Empire will adopt and spread Eastern Orthodoxy throughout their empire, abolishing any Catholic or papal influences in the area.[2]

Following the dissolution of the Roman Empire, many of the lands in France fell into chaos while the lands in Africa and up into Spain were under attack. Following the death of the prophet Muhammad in 632 CE, Islamic forces began to slowly capture lands in Middle East and moved into Africa, taking the areas north of the Sahara desert that once belonged to the Roman Empire. Their spread went as far west as Morocco, stopping their before heading North, across the Strait of Gibraltar and onto the Iberian Peninsula in 711 CE. From there, the Islamic forces captured the entire area before crossing the Pyrenees Mountains and beginning the conquest of France.[3]

The areas of France descended into upheaval following the collapse of the Roman Empire. Several tribes and other forces divided the area. The Salian Franks, under the rule of Chlodio, regarded as the first Merovingian king, attacked and defeated a Roman force in 428 CE at Cambrai, settling in Northern Gaul. Later, in 448 CE, he would be defeated and

---

[2] Gregory of Tours, Historia Froncorum Book 2 Chapter 32
[3] Collins *Early Medieval Europe* pp. 143–145

killed in Artois by General Flavius Aetius, the Roman general responsible for driving Attila the Hun out of Europe, and his Roman legions, but not before extending his land down to the Somme River. His successor, Merovich, is credited for assisting the Roman legions in turning back the Huns, and their leader, Attila, at Cataluaunian fields in Gaul. Following this assistance, the Salian Franks were legitimized as the rulers of the Franks.[4]

Merovich's grandson, Clovis the 1st, is regarded as the first true King of the Franks. He is credited for uniting the various tribes under the Merovingian rule, ensuring a single line would retain the power and rule over France for years to come. He conquered the rest of Roman Gaul at the Battle of Soissons, defeating their leader, Syagrius, and ending the last presence of Roman authority in the area. Syagrius, however, escaped and fled south to the Visigoths, who under threat of war from Clovis, handed Syagrius over for execution. Clovis continued to march, though, waging war and defeating the Visigoths at the Battle of Vouille in 507 CE. With this final capture, Clovis set the border to his kingdom at the Pyrenees Mountains.[5]

Clovis's influence was not just on the battlefield, but also in the church. Originally, Clovis was an Arian Christian, which had been ruled as heresy by the First Council of Nicea in 325 AD. These Christians had a very distinct believe to the Catholics, in that they believed that Jesus Christ was a completely separate entity from God, though subordinate to him and created by him. These Arian Christians dominated most of Clovis's kingdom, leaving Catholics as the vast minority. However, upon the insistence of his wife, Clovis

---

[4] Wood, Ian. *The Merovingian Kingdoms 450 - 751*, Pearson Education Ltd., 1994
[5] Gregory of Tours, Historia Froncorum Book 2 Chapter 41

agreed to convert. On Christmas Day in 496 CE, Clovis converted to Catholicism and was baptized.[6]

His conversion angered many of the other rulers in the area, leading to a few uneasy years of ruling. However, Clovis knew that the advantages to his conversion outweighed the possible negatives. The conversion set him apart from the other rulers and tribes in the area, namely the Visigoths and Vandals, appealing him and his kingdom to the still powerful papal center in Rome. Clovis realized that by attaching himself to the papal authority, he would ensure the future success of his heirs. Before his death, Clovis assembled the first council of Orleans, bringing thirty-three bishops to him to pass thirty-one decrees. All of these were meant to establish equality between those who conquered, and those who were subsequently conquered. Upon his death, his kingdom was partitioned into four smaller kingdoms by his four sons: The Kingdoms of Rheims, Orleans, Paris, and Soissons. These four kingdoms created disunity in the Merovingian line, ultimately leading to its abolishment in 751 CE.[7]

Over the next years, war descended upon the area as more groups fought for power with Clovis's children dividing his kingdom. The lands were rife with conflict as the Islamic forces crossed the Pyrenees Mountains. In 732 CE, Charles Martel lead Frankish and Burgundian forces into battle against the Umayyad Caliphate, one of the four Caliphate's of Islam and the conqueror of the Iberian Peninsula. This battle took place between Tours and Poitiers, offering up two different names for the same battle. The Islamic Forces, under

---

[6] *Gender and Conversion in the Merovingian Era*, Cordula Nolte, **Varieties of Religious Conversion in the Middle Ages**, ed. James Muldoon, (University of Florida Press, 1997), 88
[7] Collins, Roger, *Early Medieval Europe*

the command of Abdul Rahman Al Ghafiqi. These Islamic forces are often referred to as "the Moors."

The Moors began their assault on France in 719 CE as they took Septimania, placing a foothold into Visigoth southern France and allowing for them to move further into the area. In 720 CE, they were able to subdue Narbonne, a port city on the Mediterranean Sea that was crucial for delivering anything by a seafaring vessel to the mainland. Their leader at the time, Al-Samh ibn Malik, made Narbonne his capital in France before moving northward. They set their sights on Aquitaine, laying siege on Toulouse in 721 CE. With many cities falling to the Moors before this, Odo, Duke of Aquitaine, fought back and broke the siege, wounding ibn Malik and stopping the spread of Islam westward. Days after their retreat, Al-Samh ibn Malik died from his wounds and Abdul Rahman Al Ghafiqi took command of the Moors, allowing them to reorganize and replenish from their port base of Narbonne. Their raids turned eastward in Burgundy, going as far as Autun in 725 CE.[8]

Odo of Aquitaine's forces were weakened and depleted from various battles with the Moors over the next few years, leading to the Battle of the River Garonne in Bordeaux. Firsthand accounts recorded originally in the Mozarabic Chronicle of 754 stated that the French forces were massacred and Odo fled the battlefield; the number of dead French soldiers reached the thousands. However, even though he fled, Odo was able to reach Charles Martel in time to warn him of the impending army that was approaching. Odo surrendered control of Aquitaine to the Charles Martel and the Franks for their assistance in defeating the Moors. Also noted in the

---

[8] Ian Meadows, "The Arabs in Occitania", Arab and Islamic Culture and Connections, Saudi Aramco World

Mozarabic Chronicles of 754, was the notion that the caliphate was unaware of the true strength of the French, unaware of the Germanic tribes and assuming that none would come to the aid under fear of the Moors. It's also noted that the Moors did not scout much of Northern France, for they would have noticed how much power Charles Martel possessed. The issue surrounding Odo's defeat at Bordeaux and Garonne centered on his inability to prepare. At Toulouse, Odo was able to round up his forces away from the city while the Moors were actively attacking the city, nearly defeating it before he arrived. He caught them by surprise and was able to neutralize their offensive. At Bordeaux and Garoone, Odo was unable to gain any type of advantage, allowing him to be overrun by the Islamic army and forced to retreat. The Moors relied on heavy cavalry, using their thunderous charges to break the infantry lines. At both Bordeaux and Garonne, the Frankish lines broke within the first charge the battle was lost quickly.[9]

Charles Martel was a seasoned military veteran, having fought many battles and secured the realm from any and all potential threats prior to the Moors. He fought a civil war, uniting the people of France before turning his attention to the pagan Saxons, wars in Bavaria and Alemannia. He was a Catholic, always opting to convert the subjugated people of the realm in which he took over and expanding the influence of the papal authority. As he conquered, Charles would appoint the new kings of the area, of who would serve him. Charles devoted a great deal of time and energy to conquering the Germanic tribes, keeping them in check while expanding his power and influence.

---

[9] Isidorus Pacensis, Chronicle of 754

Once alerted, Charles began to build his army to combat the Moors. Once built, they avoided the old Roman roads and stuck to the wooded paths and trails, trying to avoid any scouts and sentries from their enemy. Charles knew that he would have to have every strategic advantage to be successful, so he made sure that the battle happened when he chose for it to be and at the location he wanted. The Moors also took a great deal of time to get to Northern France, having to stop and gather food for their horses and men. The army was stretched thin and was far away from their base in Narbonne, making it difficult for them to survive a prolonged encounter. From Odo's knowledge, Charles knew how stretched the Moors were, intending on taking a defensive position to ensure that the battle lasted for a long while. In October of 732, the Battle of Tours commenced. Charles was smart, having learned from Odo's mistakes. He placed his army under the cover of several trees and other obstructions to prevent a cavalry charge, as being in an open setting would've spelled doom for the French. With Tours at their back, Charles and his army waited patiently for the Moors to attack in a phalanx formation, which they eventually obliged.

Abdul Rahman placed a great deal of trust in his past experiences and victories on the battlefield. Knowing that his heavy cavalry lead to his many victories, especially in Bordeaux and Garonne, he ordered them to charge repeatedly at the French lines. Charles's infantry was very well trained and experienced, however, having spent many campaigns with him over the previous years. They stood tall and withstood the heavy cavalry, driving them back as the trees and hills slowed them down, preventing them from over penetrating the line. During the battle, in a move of deception, Charles sent several troops behind the Moors, sneaking into their base camp and disrupting things. They released several slaves caught during their time in France and caused quite a stir as they pillaged. Several Umayyad soldiers broke ranks and returned back to the base, fearing that their personal belongings and riches would be stolen. The rest of the line broke, fleeing with the other men and the Moors were defeated at Tours.[10]

Charles continued to fight the Moors back after the Battle of Tours. Charles attempted to take Narbonne back from the Moors in 737, only to fall short while other campaigns proved futile. Charles was able to fight the Moors back to the Pyrenees, but was unable to stop them completely from raiding and pillaging French land while trying to regain a solid foothold. While Charles tried two separate campaigns to drive the Moors completely out of France, but both ultimately failed. While he did stop the overall spread of Islam in Western Europe, he was unable to completely drive the Moors out of France. Narbonne would eventually surrender to French forces under the command of Pepin the Short, the son of Charles Martel, in 759. The Moors were driven back to the Pyrenees and were finally expelled from France.

One of the items brought by the Moors into France that revolutionized European warfare was the invention of the stirrup. The stirrup had been around for centuries, though had never reached Western Europe until the Moors, with their heavy cavalry used them to wrest control of the area. The stirrup is often credited with the birth of feudalism, having been used extensively to conquer kingdoms and create vassals. By utilizing a stirrup, mounted soldiers could stabilize their bodies long enough to swing weaponry and fire projectiles without the fear of falling off. This created an incredible advantage against basic grounded infantry, because they were

---

[10] Isidorus Pacensis, Chronicle of 754

able to attack harder and faster, utilizing the speed and power of the horse combined with the strength of the soldier.[11]

Pepin the short, of Pepin the 3rd, was the first Carolingian king of France. His father died in 741 CE, leading to his succession as Mayor of the Palace, a title given to the true ruler of the Franks while the king was more of a figurehead. He shared this title with his brother, Carloman, splitting the realm in half and ruling over each respectively. However, in 747, Carloman relinquished his title and chose a monastic life, withdrawing to life in a monastery in service of the church. With this, Pepin became the sole ruler and in 751 CE, with the assistance of Pope Zachary, Pepin deposed of the figurehead Merovingian king and anointed himself the king of the Franks. During his time, Pepin expanded his power and by growing his realm. He retook Narbonne and all of Septimania in 759, though started the campaign in 751. He waged war with the independent Aquitaine, and specifically, Waiofar, the Duke of Aquitaine. Pepin was a ferocious leader, burning and destroying villages in Aquitaine, spreading terror and mayhem while trying to capture the land. This led to their eventual surrender in 768 CE and the assassination of the Duke of Aquitaine. That year, however, Pepin died leading to the coronation of his two sons: Carloman and Charlemagne.[12]

---

[11] *Curta, Florin (2007). The other Europe in the Middle Ages: Avars, Bulgars, Khazars and Cumans. Kononklijke Brill N.Y. p. 316*
[12] Gregory of Tours, Historia Froncorum Book 2 Chapter 47

Chapter 2
The Birth and Coronation of Charlemagne as the Sole King of France

A definitive date for the birth of Charles the 1st has always been debated, though most scholars have come to agree that the date of his birth centers around the year 742 CE, though this also predates the marriage of his parents in 744 CE, making him illegitimate, though never mentioned by the scholars of the time. It's also suggested, though not validated, that he was born in Aachen, home of the Carolingian line, located in modern Germany. He was the first born of his parents, Pepin the Short and Bertrada of Laon, having many siblings but none of them stand out like his brother, Carloman. He had a sister, Gisela, who the lineage did not pass to and three brothers who died during their childhood.

It would be foolish of me to say anything about his birth and infancy, or even about his boyhood, for I can find nothing about these matters in writing, nor does anyone survive who claims to have personal knowledge of them. I have decided, therefore, to pass on to describe and illustrate his acts and his habits and the other divisions of his life without lingering over the unknown. I shall describe first his exploits both at home and abroad, then his habits and interests, and lastly the administration of the kingdom and the end of his reign, omitting nothing that demands or deserves to be recorded.[13]

Fortunately for scholars, a prominent French courtier lived during the reign of Charlemagne, providing detailed accounts of his exploits and firsthand knowledge of the times. His name was Einhard, and his work, the Vita Karoli Magni, is

---

[13] Einhard, Vita Karoli Magni, pg 12

one of the greatest pieces of literature to come out of the middle ages. Though written in Latin and translated into English, this work still provides a direct benefit into the life and exploits of Charlemagne that scholars of the middle ages treasure. Having lived from 775 CE to 840 CE, Einhard was present for much of the reign of Charlemagne, creating his work with a masterstroke of information and experience that scholars today cannot fathom.

The rise of Charlemagne can be traced to the fall of Pepin the Short in 768 CE, dying in Paris and passing down his authority to his two living sons, Carloman and Charles. Charles, thought to be around 26 at the coronation, had already been serving alongside his father in Aquitaine, gaining a firsthand knowledge of battle tactics, attrition, and recovery strategy. His brother, Carloman, was only seventeen and lacked much of the skill his brother possessed. The people of the kingdom called an assembly, declaring that both men would be king and that both would inherit the lands of their father, agreeing to split them equally with Charles taking over the lands directly owned by his father prior to him becoming the King, and his brother, taking over the lands held by his uncle before he became a monk. Both men, without fight or argument, accepted this arrangement, though not without some controversy from others in the area.

The first event the two brothers needed to handle came from Aquitaine, where their father was campaigning before his death. Rebellions and skirmishes were fought as the Franks tried to regain possession of the territory that Odo swore to Charles Martel. With their father Pepin defeating Waifer, the Duke of Aquitaine before his death, the lands in Aquitaine were split between Carloman and Charles, Two different groups, the residents of Aquitaine and the Gascons rose up in 769 CE to challenge the rule and authority of the two brothers.

Upon the Aquiatine army reaching as far north as Angouleme, they were now under the command of Hunald, a former lord in Aquitaine, turned monk, and father of Waifar. After meeting his brother, Carloman refused to go to war, retiring to Burgundy and leaving the battle to his brother. Charles, not wasting any time, immediately marched on Bordeaux, taking it and forcing Hunald to flee to Gascony. Once there, Hunald attempted to get sanctuary from Lupus II, only to have it turned down out of fear of Charles. Without any conflict, Lupus II turned Hunald over to Charles in exchange for peace, ending the rebellion of Aquitaine. Hunald, the former monk, was allowed to return to the monastery, exiled there as punishment for taking over his son's rebellion.[14]

Charles was slightly paranoid of his brother, though it proved to be futile in the end. In 770 CE, Charles married Desiderata, the daughter of King Desiderius of the Lombards, creating an alliance that surrounded all of Carloman's territories. While the pope, Stephen III, originally opposed this marriage, he would quickly realize the advantages of the Franco-Lombard alliance. At the behest of their mother, though, both kings remained civil with one another. Many men, under the rule of Carloman, attempted to drive a wedge between the two brothers and invoke them in war, but to no avail. No conflict erupted between the two brothers as they were able to rule in an uneasy harmony. Charles would send his Lombard wife away a year after their marriage, opting to marry another, much younger woman, infuriating King Desiderius.[15]

---

[14] Einhard pg 14
[15] Einhard page 32-34

However, two years after their joint coronation, on 5 December 771 CE, Carloman died of illness and his family, along with several of the nobles in the area, fled to Italy out of fear and for protection, taking up refuge in King Desiderius's court in Lombardy. Charles I was now the sole king of France.[16]

---

[16] Einhard, pg 12-15

Chapter 3
The Noble King and his Family

Charlemagne has always been regarded as a warrior king, ruthless on the battlefield and swift in his judgment. However, he also possessed a more humane, noble side that many did not get to witness often. Charlemagne was a very devout Christian and a humble man of the family, bearing many children his different wives and creating a very large, expansive line. He was regarded as polite, charming, and loathsome of anyone under the influence of alcohol, preaching temperance and moderation over self indulging with a lack of control.

Firstly, though, Charlemagne was regarded as an impressive physical specimen. He was regarded as tall, powerful, and athletic, as mentioned by the historian Einhard:

His body was large and strong; his stature tall but not ungainly, for the measure of his height was seven times the length of his own feet. The top of his head was round; his eyes were very large and piercing. His nose was rather larger than is usual; he had beautiful white hair; and his expression was brisk and cheerful; so that, whether sitting or standing, his appearance was dignified and impressive. Although his neck was rather thick and short and he was somewhat corpulent this was not noticed owing to the good proportions of the rest of his body. His step was firm and the whole carriage of his body manly; his voice was clear, but hardly so strong as you would have expected. He had good health, but for four years before his death was frequently attacked by fevers, and at last was lame of one foot. Even then he followed his own opinion rather than the advice of his doctors, whom he almost hated, because they advised him to give up the roast meat to which he was accustomed, and eat boiled instead. He constantly took exercise both by riding and hunting. This was a national habit; for there is hardly any race on the earth that can be placed on equality with the Franks in this respect. He took delight in the vapour of naturally hot waters, and constantly practiced swimming, in which he was so proficient that no one could be fairly regarded as his superior. Partly for this reason he built his palace at Aix, and lived there continuously during the last years of his life up to the time of his death. He used to invite not only his sons to the bath but also his nobles and friends, and at times even a great number of his followers and bodyguards.

Charlemagne was also a traditionalist, swearing to the customs of his people before giving way to the wills and demands of Rome. He was a servant of his people, appearing as they did and representing his kingdom.

He wore the national—that is to say, the Frankish dress. His shirts and drawers were of linen, then came a tunic with a silken fringe, and hose. His legs were cross-gartered and his feet enclosed in shoes. In winter-time he defended his shoulders and chest with a jerkin made of the skins of otters and ermine. He was clad in a blue cloak, and always wore a sword, with the hilt and belt of either gold or silver. Occasionally, too, he used a jeweled sword, but this was only on the great festivals or when he received ambassadors from foreign nations. He disliked foreign garments, however beautiful, and would never consent to wear them, except once at Rome on the request of Pope Hadrian, and once again upon the entreaty of his successor, Pope Leo, when he wore a long tunic and cloak, and put on shoes made after the Roman fashion. On festal days he walked in procession in a garment of gold cloth, with jeweled boots and a golden girdle to his cloak, and distinguished further by a diadem of gold and precious stones. But on other days his dress differed little from that of the common people.[17]

With mentions of his swimming, hunting, and other accolades, Charlemagne took amazing care of himself. He was regal in public, standing in front of his subjects in a manner that only a king should, while still having the aura of a warrior. His love of the outdoors and his ultimate refusal to adhere to anything but the traditional dress, showed a man devoted to his people and his culture, not someone who was a slave to current fashion, trends, or the will of another. Charlemagne's personality is on full display through the words of Einhard. He was a man of his people, standing for what he believed in and being a man of the French. He was an Arian Christian before converting to Catholicism later in life. He was a devout man of his God and led his people from paganism and into the church. Though sometimes ruthless, and still a barbarian, Charlemagne's devotion to his people was second to none.

Charlemagne was married several times. His first wife was Desiderata, the daughter of King Desiderius of the Lombards. With the persuasion of his mother, Bertrada, he ultimately married Desiderata for convenience and to put several allies around his brother, Carloman. He opted to divorce her shortly before their one year anniversary, creating the only documented feud he had with this mother, whom he revered, and allowing her to live with him until her death many years later. Soon after the divorce, he married Hildigard, a thirteen year old girl from Swabia, a province in modern Germany. She was of a noble line, uniting her family with Charlemagne's and giving birth to six children, three boys and three girls. After the birth of her children, Hildigard passed

---

[17] Einhard 38-39

away with Bertrada passing on shortly after, being buried with Charlemagne's father, Pepin, at St. Denis. His next wife was Fastrada from eastern France, having two daughters with her. He had other children later in life, all by concubines and outside of wedlock. His boys were: Charles, Pepin, and Ludovicus, Drago, and Hugot. His daughters were: Hroturd, Bertha, Gisla, Theoderada, Hilrud, Hruodhaid, Ruothild, Adolthurd, and Theoderic.

As a family man, Charlemange took a definite interest in the upbringing of his children, insisting on how they were educated and trained. All of his children were taught liberal studies, focusing on the arts and humanities so that they were educated and ready for a life at court. His sons, specifically, were taught how to ride as soon as they could fit on the saddle, as well as fire bows and wield swords. All of his sons were adept at hunting, learning at an early age how to track and kill their prey. His daughters, however, were not hunting, but were taught high principles, sewing, spindle, and wool work. He love for his children was unmatched. When marching, his sons, once old enough, would ride beside him while his daughters would travel in a carriage at the rear, being under heavy guard from several of his best warriors.[18]

While wanting his children to focus on the liberal arts, Charlemagne was also a master of culture and class. He was a great orator, speaking with clarity and precision. He was fluent in other languages, especially Latin, which he could speak it as well as he spoke French. He respected those who taught liberal arts, placing them in his employ to educate his children, though also taking the time to learn himself. He spent a lot of time on rhetoric, grammar, syntax, and other things related to language. He also employed Alcuin, a scholar and astronomer

---

[18] Einhard 33-36

from Britain to educate him in the stars and other astronomical things.

Arguably one of the greatest achievements was the standardization of education in his realm. While loving to learn, he ordered his scholars and scribes to standardize the method of learning for all children of nobility at recently established schools. By creating this standardization, Charlemagne was able to ensure that all of the children would receive a proper education, by his standards. This illustrates the need for an academic reform. Since the fall of the Roman Empire, schools and universities had faltered and fallen, leading to several things being taught at different institutions of learning that did not sit well with the leadership. The inability for people to read, nor be able to perform basic, mathematical equations, was viewed as a problem by Charlemagne. The root of this, was that Latin had broken down, which after nearly 400 years after the fall of the Roman Empire, was bound to happen. The fusion of Latin with the other Germanic languages in the area created a vulgar latin, which would deviate from region to region, creating very different dialects. The creation of schools helped to revolutionize the realm, bringing them into a more modern age. The trivium and quadrivium, the focuses of these schools, are still used in some places today.

To help with the language barrier, Charlemagne standardized the writing system used by the men and women in his kingdom. The Carolingian Minusculus was a system of four lines which joined capital and small letters to form words. This system was developed so that the working class would be able to understand words, phrases, and other forms of syntax in Latin. There were definite spaces between words and capital, as well as, lowercase letters. This new way of writing allowed for many religious texts to get documented, as well as many other important things that would be crucial to the realm.

One of his greatest accomplishments was having the laws of his realm, and the realms he conquered, put into writing. He broke down their legal systems, making them more streamlined and easier for his subjects to follow. He was incredibly organized and detailed, leaving nothing to chance within the legal system and drawing it out to where it subjugated everything and made it simple to follow. The biggest reason for this was that there were two legal systems in place in his realm: the Salian system and Ripuraian systems. Both systems were complex, with differing rules in place for various things, but a definite need for change was there. After a few years, and complex dictation, Charlemagne was able to repair the laws of his realm and make it easier for those to follow.

He also did a few other impressive things. The first of which was he commenced in dictating several songs and chants from his past, oral traditions that were committed to memory. Much like the Vikings, Celts, and other civilizations from the time, oral traditions were passed down from generation to generation. Charlemagne, in a move to preserve the history and culture of his people, he had the scribes and scholars of his court write down all of these stories, preserving them for posterity and civilizations to come. In another move to preserve his society, Charlemagne had French associations with all of the months of the year, giving them names that the nobles and citizens alike would recognize. By doing this, he standardized the French calendar and assisting those who could not read Greek or Latin in knowing the month of the year and seasons. He also assigned titles, in French, to the twelve cardinal directions the wind traveled, assigning another important guide to infrastructure.

Charlemagne maintained the Roman roads and buildings that had stood in France for years, helping to maintain the infrastructure that was already in place. The citizens and travelers were well versed in the lay of the land by the use of the roads that had been there for centuries, so Charlemagne took especial care in assuring that they were well maintained. With buildings, especially churches and cathedrals, Charlemagne took great care, assuring their stones laid in the foundation were secure and that the buildings would be able to stay for the longest of times. At one point, he built a church at Aix so encompassing and large; he was able to live there prior to his death and bathe regularly in the hot water and steaming vapor.[19]

Charlemagne was a very temperate man, abstaining for overconsumption while maintaining his physique and demeanor, though he did mention that fasting made people weak. While he abhorred drunkenness and anyone who drank excessive amounts of wine or mead, Charlemagne was very organized in how he consumed his food, portioning it out into courses and staying on a regiment. With the exception of the roast, brought in on a spigot from the hunters that day, Charlemange ate his meals in four distinct courses. He also would drink sparingly during dinner, not becoming over served.

Though Charlemagne was considered a temperate man, he is best known in history for two things: his love, admiration, and growth of Christianity, and his fervor for battle and conquest. With his love of God as his motivation, Charlemagne would embark on several wars in the name of Christ, retaking several pieces of land in Spain and eventually

---

[19] Einhard 38-39

going to war with the Eastern sect of the Roman Empire, the Byzantines.

Chapter 4
Charlemagne and the Church

Ah! how little do the enemies of Christ value the words of the Apostle of Christ where he says:—"All ye that are baptised in Christ, put on Christ"; and again: "Ye that are baptised in Christ are baptised in His death"; or that passage which is aimed especially at those who despise the faith and violate the sacraments: "Crucifying the Son of God afresh and putting Him to an open shame!" Oh! would that this were the case only with the heathen; and not also among those who are called by the name of Christ![20]

Regarded as one of his greatest achievements, there is no argument amongst scholars that Charlemagne was a champion for the Christianity, not just Catholicism. From the construction of vast monasteries and cathedrals, the conversion of thousands of pagans when on a campaign, Charlemagne remains one of the influential figures in the Middle Ages when it comes to Christianity. Where the various caliphs and priests did a great deal for Islam in this day and age, pushing against the Eastern Orthodox Church in Greece and Turkey, Charlemagne's expansion of the Western church is second to none. His predecessor, two generations removed, Charles Martel, fought back the Islamic forces at Tours, leading the way for Charlemagne to further the expansion of Christianity at the sake of his Islamic neighbors to South.

During the time period of Charlemagne's life, paganism, much specifically religions devoted to the moon, stars, and land, were still common place in various points across Europe. The further east you traveled, into the area of the Avars and

---

[20] Monk of St. Gall

other barbarians, one would come across several different religions. Though Christian missionaries from various sects would venture up in the region over the eight hundred year history of the religion, paganism was still prevalent in the lands not settled by the Roman Empire during its height. It's because of this, that Charlemagne's travels into the Germanic lands to his east are so significant for the spread of Christianity. By traveling as far east as modern Austria, Charlemagne was able to Christianize most of Europe, with the exception of Spain.

The lands east of Italy, including Greece and several of the empires located in the Balkan Peninsula, made the Eastern Orthodox Church, located out of the capital of the Byzantine Empire, Constantinople, their preferred religion. While the Catholic Church is centered in Rome, in 526 CE, the Byzantine Empire, under the command of Emperor Justinian, who is also the last man to go by the title, Caesar, undertook an expedition to conquer all of Italy from the recently fallen Western half of the Roman Empire. However, with the church firmly entrenched, and the fall of Northern Italy in 568 to the Lombards, the Eastern Orthodoxy could not gain a proper foothold in Western Europe.

Spain was still in the control of the Moors, the Islamic rulers who swept through Northern Africa and invaded the Iberian Peninsula. The Umayyad Caliphate, the second of the four Caliphates founded after the death of Muhammad, led the fastest conquest of land the world had seen since the days of Alexander of Macedonia. With their feet firmly entrenched in Spain, and their defeat by Charles Martel, the Moors were still focused on spreading their religion, expanding the Umayyad Caliphate even further, with the objection of overtaking Rome. However, after their defeat at Tours in 732 CE, the fires of rebellion started to ignite in the Middle East. The Caliphate, housed out of Damascus, was under attack from within during the third Muslim Civil War, as other groups tried to wrest control from them and keeping several of the troops from heading west and fortifying the campaign in France. In 750 CE, the Umayyad Caliphate fell at the Battle of Zeb in Damascus, the Umayyad capital, weakening the power they possessed in Europe. The Abbasid Caliphate, conquerors of the Umayyad, were victorious in unseating the powerful Caliphate, though could not gain a foothold among all of their possessions, namely the holdings in Iberia. Al-Andalus, the region they referred to as part of the Caliphate, would eventually become the Emirate of Cordoba in 756 CE, six years after the fall of the Umayyad Caliphate. A prince of the deposed Caliphate, Abdul al Rahman, who was to be the new Caliph upon his father's death, refused to recognize the conquering Caliphate in the Middle East, remaining loyal to the Umayyad, and elect to form his own Emirate in Spain rather than marching under the flag of the other sect. After deposing any resistance against him and unifying the various fiefdoms and vassal states, Abdul al Rahman unified Al-Andalus against the Abbasid Caliphate and formed the Emirate of Cordoba.[21]

Because of the turmoil in Spain stemming from the usurping of the previous Caliphate but refusal to join the new one, political and military unrest grew in the area. Many loyalist revolts came about, sparking a new sense of pride in the area from those who had always stood against the Caliphate and the Moors. Since the initial landing of the Islamic soldiers in 711 CE, coming across the strait of Gibraltar and onto the Iberian Peninsula, only one generation was removed. The conquered Visigoths, whose territory extended all the way through the French Riviera along the

---

[21] *Azizur Rahman, Syed.* The Story of Islamic Spain. *Goodword Books. 2001*

Mediterranean Sea, in a region known as Septimus, possessed the bulk of the land on the Iberian Peninsula. These barbarians were Catholic, swearing their allegiance to the pope in Rome. Their culture sewed the area with Christian beliefs, though the Moors were not completely intolerant. Though they taxed the Christians much heavier, they allowed them to worship at peace. However, they did convert where they could, bringing about a heavily Islamic culture to the European peninsula.

Several sects of Christendom also existed in the world during Charlemagne's reign. The first two most notable are the Catholics and the Eastern Orthodox. These two churches came about during the great schism of the Roman Empire, creating two capitals to rule the vast empire where one could not do it effectively. With Byzantium becoming the capital of the East, later to be named Constantinople by one of the future emperors, the seeds of Eastern Orthodoxy, or Greek Orthodox, were sewn. The first, and by far the largest issue is that the Eastern Orthodox Church does not recognize papal authority. They do not view the pontiff as the supreme being in the religion, and that while it is an honor to have that title bestowed upon someone, they are not the most morally upright and chosen person to lead. They feel that no man should have power or jurisdiction over the spiritual matters of anyone, much the same with many other religions around the world. Another difference is with the priests. In the Catholic faith, a married man cannot become a priest, where as currently married men can become priests in Eastern Orthodoxy, though cannot become married after ordination. These two sects, however, are very identical beyond the few differences. However, other sects have come about during the time of the Christianity that still existed during Charlemagne's days, and were regarded as heresies.

The first, and most important because Charlemagne actively practiced this faith, was Arianism, or Arian Christianity. They do not believe in the traditional, Catholic doctrine of the trinity, in that God encompasses more than one being. Essentially, they believed that God was, in fact, God with Jesus Christ being created by God and the Holy Spirit acting as an agent of God. This countered the Catholic dogma, angering those in Rome and having their founder, Arius, a scholar from Alexandria, Egypt, labeled as a heretic. With the religion having been labeled a heresy in Rome, it flourished in Constantinople, leading to several Gothic and other German leaders converting to it before heading back to their tribes and villages in Eastern Europe. This led to its spread, eventually making its way to Gaul and the conversion of the Merovingian kings.

The inhibiting and paralyzing force of superstitious beliefs penetrated to every department of life, and the most primary and elementary activities of society were influenced. War, for example, was not a simple matter of a test of strength and courage, but supernatural matters had to be taken carefully into consideration. When Clovis said of the Goths in southern Gaul, "I take it hard that these Arians should hold a part of the Gauls; let us go with God's aid and conquer them and bring the land under our dominion", he was not speaking in a hypocritical or arrogant manner but in real accordance with the religious sentiment of the time. What he meant was that the Goths, being heretics, were at once enemies of the true God and inferior to the orthodox Franks in their supernatural backing. Considerations of duty, strategy, and self-interest all reinforced one another in Clovis's mind.[22]

---

[22] Gregory of Tours

With Clovis, the great Merovingian leader taking the Arian Christian faith, the heresy as declared by the Council of Nicaea in 325 by the Nicean Creed was taking a foothold in Europe. With the Roman Empire gone, and several barbarian hordes ruling the land, the Catholic church was not in a position to fight back against the lot of Europe. Though never giving in and accepting them, several popes negotiating with Arian kings and envoys, doing what they could do influence policy and law in the land.

Thus, during Charlemagne's rule, several varying religions were in effect all around him. The Muslims were actively practicing to his south, encroaching on his borders and causing various wars with Aquitaine over his reign. The Lombards, to his South East, were practicing Catholics and very hostile at times. To his direct east were the Germanic tribes, filled with varying sects of pagans, sacrificing humans and animals and tying their lot to the connection with the land in order to appease their Gods. Charlemagne had to choose his battles with religion wisely, though his deeply imbedded faith allowed him to flourish throughout history.

Charlemagne was a devout Catholic, ruthless in methods of conversion but efficient none the less. Prior to his appointment as the Holy Roman Emperor on Christmas Day, 800 CE, Charlemagne led the realm in conversions of pagans, forcing them to submit to Catholicism or be executed, much notably the Saxon conquests in the 770s. One event stands out in history as one of the defining moments of Charlemagne's ruthless campaign against the pagans. The Massacre of Verden in 782 CE is regarded as one of the largest executions in the history of the world. In October, Charlemagne executed 4500 Saxons for their failure to convert to Catholicism and their continued upheaval. However, this massacre also prevented the Saxon's from rising up for many years, as nearly an entire generation of warriors was executed.[23]

Charlemagne also constructed beautiful churches, decorated with gold, silver, and other ornate jewels as well as marble and other precious stones:

He paid the most devout and pious regard to the Christian religion, in which he had been brought up from infancy. And, therefore, he built the great and most beautiful church at Aix, and decorated it with gold and silver and candelabras and with wicket-gates and doors of solid brass. And, since he could not procure marble columns elsewhere for the building of it, he had them brought from Rome and Ravenna. As long as his health permitted it he used diligently to attend the church both in the morning and evening, and during the night, and at the time of the Sacrifice. He took the greatest care to have all the services of the church performed with the utmost dignity, and constantly warned the keepers of the building not to allow anything improper or dirty either to be brought into or to remain in the building. He provided so great a quantity of gold and silver vessels, and so large a supply of priestly vestments, that at the religious services not even the doorkeepers, who form the lowest ecclesiastical order, had to officiate in their ordinary dress. He carefully reformed the manner of reading and singing; for he was thoroughly instructed in both, though he never read publicly himself, nor sang except in a low voice, and with the rest of the congregation.[24]

---

[23] Einhard 45-46
[24] Einhard 26

A much more in depth conversation about Aix, his magnificent temple, by another biographer of the time, the Monk of St. Gall:

When the most energetic Emperor Charles could rest awhile he sought not sluggish ease, but laboured in the service of God. He desired therefore to build upon his native soil a cathedral finer even than the works of the Romans, and soon his purpose was realised. For the building thereof he summoned architects and skilled workmen from all lands beyond the seas; and above all he placed a certain knavish abbot whose competence for the execution of such tasks he knew, though he knew not his character. When the august emperor had gone on a certain journey, this abbot allowed anyone to depart home who would pay sufficient money: and those who could not purchase their discharge, or were not allowed to return by their masters, he burdened with unending labours, as the Egyptians once afflicted the people of God. By such knavish tricks he gathered together a great mass of gold and silver and silken robes; and, exhibiting in his chamber only the least precious articles, he concealed in boxes and chests all the richest treasures. Well, one day there was brought to him on a sudden the news that his house was on fire. He ran, in great excitement, and pushed his way through the bursting flames into the strong room where his boxes, stuffed with gold, were kept: he was not satisfied to take one away, but would only leave after he had loaded his servants with a box apiece. And as he was going out a huge beam, dislodged by the fire, fell on the top of him; and then his body was burnt by temporal and his soul by eternal flames. Thus did the judgment of God keep watch for the most religious Emperor Charles, when his attention was withdrawn by the business of his kingdom.

There was another workman, the most skilled of all in the working of brass and glass. Now this man (his name was Tancho and he was at one time a monk of St Gall) made a fine bell and the emperor was delighted with its tone. Then said that most distinguished, but most unfortunate worker in brass: "Lord emperor, give orders that a great weight of copper be brought to me that I may refine it; and instead of tin give me as much silver as I shall need—a hundred pounds at least; and I will cast such a bell for you that this will seem dumb in comparison to it." Then Charles, the most liberal of monarchs, who "if riches abounded set not his heart upon them" readily gave the necessary orders, to the great delight of the knavish monk. He smelted and refined the brass; but he used, not silver, but the purest sort of tin, and soon he made a bell, much better than the one that the emperor had formerly admired, and, when he had tested it, he took it to the emperor, who admired its exquisite shape and ordered the clapper to be inserted and the bell to be hung in the bell-tower. That was soon done; and then the warden of the church, the attendants and even the boys of the place tried, one after the other, to make the bell sound. But all was in vain; and so at last the knavish maker of the bell came up, seized the rope, and pulled at the bell. When, lo and behold! down from on high came the brazen mass; fell on the very head of the cheating brass-founder; killed him on the spot; and passed straight through his carcass and crashed to the ground carrying his bowels with it. When the aforementioned weight of silver was found, the most righteous Charles ordered it to be distributed among the poorest servants of the palace.[25]

---

[25] Monk of St. Gall 34

For the church, once made the Holy Roman Emperor, Charlemagne was able to call ecumenical councils and synods, summoning bishops and holy men from around the world to converse on topics he felt to be credible. Overtime, with his authority as emperor, Charlemagne would be able to shape the foundation of Catholicism, driving a further schism between Rome and the Byzantines. On Christmas Day in 800 CE, Charlemagne traveled to Rome to seek council with Pope Leo III. According to the historian, Einhard, Charlemagne would not have entered the church on Christmas if he had known that he was going to receive this coronation. However, other historians have argued that was not the case and that his lust for more power and expansion would fuel him.

But such were not the only objects of his last visit; for the Romans had grievously outraged Pope Leo, had torn out his eyes and cut off his tongue, and thus forced him to throw himself upon the protection of the King. He therefore came to Rome to restore the condition of the church, which was terribly disturbed, and spent the whole of the winter there. It was then that he received the title of Emperor and Augustus, which he so disliked at first that he affirmed that he would not have entered the church on that day—though it was the chief festival of the church—if he could have foreseen the design of the Pope. But when he had taken the title he bore very quietly the hostility that it caused and the indignation of the Roman emperors. He conquered their ill-feeling by his magnanimity, in which, doubtless, he far excelled them, and sent frequent embassies to them, and called them his brothers.[26]

---

[26] Einhard 28

Charlemagne was known for being a very generous Christian, sending gifts and riches to the Catholics in poverty stricken areas. He dispatched emissaries to Alexandria and Carthage, both in Africa, Syria, Jerusalem, and even Greece. His love for all Christians was unmatched by any other ruler in the world. He would send the pope lavish gifts, but the greatest gift he could offer, was returning Rome to the splendor it once possessed. With the reign of Charlemagne as the leader and Emperor of the Holy Roman Empire, the Papal States would grow and Rome would once again become the center of the political world in Europe. However, Charlemagne would only visit Rome four times in his lifetime, preferring to stay in France and not venturing out into the Italian city.

His love of the church helped fuel his military conquests. From his numerous encounters with the pagan Saxons, Avars, and Bavarians, to his feuds with the Islamic Moors in Spain, Charlemagne remained ever vigilant in the spread of his faith. He was a champion for Christianity, and his army would be his weapon.

Chapter 5
The Construction of Charlemagne's Army

Charlemagne's military success is one of the things that history remembers the most about him. Though he reformed education by organizing the curriculums and constructing new schools, his highest honors still remain in his conquests and victories. The expansion of the realm was his first concern, waging several wars with various nations over time and leading over eighteen different campaigns through history, though some would argue the number is smaller because the campaigns paused and started again at a later date. Never the less, Charlemagne's armies were usually in the fields, dominating opponents while expanding his territory and power.

His battle techniques, while effective, were not revolutionary. He did not change warfare by inventing a new formation or stance, much like the Greeks or Romans, but instead focused on what he could to be successful. As noted earlier by how effective Charlemagne was at organizing his realm and reforming several areas of his culture at home, he took the same acumen one the battlefield. The men at his disposal were well seasoned, Frankish warriors, descended from the army of Charles Martel and even further. These men swore an oath of fealty to Charlemagne, opting to serve when his command called.

With the rise of the Carolingians, and especially Charlemagne, the feudal institutions in Europe were established. The land holding nobility, usually a knight or other lord, swore an oath of fealty and agreed to serve the king whenever he called. The land owner would then subdivide his land amongst his vassals, with many of them serving in the private battalion and regiment of the land owner. These men would also come when the land owner was summoned and even men who served the second land owner. The vassals or tenants would usually not take up arms directly, instead serving as craftsmen and laborers, or even siege weapon specialists.

The knights at Charlemagne's disposal are regarded in history as some of the greatest short ranged fighters to have ever lived. With thick, iron armor and chain mail, these men would enter the battlefield and engage in close combat with their foes. Swinging heavy, iron swords and equipped with sturdy, iron shields, the knights would walk onto the battlefield in formation, crushing resistances with relative ease. Many knights, however, chose to ride horses onto the battlefield. While the stirrup was making its way into the Europe, the use of it was not completely widespread. However, by arming them with a large pike, Charlemagne was able to have an expansive heavy cavalry at his disposal, much like the Moors during the invasion of Aquitaine and the conquest of Bordeaux.

His armies, however, were likely not very large, consisting of maybe ten thousand at a time. Because of the campaigns he was fighting, especially in Eastern Europe, there was no requirement for a large, engrossing army. Several reasons exist for the army remaining small. With the bulk of the manpower coming from estates with farmlands, men needed to be available to till the ground, plant the fields, and harvest the crops. Peasants had to be able to work and serve their land owner, or else the land owner would not have the money to continue to live his lifestyle. Also, in the time of Charlemagne, the populations in the area were not very dense, with the exception of the larger cities in the realm: Bordeaux, Orleans, Paris, Aachen, and a few others. Feeding a large army, as well as the horses and other livestock, were simply not an option. So, while text from the contemporaries of the time mention that Charlemagne amassed large armies, it is more likely that they were quite small, though still incredibly larger in comparison to the armies they were fighting.

The equipment of the army was second to none of the time, as the knights would personally ensure that they had the sharpest swords and sturdiest shields. Bows and crossbows were common place in the ranks of the army. The bows were typically made of wood, though some composite bows did find their way through the ranks. A composite bow is made from wood, bone, and metal and is held together by animal sinew to ensure its sturdiness. These bows were effective from long range, able to clear walls and inflict casualties from a distance. The crossbows originated in Greece and were typically used more by the Islamic forces on the Iberian Peninsula, however, a few records of crossbow use from various knights was recorded by the Monk of St. Gall. Other small, ranged weapons emerged on the battlefield: slings, javelins, and throwing axes.

One of the largest advantages Charlemagne had was the time in which he lived. Because of the success of his grandfather, Charles Martel, and his father, Pepin the Short, Charlemagne entered into ruling in a time of great advantage. Unless he was waging a war in the south with the Spanish, Charlemagne possessed a military advantage over any of his potential foes. The use of heavy cavalry was not widespread in Europe, as only Charlemagne effectively utilized it. With these horses at his disposal, he would crush enemy lines and end the battle before it became too long, drawn out, and costly.

Cities across Europe were fortified by large, encompassing walls. In order to invade, the walls would need to be broken down or another way to enter had to be devised. The walls in Northern and Western Europe were generally constructed of wood and built to repel small forces. This also lends to the suggestion that the armies of the time were not terribly large. Archer towers, often referred to as watchtowers, were starting to become the norm in most of the cities during Charlemagne's time. These towers would hold several archers, all equipped with bows capable of raining arrows down on an invading army.

To counter the large walls and defenses, Charlemagne turned to siege weaponry. While the battering ram had been around for thousands of years, Charlemagne needed a weapon he could fire at a distance. The ballista, the primary weapon of the Roman Empire, was no longer practical as the resources required to construct these machines was no longer easy to come by. The catapult had become the tool used to crush the opposition at range. Several models existed, though Charlemagne used the Mangonel, a device that fired projectiles from a bowl shaped portion at the end of a large section. With wheels at the base to help it move, several men would pull the large arm back to lock in place. They would load the bowl and release a lever, firing the projectile upwards of 1300 feet. Stones, carcasses, and fiery objects would be used to inflict terrible structural damage on the city, as well as psychological damage to its inhabitants.

Another important aspect for the armies of Charlemagne was the use of large ships for naval combat. Though not tactically advanced as the ships in the feudal period during the high middle ages, these ships were powered by men. Naval technology had not advanced a great deal since the days of the Romans or Greeks, though the use of cloth to catch the wind was in place. While the Vikings appeared during the times of Charlemagne, utilizing small, quick man powered boats to pillage and plunder the seas.

He built a fleet, too, for the war against the Northmen, constructing ships for this purpose near those rivers which flow out of Gaul and Germany into the northern ocean. And because the Northmen laid waste the coasts of Gaul and Germany by their constant attacks he planted forts and garrisons in all harbours and at the mouths of all navigable rivers, and prevented in this way the passage of the enemy. He took the same measures in the South, on the shore of Narbonne and Septimania, and also along all the coasts of Italy as far as Rome, to hold in check the Moors, who had lately begun to make piratical excursions. And by reason of these precautions Italy suffered no serious harm from the Moors, nor Gaul and Germany from the Northmen, in the days of Charles; except that Centumcellæ, a city of Etruria, was betrayed into the hands of the Moors and plundered, and in Frisia certain islands lying close to Germany were ravaged by the Northmen.[27]

The greatest thing Charlemagne could do for his army was the efficient use of the supply chain and a keen sense of logistics. With his armies spread out, usually far from home, Charlemagne remained focused and vigilant on keeping his armies rested and fed. The use of supply chains allowed his men and his horses to stay well fed in shape, not having to worry with hunger pains or weakness. However, supply chains became the target of Charlemagne's opposition. By eliminating the supply of food and other resources, the army would become weak and the morale would sink. But, by not allowing for large campaigns, drawn out campaigns, the fall of a supply

---

[27] Einhard 31

line was never a deathblow. Because the armies would only wage wars in the summer, typically, they would only have to have six months of rations. Thus, the supply chain was effective, and if it were to break down, death was not inevitable.[28]

These, then, are the wars which this mighty King waged during the course of forty-seven years—for his reign extended over that period—in different parts of the world with the utmost skill and success. By these wars he so nobly increased the kingdom of the Franks, which was great and strong when he inherited it from his father Pippin, that the additions he made almost doubled it. For before his time the power of the Frankish kingdom extended only over that part of Gaul which is bounded by the Rhine, the Loire, and the Balearic Sea; and that part of Germany which is inhabited by the so-called eastern Franks, and which is bounded by Saxony, the Danube, the Rhine, and the river Saal, which stream separates the Thuringians and the Sorabs; and, further, over the Alamanni and the Bavarians. But Charles, by the wars that have been mentioned, conquered and made tributary the following countries:—First, Aquitania and Gascony, and the whole Pyrenean range, and the country of Spain as far as the Ebro, which, rising in Navarre and passing through the most fertile territory of Spain, falls into the Balearic Sea, beneath the walls of the city of Tortosa; next, all Italy from Augusta Prætoria as far as lower Calabria, where are the frontiers of the Greeks and Beneventans, a thousand miles and more in length; next, Saxony, which is a considerable portion of Germany, and is reckoned to be twice as broad and about as long as that part of Germany which is inhabited by the Franks; then both provinces of Pannonia and Dacia, on one

[28] Hooper, Nicholas / Bennett, Matthew. *The Cambridge illustrated atlas of warfare: the Middle Ages* Cambridge University Press, 1996

side of the river Danube, and Histria and Liburnia and Dalmatia, with the exception of the maritime cities which he left to the Emperor of Constantinople on account of their friendship and the treaty made between them; lastly, all the barbarous and fierce nations lying between the Rhine, the Vistula, the Ocean, and the Danube, who speak much the same language, but in character and dress are very unlike. The chief of these last are the Welatabi, the Sorabi, the Abodriti, and the Bohemians; against these he waged war, but the others, and by far the larger number, surrendered without a struggle.[29]

The army was led, when Charlemagne was not present, by various nobles and other land holders, whether counts, dukes, or lords. These men were held to a very high standard, flexing the power and will of the king while making sure to conform to his standards. These men were trained and served alongside Charlemagne, being summoned at his command to lead them into battle. He required his nobles to be brave, though not foolish or reckless, informing that they lead their armies for the good of his majesty.

When he found that the nobles of his army were accustomed in secret to speak contemptuously of him, he ordered one day a huge and ferocious bull to be brought out; and then a savage lion to be let loose upon him. The lion rushed with tremendous fury on the bull, seized him by the neck and cast him on the ground. Then the king said to those who stood round him: "Now, drag off the lion from the bull, or kill the one on the top of the other." They looked on one another, with a chill at their hearts, and could hardly utter these words amidst their sobs:—"Lord, what man is there under heaven, who dare attempt it?" Then Pippin rose confidently from his

---

[29] Einhard 15

throne, drew his sword, and at one blow cut through the neck of the lion and severed the head of the bull from his shoulders. Then he put back his sword into its sheath and sat again upon his throne and said: "Well, do you think I am fit to be your lord? Have you not heard what the little David did to the giant Goliath, or what the child Alexander did to his nobles?" They fell to the ground, as though a thunderbolt had struck them, and cried: "Who but a madman would deny your right to rule over all mankind?"[30]

Charlemagne's campaigns were effective, taking over a great portion of Europe systematically and eventually, creating the second Roman Empire. His wars in Saxony, however, have defined him as ruthless, aggressive, but incredibly efficient.

---

[30] Monk of St.Gall

Chapter 6
The Conquest, Rise, and
Massacres in Saxony

Wars in Saxony became a commonplace during the reign of Charlemagne. For more than thirty years, spanning from 772 to 804, Charlemagne was forced to wage a constant war with the villagers and tribesmen of the area.

When this war was ended the Saxon war, which seemed dropped for a time, was taken up again. Never was there a war more prolonged nor more cruel than this, nor one that required greater efforts on the part of the Frankish peoples. For the Saxons, like most of the races that inhabit Germany, are by nature fierce, devoted to the worship of demons and hostile to our religion, and they think it no dishonour to confound and transgress the laws of God and man. There were reasons, too, which might at any time cause a disturbance of the peace. For our boundaries and theirs touch almost everywhere on the open plain, except where in a few places large forests or ranges of mountains are interposed to separate the territories of the two nations by a definite frontier; so that on both sides murder, robbery, and arson were of constant occurrence. The Franks were so irritated by these things that they thought it was time no longer to be satisfied with retaliation but to declare open war against them.

So war was declared, and was fought for thirty years continuously with the greatest fierceness on both sides, but with heavier loss to the Saxons than the Franks. The end might have been reached sooner had it not been for the perfidy of the Saxons. It is hard to say how often they admitted themselves beaten and surrendered as suppliants to King Charles; how often they promised to obey his orders, gave without delay the required hostages, and received the ambassadors that were sent to them. Sometimes they were so cowed and broken that they promised to abandon the worship of devils and willingly to submit themselves to the Christian religion. But though sometimes ready to bow to his commands they were always eager to break their promise, so that it is impossible to say which course seemed to come more natural to them, for from the beginning of the war there was scarcely a year in which they did not both promise and fail to perform.

But the high courage of the King and the constancy of his mind, which remained unshaken by prosperity and adversity, could not be conquered by their changes nor forced by weariness to desist from his undertakings. He never allowed those who offended in this way to go unpunished, but either led an army himself, or sent one under the command of his counts, to chastise their perfidy and inflict a suitable penalty. So that at last, when all who had resisted had been defeated and brought under his power, he took ten thousand of the inhabitants of both banks of the Elbe, with their wives and children, and planted them in many groups in various parts of Germany and Gaul. And at last the war, protracted through so many years, was finished on conditions proposed by the King and accepted by them; they were to abandon the worship of devils, to turn from their national ceremonies, to receive the sacraments of the Christian faith and religion, and then, joined to the Franks, to make one people with them.

In this war, despite its prolongation through so many years, he did not himself meet the enemy in battle more than twice— once near the mountain called Osning, in the district of Detmold, and again at the river Hasa—and both these battles *were fought in one month, with an interval of only a few days. In these two battles the enemy were so beaten and cowed that they never again ventured to challenge the King nor to resist his attack unless they were protected by some advantage of ground.*[31]

Saxony, currently located in modern Germany, was comprised of four distinct regions. The closest to the Franks was Westphalia, a region centered between the Rhine and Weser rivers. Considered to be the region most associated with the Saxon wars, the leader of the revolts, Widukind, hailed from there. To the east of Westphalia was Angria, located above the Rhine River and along the Weser River. To its east was Eastphalia, the furthest kingdom east in all of Saxony. It bordered the River Leine in the west, neighboring it with Angria, and the Elbe and Salle to its east. Finally, the fourth administrative region for Saxony was Nordalbingia, north of Eastphalia and bordering the Elbe River.

As a civilization, the Saxons are regarded as one of the founding tribes to settle Britain. According to Greek philosopher Ptolemy, in his work, *Geographia*, written in the second century CE, mentions the origins of the Saxons to be from the area around the Elbe River, linking their origin to Europe.[32] However, in the Ecclesiastical History of the English People, Bede notes that their ancestors, the Saxons, hailed from an area near the Rhine River.[33] The Saxons were definitively mentioned in Roman annals, where in 365 CE, the Roman Emperor Julian linked them to a rival emperor in Gaul. With attacks by land and sea, the Romans were forced to

---

[31] Monk of St. Gall
[32] Ptolemy, Geographia
[33] Bede, Ecclesiastical History of the English People

fortify both sides of the English Channel to defend against their ongoing raids.

The Saxon Wars began in January, 772 CE when a Saxon regiment razed a church at Deventer, a small city in France. With their pagan roots, the Saxons burnt down the Christian church and defiled Charlemagne's religion. Reacting quickly, Charlemagne organized his army marched into Saxon territory a few months later. He immediately subjugated the citizens upon his invasion Charlemagne marched on Saxony for religious revenge, enacting this by destroying a pagan idol, the Irminsul, at Eresburt in 773 CE. This idol, a common theme in Germanic paganism, symbols the connection between the land and the sky and was looked upon as the primary source of religion. Thus, Charlemagne actively attacked the pagan religion while invading Saxony.[34]

His initial campaign leveled several Saxon cities and fortresses and went as far east as the Weser River. During the march, he took several hostages to gain a foothold in future negotiations. Shortly upon reaching the river, several nobles approached Charlemagne under a flag of truce. After quick negotiations, Charlemagne agreed to return the hostages and return to France, not asking for more concessions as a war with the Lombards had just begun in Northern Italy.

The war was not over though, as Charlemagne lead a second campaign against into Saxony in 775. Shortly after leaving Saxony to tend to the wars with the Lombards, a peasant from Westphalia, Widukind, lead an army of Saxons to pillage Frankish lands along the Rhine. Conflicts continued as Charlemagne was away, with Widukind leading his troops into constant battles with the local Frankish nobility. Once

---

[34] Royal Frankish Annals

Charlemagne reentered Westphalia, he conquered the fort of Sigburg, weakening the Saxon grip on the area. He went all the way through to Eastphalia, deposing the leader, Hessi, and forcing his conversion to Christianity. Upon his return to France, he marched through Engria, leaving encampments of soldiers in Sigburg and Eresburg. With his second campaign, Charlemagne effectively controlled all of Saxony, with the exception of Nordalbingia. The armed confrontations stopped briefly, though Saxony would rise again a year later. In 776, rebels, still under the command of Widukind, destroyed his fortress at Eresburg, killing several soldiers and razing the structure. After rushing to Saxony from Lombardy, Charlemagne's forces quelled the rebellion, forcing Widukind to flee to Denmak. Noticing the trouble and turmoil brewing, Charlemagne opted to call a diet, a meeting to discuss bringing Saxony into the kingdom of the Franks. In 777 CE, this union happened. Several Saxons were baptized, denouncing their pagan beliefs while Saxony was brought into the kingdom of Charlemagne. The purpose of the diet was more for the spread of Christianity than for the claiming of territory. With the Saxons still immensely Pagan, Charlemagne opted to recruit several Anglo-Saxon missionaries from England to assist in the conversion. He issued several decrees, all designed to weaken any Saxon resistance and punish any acts of heresy with death. His harsh treatment of the Saxons earned him the moniker, "butcher of Saxons."

The war was not over though, as Charlemagne led the assaults against the Pagan resistance, refusing to convert to Christianity and staying true to their heritage. Alcuin, one of Charlemagne's advisors and friends, urged the king to stop spreading Christianity by violence, instead leaning on peaceful persuasion. However, he did not take this position. In 779 CE, Charlemagne marched his armies across Westphalia, Engria, and Eastphalia again, quelling rebellions and conquering the Pagans. In 780 CE, following the conclusion of his march, Charlemagne called the diet of Lippspringe, dividing the three regions into Frankish counties and missionary locales. With Saxony firmly in his grasps, he turned his attention to Lombardy, leaving Saxony for three years.

The second Saxon war began in 782 CE as Widukind returned from Denmark with a large army and attacked several missionaries, convents, and churches. The laws of the time were strict on Paganism, allowing Widukind the ability to amass a large army under the strict confines of the Charlemagne's government. A renewal of the tension and war emerged, reminding the suppressed people of what they had before Charlemagne. With Charlemagne away elsewhere campaigning, Widukind lead an army against the Franks at Suntel. Without much organization, the Franks were defeated handily, though retribution would be swift and harsh from Charlemagne.

When the king heard of this disaster he decided not to delay, but made haste to gather an army, and marched into Saxony. There he called to his presence the chiefs of the Saxons, and inquired who had induced the people to rebel. They all declared that Widukind was the author of the treason, but said that they could not produce him because after the deed was done he had fled to the Northmen.

But the others who had carried out his will and committed the crime they delivered up to the king to the number of four thousand and five hundred; and by the king's command they were all beheaded in one day upon the river Aller in the place called Verden. When he had wreaked vengeance after this fashion, the king withdrew to the town of Diedenhofen.[35]

In October of 782, Charlemagne, enraged from the Saxon uprising, quickly organized his troops and marched to Verden and slaughtered all those responsible for the defeat of his army, with the exception of Widukind, who again fled to Denmark. War raged on for three more years, as Charlemagne led his army across the region, quelling rebellions and squashing any pagan resistance he came across. Finally, in 785 CE, the leader of the rebellions, Widukind surrendered at Bardengau, swore fealty to Charlemagne and was baptized into Christianity with Charlemagne as his Godfather.

The third and last phase of the war started in 792 CE after seven years of peace. The Westphalias, located closest to the Franks, rebelled against Charlemagne for their forced recruitment into service of the army. With the other regions slowly joining, the final phase didn't have the power of the first two. The missionaries and priests had done an excellent job with controlling the area and suppressing paganism. Many of the citizens in the area did not want to go back to war with Charlemagne as they now shared a common religion with him. Another rebellion occurred in 796 in Engria, though it was also quickly quelled and did not amount to anything. Though they rise up one last time in 804 CE, the wars in Saxony were waning to a conclusion, thirty years after they had started.

After the insurrection in Engria in 796 CE, Charlemagne knew that he would have to change his approach in handling the Saxons or war would continue. In 797, Charlemagne relaxed the special laws designed to persecute the pagans. Though still encouraging their conversion, capital

---

[35] Einhard 57

punishment was no longer required for someone actively practicing. He would go a step further in 802, codifying the Saxon law and established ecclesiastic structures that were created with the sole purpose of securing the conversion of the Saxon people.

The entire conflict over the span of thirty-two years was based on religion. Charlemagne's devotion to Christianity led his rage and desire to conquer the pagans in Saxony and bring them under the guidance of Rome. Recruiting priests from England, men who shared a common ancestry with the Saxons, helped ease the process and brought some familiarity to the conquered people. While incredibly bloody, this war shows how tenacious Charlemagne was. His drive to spread Christianity was unmatched by anyone and his ability to quickly move from one battlefield to another shows how flexible of a commander he was. The results of the conflict were absolute though. The people of Saxony were now united under Frankish rule and all of its citizens must convert to Christianity and accept its sacraments, denouncing any of their previous tribal paganism and customs.

Chapter 7
The Wars with Lombardy

Charlemagne's conquests with the Saxons and Lombards intertwined through the years prior to 800 CE. Though his wars with the Lombards are not regarded for their bloodshed or massacres, they did, however, plant the seeds for his future ascension the emperor of the West. Regarded as one of his most decisive campaigns, the conquest of Lombardy is one of the few times that Charlemagne assumed the crown after taking over the kingdom and forced the nobility to pay homage to him.

When the Aquitanian trouble was settled and the war finished, when, too, his partner in the kingdom had withdrawn from the world's affairs, he undertook a war against the Lombards, being moved thereto by the entreaties and the prayers of Hadrian, Bishop of the City of Rome. Now, this war, too, had been undertaken by his father at the supplication of Pope Stephen, under circumstances of great difficulty, inasmuch as certain of the chiefs of the Franks, whose advice he was accustomed to ask, so strongly resisted his wishes that they openly declared that they would leave their King to return home. But now Charles undertook the war against King Haistulf, and most swiftly brought it to an end. For, though his reasons for undertaking the war were similar to, and, indeed, the same as those of his father, he plainly fought it out with a very different energy, and brought it to a different end. For Pippin, after a siege of a few days at Pavia, forced King Haistulf to give hostages, and restore to the Romans the towns and fortresses that he had taken from them, and to give a solemn promise that he would not attempt to regain what he had surrendered. But King

Charles, when once he had begun the war, did not stop until he had received the surrender of King Desiderius, whom he had worn down after a long siege; until he had forced his son Adalgis, in whom the hopes of his people seemed to be centred, to fly not only from his kingdom but from Italy; until he had restored to the Romans all that had been taken from them; until he had crushed Hruodgausus, Præfect of the Duchy of Friuli, who was attempting a revolution; until, in fine, he had brought all Italy under his rule, and placed his son Pippin as king over the conquered country. I should describe here the difficulties of the passage of the Alps and the vast toil with which the Franks found their way through the pathless mountain ridges, the rocks that soared to heaven, and the sharply-pointed cliffs, if it were not that my purpose in the present work is rather to describe Charles's manner of life than to chronicle the events of the wars that he waged. The sum of this war was the conquest of Italy, the transportation and perpetual exile of King Desiderius, the expulsion of his son Adalgis from Italy, power taken from the kings of the Lombards and restored to Hadrian, the Ruler of the Roman Church.[36]

Issues with the Lombards existed prior to the coronation of Charlemagne. His father, Pepin the Short, declared war on the Lombards for their invasion of the duchy of Rome and their acquisition of the Exarchate of Ravenna from a prolonged war with the Byzantines. The exarchate was the farthest territory west under the control of the Byzantine Empire and surrounded Rome, the seat of the west. Through constant battle, in 751 CE, King Aistulf of the Lombards conquered the Exarchate and surrounded Rome. At the behest of Pope Stephen II, Pepin the Short marched his French army into the Ravenna and usurped Aistulf, conquering the lands

---

[36] Einhard 14-16

and removing the Lombards in 756 CE. Following the conquest, in a gracious move to gain favor with the papacy, Pepin donated the lands conquered from Lombards to the papacy, effectively creating the Papal States, the first building block of the Holy Roman Empire that would be formed in two hundred years.

In 772 CE, King Desiderius of the Lombards invaded the Papal States, insisting on conquering the lands his father lost in 756 CE. Under duress, Pope Adrian I contacted Charlemagne for assistance in removing the foreign threat from his borders. In 756 CE, the papacy became terrestrial leaders, as well as spiritual ones, but without much of a standing army, the Papal States were ripe for the picking. Immediately assaulting and overtaking the Pentapolis, Desiderius had his sights set on Rome, posing an imminent and dangerous threat to Pope Adrian I. Though originally acting as an arbitrator between the two parties, meeting with them at Thionville, Charlemagne ruled in favor of the pope and ordered Desiderius withdraw from the papal territory given to the papacy by his father, Pepin. Scoffing at his demands, Desiderius did not comply and Charlemagne was forced into war to defend the papacy.

Historically, when scholars have studied Charlemagne, they always discuss how he was a devout champion of Christianity, especially Catholicism. With this in mind, scholars are able to see the passion and devotion he put into this campaign, defending the papacy as only he felt he could. Charlemagne defended his religion and those who chose to assault it, attacking the lands that belonged to the Pope. It also worth mentioning that King Desiderius did not have a pleasant relationship with Charlemagne. As mentioned earlier, Desiderius's daughter married Charlemagne prior to this war at the urging of his mother and to create an ally with someone who neighbored his brother's kingdom. However, after divorcing her after just under a year of marriage proved to be the death knell in their relationship, making it impossible for them to come to terms peacefully.

In 773, Charlemagne invaded Lombardy, crossing the Alps and pushing back the Lombards with relative ease. With the assistance of his uncle, Bernard, the army evaded a Lombard fortification and out flanked their enemy, crushing them and forcing them to flee the heavily fortified city of Pavia, just south of Milan in Northern Italy. The army Charlemagne brought was vastly large, able to surround the entire city and siege it from all sides. As the city was besieged, Charlemagne traveled to Rome to seek an audience with the pope in 774. Once there, he acknowledged the papal claims of the dominion over those lands, while also granting him the rights to several other pieces of land around the former Exarchate of Ravenna: Tuscany, Emila, Venice, and Corsica. This move granted him extreme favor with the pope as he granted the title of patrician to Charlemagne.

The siege lasted until June when the Lombards finally surrendered. In exchange for their lives, Desiderius and his heirs were deposed and exiled from Lombardy, being sent to live in various abbeys or in Constantinople. The line of the Lombard kings ended at the Siege of Pavia. With their vicious and unfriendly history, as well as their direct attack on the church through the invasion of their lands, Charlemagne did not show mercy. While he allowed them to live, the former Lombard leaders were forced to acknowledge Charlemagne as the new King of Lombardy, watching as he took the Iron Crown from Desiderius and anointing himself the new ruler of the territory. The nobles and magnates in Pavia were forced to kneel before him, paying homage to him as their new leader.

The conquest of Lombardy was a staple of Charlemagne's reign. While not his most lavish or famous, it is still one of the lynch pins that holds his story together. Without the conquest of Lombardy and the defense of the Papal States, Charlemagne would not have been able to continue his expansion of his empire. By defending the Papal States, and awarding them more territory, Charlemagne was able to secure papal favor in future expeditions, while also sowing the seeds for his ascension to emperor.

Chapter 8
The Recocnquista Begins

Charlemagne's faith was his most prized possession, hanging on the words of St. Augustine and other religious texts while storming various battlefields and creating an Empire for him to be proud of and leave for his children. An area that would prove to be pivotal to his reign was the region south of France, toward Basque areas and into the Pyrenees Mountains, crossing over into the Iberian Peninsula. The issues that stemmed from Charlemagne's problems with the Moors came about over nearly a century of division. Though stopped by Charles Martel at the Battle of Tours, the Moors were still an aggressive military and political entity into the days of Charlemagne. Simply put the fact that Charles Martel was able to stop them, combined with the systematic destruction of the Umayyad Caliphate in Damascus, crippled their internal infrastructure and government. While the Umayyad Caliphate and its leaders created Al-Andulus from the Roman remnants on the Iberian Peninsula, their demise back in Syria changed the way that the region operated, making it more difficult to maintain peace throughout the region.

However, even after the Battle of Tours and the Islamic pushback, the Moors were still marauding through Septimania and Aquitaine. Their ability to continue their assault on the French land, even after they were badly defeated, was because of the port of Narbonne. In 751 CE, Pepin the Short, who already amassed a very powerful empire and crowned himself King of the Franks, formed an alliance with the Abbasid Caliphate, the new regime which emerged after the fall of the Umayyads. Emissaries were sent to Baghdad, the seat of the

Abbasid Caliphate and trade relations commenced, with Arab gold becoming a very heavily sought after commodity in the western world. The Abbasid Caliphate did not have control over the remnants of the Umayyad Caliphate's territories on the Iberian Peninsula, making it practical for Pepin the Short to continue his assault on the remnants of the Moor's stronghold near the Mediteranean Sea. With this, Pepin continued to his war with Al-Andulus and the Emirate of Cordoba. With the conquering of Narbonne in 759 CE, Pepin expelled the Islamic threat and pushed it back over the Pyrenees Mountains where he could focus his attention on Aquitaine.

Whilst the war with the Saxons was being prosecuted constantly and almost continuously he placed garrisons at suitable places on the frontier, and attacked Spain with the largest military expedition that he could collect. He crossed the Pyrenees, received the surrender of all the towns and fortresses that he attacked, and returned with his army safe and sound, except for a reverse which he experienced through the treason of the Gascons on his return through the passes of the Pyrenees. For while his army was marching in a long line, suiting their formation to the character of the ground and the defiles, the Gascons placed an ambuscade on the top of the mountain—where the density and extent of the woods in the neighbourhood rendered it highly suitable for such a purpose—and then rushing down into the valley beneath threw into disorder the last part of the baggage train and also the rearguard which acted as a protection to those in advance. In the battle which followed the Gascons slew their opponents to the last man. Then they seized upon the baggage, and under cover of the night, which was already falling, they scattered with the utmost rapidity in different directions. The Gascons were assisted in this feat by the lightness of their armour and the character of the ground where the affair took place. In this battle Eggihard, the surveyor of the royal table; Anselm, the Count of the Palace; and Roland, Præfect of the Breton frontier, were killed along with very many others. Nor could this assault be punished at once, for when the deed had been done the enemy so completely disappeared that they left behind them not so much as a rumour of their whereabouts. [37]

Charlemagne's wars in Spain are what many historians credit to the beginning of his incredible portfolio of achievements and accomplishments, whether diplomatically or militarily. The overall significance of his campaign, though incredibly bloody with many pitfalls and short comings, is crucial to Spain gaining their independence in 1492. With his eventual victory, led by his son, Louis the Pious, Charlemagne created a definitive wall of resistance that the Moors could not break. Though crowned King of Aquitaine at the age of 3, Louis would grow to become a successful ruler and would be the primary reason the Moors would never go further than Bordeaux again.

With the Moors pushed back, Charlemagne knew that they would not stay away for long and that he would need to be proactive in his defense to keep them at bay. Similar to what the Moors did in making Narbonne their base of operations for their continued assault on the French mainland, Charlemagne made Toulouse his. After his first incident as king, subduing the Aquitaine rebellion without the assistance of his brother, Charlemagne reorganized the kingdom, appointing several counts and lords who were all loyal to him to keep a rebellion from emerging. Also, with the church firmly at his side, the people of Aquitaine were loyal to his cause. The stability in this

---

[37] Einhard 20-22

region would allow Charlemagne to focus on things not pertaining to whether this portion of his kingdom would rebel again. By creating an infrastructure filled with people loyal to him and the church, it made it prudent for him to denote Toulouse as his primary defense against the Moors.

Fortunately for Charlemagne, the area of Northern Spain was in a state of civil war. The areas of Barcelona, Girona, Huesca, and Zaragoza were known enemies of the Emirate leader, Abdul al Rahman. While at the Diet of Paderborn in Saxony, Charlemagne received envoys from Spain alerting him of the constant state of civil war and the request for aide, which he granted in exchange for their sworn allegiance. Sulayman al-Arabi, the governor of Barcelona and Girona, personally guaranteed the surrender of his two states, as well as Zaragoza and Huesca, claiming the leaders already agreed to the terms under the threat of the Umayyad advancement. Charlemagne was gifted an opportunity to further push the Muslims out of Europe, serving two of incredibly important things to him. The first, it was a war against a different religion, one being fought since the emergence of Islam and the aggressive expansion that followed. The second, it secured his borders even further. Charlemagne was aware of the battles his father, Pepin, fought in the southern parts of France, as well as the stories of his grandfather at Tours. For Charlemagne to put more distance between France and the Moors would be an incredible coup. In 778 CE, Charlemagne marched his armies across the Pyrenees into Muslim Spain.

Unfortunately, the king of the Franks was given false information while at Paderborn regarding the autonomous Spanish kingdoms. Charlemagne reached Zaragoza and was greeted as a king. However, Husayn, the leader of Zaragoza, denied sending an emissary to request aid from Charlemagne or agree to surrender his city to him, even though Sulayman spoke on his behalf. A few months prior to this, Husayn defeated the Moors, ensuring that they could hold on to their autonomous state and not have to surrender to the Moors and the remnants of the Umayyad Caliphate. Enraged, Charlemagne attacked Zaragoza, laying siege upon the city for over a month. Husayn defended the city admirably, forcing Charlemagne to give up and return back to France, imprisoning Sulayman for his perceived lies and taking several hostages. In negotiations, Husayn agreed to give Charlemagne a vast sum of gold in exchange for many of the prisoners he took, though Sulayman was not one of the men he bartered for. On his march out, Charlemagne attacked and conquered the city of Pamplona, tearing down the walls and pillaging the city before continuing his march back to France. However, in retaliation for his attack of Pamplona, a large Muslim army ambushed Charlemagne's rear guard, leading to the Battle of Roncevaux Pass.

The Battle of Ronceaux Pass was a very deadly battle and one of the biggest defeats ever for Charlemagne. Led by the children of Sulayman, who had allied with the Muslims upon learning of Charlemagne capturing their father, the Battle of Roncevaux Pass proved to be pivotal in the overall campaign against the Moors.

Having decided to return, [Charlemagne] entered the mountains of the Pyrenees, in whose summits the <u>Vascones</u> *had set up an ambush. They attacked the rearguard, causing confusion which spread to all the army. And, while the Franks were superior to the Vascones both in armament and in courage, the roughness of the terrain and the difference in the style of combat made them generally weaker. In this battle were killed the majority of the paladins that the King had placed in command of his forces. The baggage was sacked, and suddenly the enemy vanished, thanks to their knowledge of the terrain. The memory of the injury so produced overshadowed in the King's heart that of the feats done in Hispania.*[38]

The Vascones had an incredible advantage in this encounter, stemming from their knowledge of the terrain, placement of their soldiers, and the element of surprise. Their soldiers fought primarily in a guerilla like manner, attacking quickly before retreating and then attacking again, only attacking when their opponent was pinned back and at an incredible disadvantage. These warriors were armed with short spears, daggers, and javelins to toss at their enemies from range. Many of these warriors were peasants, motivated by greed and theft to amass incredible riches at the cost of a foreign leader. However, national pride also motivated these men, as Charlemagne tore down the walls of their capital in Pamplona.

The leader of the region, Lupo II of Gascony, did not have a great relationship with Charlemagne. Though swearing fealty and paying homage to the French leader, Lupo possessed a key dispute with him over the territory. With the attack taking place in his territory, and with his trade allegiance to the Basques, there is motivation for Lupo to have sanctioned the surprise attack on Charlemagne and his army, though this is only speculation and never proven.

On 15 August 778 CE, Charlemange's army was attacked as they marched home through the Pyrenees Mountains. Though at the front, Charlemagne was able to escape, the rear guard and baggage train did not escape. The Basque soldiers cut off and isolated this train, slaughtering all

---

[38] Royal Frankish Annals

of the soldiers and plundering the goods. While he tried to get his soldiers to regroup and fight back against the attackers, it was to no avail. Their superior position, combined with their knowledge of the terrain made it incredibly difficult for Charlemagne and his army to counter. The losses were incredible. One of the losses was a man named Roland, one of Charlemagne's chief allies in handling affairs. He helped conquer the Bretons a few years before his death and unified many parts of France before heading to Zaragoza with Charlemagne. His death was cherished by the people of France, turning it into one of the oldest epic poems in the world, The Song of Roland. In this, Roland is leading the rear guard of Charlemagne and holds out for as long as possible so that his king can escape with his life. Prior to his death, he blew a magnificent horn, bursting his temples with the pressure he emitted, killing him shortly thereafter. His pride was sung about for years, until in 1098, it was compiled and kept for generations.

However, Charlemange's assaults on the Moors were not finished. Under the direction of his son, Louis, the Carolingians continued their wars in Northern Spain. Many of the leaders in Northern Spain did not side with the Moors, opting instead of rebel and enlist the aid of the French where possible. Once several campaigns and conquests of the smaller areas were done, as well as several allies in other areas of the Basque country, Charlemagne was able to create the buffer zone he required. This zone was referred to as the Marca Hispania and it served as a separation between his two regions. As a leader, Charlemagne would never return to Spain, only sending his generals and other leaders, including his son, to handle the affairs of the state. This area would consist of the Duchies of Aquitaine and Gascony, as well as Septimania. These areas would serve as the buffer protecting the heart of Carolingian France and the remnants of the Umayyad Caliphate, keeping them at bay so that the two regions could prosper separately. Also, to ensure the safety of any French army traveling through the region, Charlemagne realigned the territory on the southern border of the mountains, creating the kingdoms of Catalonia, Pamplona, and Aragon. Catalonia was incredibly important, as it also secured the sea side border when marching through.

In 797 CE, the greatest domino in Spain fell for Charlemagne. The greatest city in the region, Barcelona, fell to the marauding French. Their governor, Zeid, rejected the Moors and handed the city over to the French, surrendering it without a battle. This would not last; however, as the Umayyad army recaptured the city two years later, ending the rebellion and deposing of Zeid. With a foothold already in the area, Louis of Aquitaine, Charlemagne's son, marched his entire army over the Pyrenees and laid siege upon the city for two years. Once overtaken, Louis continued to march his army toward the Ebro River, eventually gaining access to Valencia, an immensely important port in the Mediterranean. In 813 CE, the Emir al-Hakam I was forced to recognize the conquests of the French and relinquish any claims to the territories. Though bloody, ferocious, and staggering, the wars with the Spanish were over.

Many historians look back at this long, drawn out campaign and point to it as the first start of the Reconquista, the event where Spain would eventually gain its independence from the Moors and establish themselves as a country. With the Moors not forcing the Christians in the area to convert, allowing them to practice their religion in peace, though in private, and to pay a much larger tax than the Muslims, Christianity was still able to survive in Spain. Though it did not thrive, and in many pockets it did die out as several rulers converted to Islam, several Christian sects survived. Had they forced the conversion, much like how Charlemagne did with the pagans in Saxony, the Reconquista could have ended differently and been a much tougher endeavor. Also, by the Umayyad Caliphate failing in capturing all of Northern Spain, losing battles and allowing them to keep their autonomy, they essentially could never fully control the area. That's not to say that the Moors did not have authority, but without their leadership in place, the threat of rebellion against them was always there. Having positive relationships with the Moors, for the sake of trade and diplomacy, was crucial for the autonomous kingdoms in Northern Spain. The Moors army was incredibly large, and while many of them were able to stand their ground and withstand various sieges, they could not compete with them in an open war. By aligning themselves, eventually, with the French, they were able to keep their autonomy while being subjected by the French. These two factors are the reasons that the Reconquista happened. Without nations that were free from the rule of the Moors and citizens under the rule of the Moors being allowed to practice Christianity, reestablishing Christianity as a dominant religion after the expulsion of the Moors was possible.

Chapter 9
Bavaria and the Slavic States

Another area of concern for Charlemagne was the region of Bavaria. Though not regarded as one of his greater campaigns, taking control and subjecting Bavaria proved to be important from a regional stand point, as they were the key component in the next war Charlemagne would need to fight. The key sticking point in this conflict, however, was that the ruler of Bavaria was married to the daughter of the former king of Lombardy, Desiderius. Thus, tension was already there, still brimming with malice after the treatment of her father.

A fearful foe resided on the other side of the Bavaria, one who has already assaulted and pillaged their way through the Roman Empire before and wreaked havoc on Byzantine. The Huns, or Avars, were nestled on the opposite side of Bavaria and Charlemagne knew that eventually, if he wanted to expand his reach, he would have to battle and conquer them. However, to get there, he needed Bavaria to establish the foothold that would allow him access to the area. In the past, Bavarian dukes were granted autonomy from the Merovingian rulers, allowing them to rule and lead their people as they saw fit. This autonomy was the reason Charlemagne needed to quell them, stripping them of it before attacking.

Then the Bavarian war broke out suddenly, and was swiftly ended. It was caused by the pride and folly of Tassilo, Duke of Bavaria; for upon the instigation of his wife, who thought that she might revenge through her husband the banishment of her father Desiderius, King of the Lombards, he made an alliance with the Huns, the eastern neighbours of the

Bavarians, and not only refused obedience to King Charles but even dared to challenge him in war. The high courage of the King could not bear his overweening insolence, and he forthwith called a general levy for an attack on Bavaria, and came in person with a great army to the river Lech, which separates Bavaria from Germany. He pitched his camp upon the banks of the river, and determined to make trial of the mind of the Duke before he entered the province. But Duke Tassilo saw no profit either for himself or his people in stubbornness, and threw himself upon the King's mercy. He gave the hostages who were demanded, his own son Theodo among the number, and further promised upon oath that no one should ever persuade him again to fall away from his allegiance to the King. And thus a war which seemed likely to grow into a very great one came to a most swift ending. But Tassilo was subsequently summoned into the King's presence, and was not allowed to return, and the province that he ruled was for the future committed to the administration not of dukes but of counts.[39]

Charlemagne marched his troops into Bavaria to attack the territories under Duke Tassilo III, who had aligned himself with the Lombards. In 788, Charlemagne prepared for what could have been the longest war in his career as the leader of the Franks, thinking that it would last for years, just like the wars with the Saxons had. However, this was not the case. The war was incredibly brief and Bavaria submitted to Charlemagne, allowing him to focus his attention on the threat to the east. In 794, Duke Tassilo III renounced his claims to any land or power in Bavaria, essentially stripping him of power

---

[39] Einhard 11

While this war was brief, it served a purpose. Every conquest, whether small or large, was a part of a great plan set forth by Charlemagne. His vision of Europe involved driving out the Huns, subjugating them into the realm and removing any hint of problems or rebellions. Charlemagne, ultimately, wanted a peaceful realm. However, he knew he would have to conquer his enemies in order to achieve it. As Europe changed following the fall of the Western Roman Empire, Charlemagne arose to reunite it, conquering the smaller territories to fit them into a large body, all with a much larger purpose. All while fighting these battles in Bavaria and preparing to fight the Huns, he was still having to battle with Saxons and the Spanish. For Charlemagne to create a peaceful border, he knew that he would have to fight on all fronts to achieve it. Using armies from his conquered realms, he was able to have a great number of soldiers at his disposal, though not having to march them all in one massive army. He could have armies in Spain and armies in Saxony because of his organization and conquests. With the feudal systems in place and by appointing lords and vassals loyal to him in the conquered territories, Charlemagne's people supply was impressive.

When these troubles had been settled he waged war against the Slavs, whom we are accustomed to call Wilzi, but who properly—that is, in their own tongue—are called Welatabi. Here the Saxons fought along with the other allied nations who followed the King's standards, though their loyalty was feigned and far from sincere. The cause of the war was that the Wilzi were constantly invading and attacking the Abodriti, the former allies of the Franks, and refused to obey the King's commands to desist from their attacks. There is a gulf stretching from the western sea towards the East, of undiscovered length, but nowhere more than a hundred miles in breadth, and often much narrower. Many nations occupy the shores of this sea. The Danes and the Swedes, whom we call the Northmen, hold its northern shore and all the islands in it. The Slavs and the Aisti and various other nations inhabit the eastern shore, amongst whom the chief are these Welatabi against whom then the King waged war. He so broke and subdued them in a single campaign, conducted by himself, that they thought it no longer wise to refuse to obey his commands.[40]

Charlemagne also fought wars all over the Slavic states, essentially unifying the territory before launching his next full scale campaign. The first of his Slavic expeditions came in 789 CE, when, upon learning of their pagan influence upon the region and the constant raids, Charlemagne marched his army across the Elbe River and put the Wiltzes to the sword, taking several hostages before continuing his march toward the Baltic Sea. This was one of the quickest and most effective campaigns of Charlemagne's rule, as it concluded quickly and he was able to gain vast stretches of land without the exertion of much manpower. The Wiltzes fell quickly, agreeing to pay homage to Charlemagne and allow Christian missionaries into the region without the fear of death.

---

[40] Einhard 12

Chapter 10
The Invasion of the Huns

The Avar Khaganate was an incredible foe, proving to be difficult for Charlemagne, as well as the rest of the world. A group of Eurasian nomads, known as the Huns, traveled from parts of Mongolia and Asia in the early first century CE. These men would ravage, pillage, and plunder their way across areas as they traveled from town to town. They were nomadic, refusing to settle, and instead, following their sources of food and taking it from villages. During the fifth century, the Huns migrated to Europe. During this time, the Huns waged wars against the Roman Empire, battling their legions and holding their own, showing their superiority on the battlefield. Lead by one of the greatest barbarian kings in the history of the world, Attila, the Huns would repeatedly defeat the Romans and pillage the cities. In 450 CE, Attila would lead his army into Gaul, attacking several villages and bringing in several Goths, Franks, and Burgundians into his command. After a year of marching, he attacked Orleans, laying siege upon the city.

The Romans were forced to ask, sending one of their most prominent generals, Favlius Aetius, who at one time, had a personal allegiance with Attila, to subdue him and push him out of Roman territory. The Battle of the Catalaunian Plains took place in 451 and proved to be a costly defeat for Attila. According to Saint Sidonius Apollinaris, General Aetius was leading a group of soldiers consisting primarily of auxiliary troops without any career soldiers. However, he, along with the a Visigothic army lead by King Theodoric, defeated Attila and drove the Huns back out of Roman territory, where they eventually settled to the east of the Danube River. The Huns used mounted archers, though not completely effective without the use of a stirrup. They would pillage cities and only fight when they saw it advantageous. They would continue to marauder and pillage the land, but, their new homeland would eventually be referred to as the Avar Khaganate.

Using the rich, fertile soil around the Danube River, the Avars were able to sustain a civilization, though still holding onto the traditions of their past. They would pillage, plunder, and attack their neighbors, staying involved militarily and ravaging when they could. With their passion for warfare, they were able to subdue any of the threats around them, with the exception of the Byzantines to their south. Still holding a grudge after three centuries, the Avars were motivated to destroy anything Roman in the world. Wars would them would wage for hundreds of years, eventually leading the siege of Constantinople in 626 CE, which would ultimately prove to be their undoing.

With the assistance of the Persians, the Avars chose to deliver a crushing blow to the empire and bring Constantinople to its knees. On 29 June, 626 CE, eighty thousand Avar and Persian soldiers attacked Constantinople, firing on its walls in an attempt to tear them down. Under the defense of Patriarch Sergius and the patrician Bonus, the Byzantine soldiers behind the walls, mostly dismounted cavalry, were charged with defending the city. The Avars brought to the battlefield massive siege equipment, propelling fiery boulders and large pieces of stone at the thick walls of the city. However, with the Patriarch preaching how the Byzantines possessed divine favor, and how God will not let them fall at the hands of the heathens, the morale of the army remained high. Every attack proved futile. The Avar and Persian ships that attempted to bombard the city or ferry troops from one side of the sea to the other were sunk by the Byzantine navy. Every assault failed dramatically, breaking the will of the Avars and forcing their retreat. Their aggressive tendencies put them at a disadvantage and Constantinople was able to defend itself successfully. The Avars returned to the Khaganate to never go near Constantinople again, though still remaining aggressive in the rest of Europe.

The Khaganate changed over time. While still conquering areas around them, namely the Slavic areas around Bohemia, the Avars started to develop a culture away from warfare, breaking from their history as Huns. Farming became a part of their everyday lives, utilizing their geography along the Danube to create bountiful crops. The nomadic tendencies of their past was over and the new focus was on turning the Khanagate into a powerful, yet regional, civilization. Their powerful, militaristic culture fused with the Slavic cultures of the area, combining their languages and creating a unique, linguistic culture that is still around. The Avars became great at pottery, using a wheel to create beautiful clay sculptures and vessels. They would decorate them ornately, creating a beautiful motif of jewels and vibrant colors.

The greatest of all his wars, next to the Saxon war, followed this one—that, namely, which he undertook against the Huns and the Avars. He prosecuted this with more vigour than the rest and with a far greater military preparation. However, he conducted in person only one expedition into Pannonia, the province then occupied by the Avars; the management of the rest he left to his son Pippin, and the governors of the provinces, and in some cases to his counts and lieutenants. These carried on the war with the greatest energy, and finished it after eight years of fighting. How many battles were fought there and how much blood was shed is still shown by the deserted and uninhabited condition of Pannonia, and the district in which stood the palace of the

Kagan is so desolate that there is not so much as a trace of human habitation. All the nobles of the Huns were killed in this war, all their glory passed away; their money and all the treasures that they had collected for so long were carried away. Nor can the memory of man recall any war waged against the Franks by which they were so much enriched and their wealth so increased. Up to this time they were regarded almost as a poor people, but now so much gold and silver were found in the palace, such precious spoils were seized by them in their battles, that it might fairly be held that the Franks had righteously taken from the Huns what they unrighteously had taken from other nations. Only two of the nobles of the Franks were killed in this war. Eric, the Duke of Friuli, was caught in an ambuscade laid by the townsmen of Tharsatica, a maritime town of Liburnia. And Gerold, the Governor of Bavaria, when he was marshalling his army to fight with the Huns in Pannonia, was killed by an unknown hand, along with two others, who accompanied him as he rode along the line encouraging the soldiers by name. For the rest, the war was almost bloodless so far as the Franks were concerned, and most fortunate in its result although so difficult and protracted.[41]

In 788 CE, the Avars invaded Bavaria. Though preoccupied with battles elsewhere, namely Saxony and Spain, Charlemagne took note of the invasion. In 790 CE, Charlemagne retaliated, marching his troops into Bavaria to attack the Avars. As he marched down the Danube River, he razed structures and burnt Avar towns to the ground. Charlemagne continued his trend of being ruthless, especially to those who he didn't believe to be Christians. Not much is known about the religion of the Avars, but reports from various historians of the time mention that they were pagan,

---

[41] Einhard 16

which would explain why Charlemagne would, in fact, destroy their towns and villages. Stories were also passed down from the Huns invasion of Gaul and the siege of Orleans, which could have also fueled Charlemagne's ambition to destroy any and everything he could find regarding the Avars. The area of Pannonia, which was where the Avars made their home, was decimated by the invasion of Charlemagne. However, as fortune would have it, the Avars were reprieved as another war broke out requiring Charlemagne's immediate attention. Saxony revolted for the final time, pulling Charlemagne away from the Avars briefly to quell the rebellion. With Charlemagne in Saxony, his son, Pippin, and Duke Eric of Friuli, one of the many trusted soldier's in his command, took control over the campaign.

The Avars possessed a unique architectural advantage when it came to their fortresses and fortifications. Instead of creating garrisons and fortresses with points, in almost triangle and pentagram shapes to allow their archers to flank the oncoming army, the Avars built their structures in a complete ring, allowing no points. There were several advantages and disadvantages to this design. The first disadvantage is that the Avars weren't offered any kind of offensive advantage from this structure. With normal, traditional fortresses, the walls jetting out and forming a series of triangles allowed the defenders a key advantage when the offensive army comes inside the walls, having to expose their flank to archers and spearmen in order for them to penetrate their walls. With the circular design, the enemy doesn't ever have to expose their flanks. An advantage, however, is that there are no soft spots in the walls. With the traditional setup, the inward point can be considered a soft spot, and with enough force, can break the wall. With a circular design, there is no soft spot or target point for the offensive army to hit.

Also, another advantage of a round structure is how it will allow the troops to move on the inside, allowing them to fortify locations quicker due to less ground to cover. The ringed structure allowed the Avars to concentrate the bulk of their soldiers in one location, fortifying it quickly when they fell. The sacrifice of a sure flank gave way to the advantage of increased mobility.

Pippin and the Duke of Friuli conquered the capital city of the Avars with Charlemagne away in Saxony and brought the Avars to their knees. Riches and rewards were sent to Charlemagne's capital in Aachen as the two conquerors celebrated as heroes. The leaders of the Avars, broken and beaten, traveled to Aachen for an audience with Charlemagne. There, the leaders surrendered, agreeing to be baptized in the Christian faith. One of the leaders, renamed Abraham by Charlemagne after his Baptism, returned to the Avars as their leader, though a vassal of Charlemagne. This would only prove to be temporary, however, as a Bulgarian by the name of Khan Krum would attack the remnants of the Avars in an attempt to bring them under his banner. Charlemagne would send an army into Bavaria to finish destroying the remains of the Avar Confederation in 803 CE. Though Charlemagne would never go to war with the Bulgarian Khan, tensions were somewhat uneasy. In 805 CE, several Avar leaders requested the permission of Charlemagne to reestablish their territory elsewhere and remain vassals under his stewardship. He granted them the land southeast of Vienna, creating a crucial territory in the Transdanubian region.

Historically speaking, with the exception of the Byzantines, the Avars posed the biggest threat to Charlemagne's empire. Had he not put them into check when they invaded Bavaria, the likelihood is that they would have continued to expand into Saxony and eventually into France.

The Avars, unlike any other army Charlemagne would wage war with, attacked his territory first without provocation. Though prepared, because he knew where they were and their history of violence and warmongering, the Avars struck first and Charlemagne made them pay on an epic level.

The territories acquired by Charlemagne effectively linked up most of Europe under his banner. With the papacy in his pocket and the effective setup of feudal duchies and kingdoms, Charlemagne organized his empire so that it could withstand many issues that arose in other areas. The leaders were all loyal to him, helping him to keep the area free of any types of harmful interactions and internal strife. Charlemagne was able to focus on the many wars simultaneously because of his strong, effective, and organized domestic arrangement within the beginnings of the feudal system.

Chapter 11
The New Emperor

Charlemagne's unification of Europe, to this day, is still his greatest achievement. By essentially recreating the Western Roman Empire, Charlemagne brings the bulk of Europe into the papacy and under the crown of the church. One of the most essential things in the middle ages was the Catholic Church. Though pitted with various incidents of papal corruption and bad leadership, the Catholic Church was the central focal point that remained unchanged throughout the time. Because of their ties on the spiritual world, barbarians would often listen to the pope over their own ruler, which would in turn upset the ruler. However, many rulers also swore an oath to Rome, making them the dominant power in Europe. Charlemagne viewed himself as the defender of Rome, protecting the papacy and spreading the divine word of Christ to the heathens around him. He felt it was his duty as a Christian leader to sow the seeds of the faith amongst the godless men and women across the Rhine and Elbe Rivers, and to crush out the Islamic forces in Spain. Charlemagne took it upon himself to defend the church that he was waged wars with other powers over how they treated the church. The war with Lombardy was over their invasion of the Papal States. With Desiderius of Lombardy invading Ravenna, Charlemagne felt it was his obligation to the papacy to end any threat that was imminent and maintain the sanctity of the church. Often, Charlemagne would send deposed leaders to monasteries, forcing them to live out the rest of their days in the servitude of God.

Pope Leo III was not a very good pope in the grand scheme of things, though he was unofficially canonized by Pope Clement X in 1673, though was eventually renounced in 1953 by Pope Pius XII. He was elected Pope on 26 Dec. 795 CE, the day that Adrian I was entombed. Many of the Cardinals and Bishops in Rome feared Charlemagne and that his influence would ultimately affect the outcome of the election, thus, haste was in order. Leo III ascended to the papacy shortly after the death of Adrian I without a hint of dissent or other incidents coming from Rome.

In his territories, Charlemagne directly controlled the appointing of the clergy. He would recruit from all over the continent, requesting monks from modern day England, Italy, and other parts of France to take a position inside the church within his borders. Charlemagne thought it best to have the best and brightest clergymen operating within his realm. One of his most loyal advisors, Alcuin, was recruited form York to serve. In the period following the collapse of the Roman Empire, the church was the center for all thought and knowledge, controlling the schools and universities. With his obsession for thought and knowledge, as well as broadening and expanding his own horizons, Charlemagne sought out the best and brightest to help him expand his church, increase the knowledge of his children and citizens, and ultimately, helped him start the Carolingian Renaissance.

He would give orders about how the services were to be commenced, informing the clergy of the days and times the services were to be held, and in the manner in which they were to be conducted. Though a servant of God and an ally of the papacy, Charlemagne controlled how his loyal subjects listened to the word of God. Charlemagne ultimately micromanaged the church while it operated within his borders. Thought not changing and altering ecclesiastical policies passed down from Rome, he would alter the policies locally to adhere to his people, ensuring that they attended mass unabated and could worship without much hindrance. The diocese inside Charlemagne's territory was largely appointed by him, though still worked with the Cardinals and Bishops in Rome. Peace was maintained and relationships rarely, if ever, broke down between Charlemagne and the Catholic Church.

Once that most religious Emperor Charles gave orders that all bishops throughout his wide domains should preach in the nave of their cathedral before a certain day, which he appointed, under penalty of being deprived of the episcopal dignity, if they failed to comply with the order.—But why do I say "dignity" when the apostle protests: "He that desires a bishopric desires a good work"? But in truth, most serene of kings, I must confess to you that there is great "dignity" in the office, but not the slightest "good work" is required. Well, the aforementioned bishop was at first alarmed at this command, because gluttony and pride were all his learning, and he feared that if he lost his bishopric he would lose at the same time his soft living. So he invited two of the chiefs of the palace on the festal day, and after the reading of the lesson mounted the pulpit as though he were going to address the people. All the people ran together in wonder at so unexpected an occurrence, except one poor red-headed fellow, who had his head covered with clouts, because he had no hat, and was foolishly ashamed of his red hair. Then the bishop—bishop in name but not in deed—called to his doorkeeper or rather his scario (whose dignity and duties went by the name of the ædileship among the ancient Romans) and said: "Bring me that man in the hat who is standing there near the door of the church." The doorkeeper made haste to obey, seized the poor man and began to drag him towards the bishop. But he feared some heavy penalty for daring to stand in the house of God with covered head, and struggled with all his might to avoid being brought before the tribunal of the terrible judge. But the bishop, looking from his perch, now addressing his vassals and now chiding the poor knave, bawled out and preached as follows:—"Here with him! don't let him slip! Willy-nilly you've got to come." When at last force or fear brought him near, the bishop cried: "Come forward; nay, you must come quite close." Then he snatched the head-covering from his captive and cried to the people:—"Lo and behold all ye people; the boor is red-headed." Then he returned to the altar and performed the ceremony, or pretended to perform it.

When the mass was thus scrambled through his guests passed into his hall, which was decorated with many-coloured carpets, and cloths of all kinds; and there a magnificent banquet, served in gold and silver and jewelled cups, was provided, calculated to tickle the appetite of the fastidious or the well-fed. The bishop himself sat on the softest of cushions, clad in precious silks and wearing the imperial purple, so that he seemed a king except for the sceptre and the title. He was surrounded by troops of rich knights, in comparison with whom the officers of the palace (nobles though they were) of the unconquered Charles seemed to themselves most mean. When they asked leave to depart after this wonderful and more than royal banquet he, desiring to show still more plainly his magnificence and his glory, ordered skilled musicians to come forward, the sound of whose voices could soften the hardest hearts or turn to ice the swiftly flowing waters of the Rhine. And at the same time every kind of choice drink, subtly and variously compounded, was offered them in bowls of gold and gems, whose sheen was mixed with that of the flowers and leaves with which they were crowned:

but their stomachs could contain no more so that the glasses lay idle in their hands. Meanwhile pastry cooks and sausage makers, servers and dressers offered preparations of exquisite art to stimulate their appetite, though their stomachs could contain no more: it was a banquet such as was never offered even to the great Charles himself.

When morning came and the bishop returned some way towards soberness, he thought with fear of the luxury that he had paraded before the servants of the emperor. So he called them into his presence, loaded them with presents worthy of a king, and implored them to speak to the terrible Charles of the goodness and simplicity of his life; and above all to tell him how he had preached publicly before them in his cathedral.

Upon their return Charles asked them why the bishop had invited them. Thereupon they fell at his feet and said: "Master, it was that he might honour us as your representatives, far beyond our humble deserts." "He is," they went on, "in every way the best and the most faithful of bishops and most worthy of the highest rank in the Church. For, if you will trust our poor judgment, we profess to your sublime majesty that we heard him preach in his church in the most stirring fashion." Then the emperor who knew the bishop's lack of skill pressed them further as to the manner of his preaching; and they, perforce, revealed all. Then the emperor saw that he had made an effort to say something rather than disobey the imperial order; and he allowed him, in spite of his unworthiness, to retain the bishopric.

Shortly after a young man, a relation of the emperor's, sang, on the occasion of some festival, the Alleluia admirably: and the Emperor turned to this same bishop and said: "My clerk is singing very well." But the stupid man, thought that he was jesting and did not know that the clerk was the emperor's relation; and so he answered: "Any clown in our countryside drones as well as that to his oxen at their ploughing." At this vulgar answer the emperor turned on him the lightning of his flashing eyes and dashed him terror-stricken to the very ground.[42]

The situation around Europe in 800 CE was much different from when Charlemagne took over as King of the Franks in 774 CE. At home, all of France was united, including Septimania, Gascony, and Aquitaine, which had been raging various wars since the fall of the Roman Empire. By appointing his son, Louis, king of Aquitaine, Charlemagne stabilized the region and allowed for the buffer region, the Spanish March, to be created. Also, by appointing his son, the local nobility stepped in line and essentially swore fealty to Charlemagne. This assisted in ensuring the stability in the region and allowing for it remain peaceful for the rest of his lifetime. This also allowed his son to continue to defend the borders against the Moors, eventually leading to their surrender and establishment of French territory. Saxony has essentially fallen, with the people being annexed into the French population and the bloody uprisings over. The conquest of the Avars was complete, eventually leading to their expansion into the areas southeast of Vienna and expanding the boundaries of Charlemagne's empire without much of a fuss. The Lombards were conquered and subjugated after attempting to muscle around the church, invading Ravenna and trying to capture land that was given to the papacy by Charlemagne's father, Pepin the Short.

---

[42] Monk of St. Gall

Because of his efforts, devotion, and ambition, Charlemagne was regarded as the dominant figure in Europe. His kingdom was looked on by those, not subjugated, as powerful and awe inspiring. The Byzantine Empire with their capital city, Constantinople, took note of the Charlemagne's power and drive, respecting him while he remained firmly entrenched away from their territory, though this would not be the case forever. Following the split of the Roman Empire, Constantinople and Rome were regarded as the two great seats of power in the western world. With the sacking of Rome by the Huns, Visigoths, and Vandals essentially toppling it as a power, the emperor of Constantinople was essentially the de facto leader of the Roman Empire. After years of succession, the crown continued to pass on, even though they eventually dropped the title Caesar. Because of this connection, tensions would eventually arise after Charlemagne's coronation as Emperor with the Byzantine's questioning the legitimacy of his ascension.

Now since envy always rages among the envious so it is customary and regular with the Romans to oppose or rather to fight against all strong Popes, who are from time to time raised to the apostolic see. Whence it came to pass that certain of the Romans, themselves blinded with envy, charged the above-mentioned Pope Leo of holy memory with a deadly crime and tried to blind him. But they were frightened and held back by some divine impulse, and after trying in vain to gouge out his eyes, they slashed them across the middle with knives. The Pope had news of this carried secretly by his servants to Michael, Emperor of Constantinople; but he refused all assistance saying: "The Pope has an independent kingdom and one higher than mine; so he must act his own revenge upon his enemies." Thereupon the holy Leo invited the unconquered Charles to come to Rome; following in this the ordinance of God, that, as Charles was already in very deed ruler and emperor over many nations, so also by the authority of the apostolic see he might have now the name of Emperor, Cæsar and Augustus. Now Charles, being always ready to march and in warlike array, though he knew nothing at all of the cause of the summons, came at once with his attendants and his vassals; himself the head of the world he came to the city that had once been the head of the world. And when the abandoned people heard of his sudden coming, at once, as sparrows hide themselves when they hear the voice of their master, so they fled and hid in various hiding-places, cellars, and dens. Nowhere however under heaven could they escape from his energy and penetration; and soon they were captured and brought in chains to the Cathedral of St Peter. Then the undaunted Father Leo took the gospel of our Lord Jesus Christ and held it over his head, and then in the presence of Charles and his knights, in presence also of his persecutors, he swore in the following words:—"So on the day of the great judgment may I partake in the promises, as I am innocent of the charge that is falsely laid against me." Then many of the prisoners asked to be allowed to swear upon the tomb of St Peter that they also were innocent of the charge laid against them. But the Pope knew their falseness and said to Charles: "Do not, I pray you, unconquered servant of God, give assent to their cunning; for well they know that Saint Peter is always ready to forgive. But seek among the tombs of the martyrs the stone upon which is written the name of St Pancras, that boy of thirteen years; and if they will swear to you in his name you may know that you have them fast." It was done as the Pope ordered. And when many people drew near to take the oath upon this tomb, straightway some fell back dead and some were seized by the devil and went mad. Then the terrible Charles said to his servants: "Take care that none of them escapes." Then he condemned all who had been

94

taken prisoner either to some kind of death or to perpetual imprisonment.

As Charles stayed in Rome for a few days, the bishop of the apostolic see called together all who would come from the neighbouring districts and then, in their presence and in the presence of all the knights of the unconquered Charles, he declared him to be Emperor and Defender of the Roman Church.[43]

Dissension in Rome came after his ascension to the papacy for Leo III. Though appointed in a very swift manner, to avoid any outside influence from Charlemagne or the Byzantines, enemies appeared from all around, mostly linked to the allies, friends, and descended family of Adrian I, the recently deceased pope. Under the claims that he was an adulterer, fornicator, and liar, the accusations that Leo III was unfit mounted and became enormous. Though in a position of ultimate power, the jealousy and dissent motivated several people of Rome to unite against him. Fortunately for Leo III, upon his ascension, he allied himself with Charlemagne, sending envoys to meet him with and bestowing upon him the keys of the Confession of St. Peter and the standard to the city of Rome. He looked upon the Frankish king as his largest ally, which in truth was correct. Charlemagne bestowed upon the new pope letters congratulating on his appointment and several treasures acquired from his conquest of the Avars. Motivated by a number of things, Leo III was assaulted as he marched to the Flaminian Gate in Rome on 25 April, 799. The attackers, all armed, drove the pope to the ground and attempted to gouge his eyes out and remove his tongue, rendering it impossible for him to continue his job as the leader of the Catholic Church.

---

[43] Monk of St. Gall

Though injured, he managed to escape with his life, eyes, and tongue intact. The duke of Spoleto, an important ally of Charlemagne, gave the pope refuge while he recovered from his minor injuries until he could return to Rome. After his brief recovery, Leo III marched, with a heavily armed guard, to Paderborn were Charlemagne was camped. With an immaculate reception for the pontiff upon his arrival in the German city, Charlemagne was enraged at how this could have happened to the man in the seat of Christendom. He summoned the dissenters to Paderborn, electing to protect the pope and to act as an arbitrator, hoping to settle the issue and allow the pope to return to Rome unscathed. With the leaders, summoned, Charlemagne could not come to a decision, and instead, ordered the talks to continue in Rome. Under the advice of Alcuin, he personally escorted Leo III back to Rome, marching over the Alps and through Northern Italy before depositing him safely at his home.

On 1 December, 800 CE, Charlemagne started listening to the claims and accusations from the various accusers. He listened as they declared that he was unfit for the papacy and how he was a liar, perjurer, and adulterer. He listened as the various accusers told stories of his personal life and how the Catholic Church should remove him from power, denounce him personally, and excommunicate him from their blessed church. Charlemagne was fair and true, listening to everyone before coming to his own judgment. On 23 December 800 CE, Pope Leo III took an oath of purgation in regards to the accusations brought forth against him. This oath put the fate of Leo III firmly in the hands of his creator. If he lied about his innocence, there would be no repentance and he would serve his punishment in the afterlife. In this age, swearing an oath to God was the ultimate decider in claims, because in essence, the accused is sacrificing his everlasting soul if he is not telling the truth. This was big because of how large God played in the culture of the times. God was the keystone for all thought and decisions during this age, so, with Leo III making an oath of purgation, he was exonerated of all charges brought against him. The accusers were left in a rotten position, as with the oath satisfied, Charlemagne ruled in favor of Leo III. All of the accusers were exiled from Rome, allowing Leo III to rule the Catholic Church without the constant fear of being overthrown.

But such were not the only objects of his last visit; for the Romans had grievously outraged Pope Leo, had torn out his eyes and cut off his tongue, and thus forced him to throw himself upon the protection of the King. He therefore came to Rome to restore the condition of the church, which was terribly disturbed, and spent the whole of the winter there. It was then that he received the title of Emperor and Augustus, which he so disliked at first that he affirmed that he would not have entered the church on that day—though it was the chief festival of the church—if he could have foreseen the design of the Pope. But when he had taken the title he bore very quietly the hostility that it caused and the indignation of the Roman emperors. He conquered their ill-feeling by his magnanimity, in which, doubtless, he far excelled them, and sent frequent embassies to them, and called them his brothers.[44]

On 25 December 800 CE, Charlemagne was crowned emperor of the Romans, effectively becoming the first emperor of the Holy Roman Empire (what it would be referred to in 932 CE). By doing this, Pope Leo III denounced the rule of the Empress in Constantinople, ending the legitimacy of her claims to the Roman throne. Because of this, there were, as it

---

[44] Einhard 28

was when the Roman Empire split, two emperors of the defunct Roman Empire. His coronation started two centuries of on and off warfare that would shape the modern world.

Many historians have had arguments, debates, and other discussions over whether or not Charlemagne was aware of this move from the pope. While Einhard, his biographer, denies the claims that Charlemagne was aware of this coronation and that he would not have been in Rome that day had he known, others looking back at Charelmagne's historical trends and power grabs think otherwise. With his constant lust for expansion, though motivated by his devotion to the church, it is feasible to think and believe that he was aware of what was transpiring, even pushing Leo III as far as to suggest this. However, he possessed allies in Constantinople, so it is could be reasonable to believe that he did not want to push them to a possible, though inevitable, war.

Charlemagne was a very cautious planner, though incredibly aggressive. To think that he was unaware of the pending coronation is naïve, even if he wanted to maintain peace with the Byzantines. However, he was aware that a war with the Byzantine Empire was inevitable, much like with the Avars. With his unabated willingness to expand the reach of Catholicism, invading a capturing Constantinople, pushing the boundaries of Catholicism seemed like a reasonable goal. His army was massive and he was a very patient, strategic planner. With the right collection of forces, Charlemagne potentially thought that he could overtake the Byzantines and siege Constantinople, something that no one had ever done. The Byzantine historian Theophanes believed that Charlemagne's coronation was only the first step in his plan for uniting the two regions. He believes that Charlemagne's intentions were to marry Empress Irene in Constantinople and take the throne for himself, which he admits that the queen seemed favorable to the idea, though it never came to fruition.

At the time, the Pope firmly believed that there was no living connection to the former Roman Empire, with the Byzantine claims already being denounced. Since 727 CE, Rome was in a disagreement with Constantinople about the legitimacy of their line in relation to the true lineage of the Roman Empire. This disagreement was further pushed by the claims of iconoclasm from the Eastern Church, driving a wedge between the two. With Leo III crowning Charlemagne the Emperor of the Romans, he further claims that the Byzantine line is illegitimate and that he alone is capable of extending the line of Roman rulers. The Pope makes the claim that he is the sole power of Rome and the former empire and that the Byzantines have no claim to the title or the throne. This would ultimately prove to be fatal for their ongoing relationship, because this would unfortunately, heave them into awkward diplomatic situation.

Iconoclasm remained a sticking point for Charlemagne and the Catholic Church regarding their division with the Byzantine Empire and the Eastern Orthodox Church. The use of icons, or idols, for worship was a pagan tradition that was incorporated into several aspects of Christianity, though was outlawed as heresy by the Catholic Church. At the second council of Nicaea in 787 CE, the use of idols in the veneration of worship was discussed and, at the behest of the Empress, allowed into practice in the Eastern Church, removing the heresy label placed on it by the Catholics. The bishops in Constantinople agreed that there was a definite separation between the idols used and God himself, admitting that the idols were not direct representations of God, but merely symbols. They also agreed that every religious alter should bear a symbol or a relic while also restricting several acts that men and women in monastic orders could partake in.

As the sacred and life-giving cross is everywhere set up as a symbol, so also should the images of Jesus Christ, the Virgin Mary, the holy angels, as well as those of the saints and other pious and holy men be embodied in the manufacture of sacred vessels, tapestries, vestments, etc., and exhibited on the walls of churches, in the homes, and in all conspicuous places, by the roadside and everywhere, to be revered by all who might see them. For the more they are contemplated, the more they move to fervent memory of their prototypes. Therefore, it is proper to accord to them a fervent and reverent adoration, not, however, the veritable worship which, according to our faith, belongs to the Divine Being alone — for the honor accorded to the image passes over to its prototype, and whoever venerate the image venerate in it the reality of what is there represented.[45]

The emperor of Byzantine at the time was Nicephorus I, a descendent of Empress Irene. In 803 CE, the two leaders attempted to hash out any border disputes, drawing up defined boundary lines while remaining peaceful with one another. This proposed *Pax Nicephoria* was the failed attempt to create a peaceful solution in regards to the territory divisions. Though agreements were loosely made regarding the territory, the breaking issue, Charlemagne's imperial authority, was not recognized. For three more years, the relations between the two leaders would sour. Venice, which was occupied by the Byzantines, defected and joined the kingdom of the Franks, angering Nicephorus and prompting him to attack. With an incredible navy, Nicephorus opened fire

---

[45] Translated quote from the documents regarding the 2nd Council of Nicaea
Accessed through http://www.ccel.org/ccel/schaff/npnf214.xvi.html

on Venice in 806 CE, opting to attack Charlemagne by sea. This conflict lasted until 810 CE, when the Byzantine loyalists in Venice revolted; retaking the city and granting it back to the Byzantines. Nicephorus, unfortunately, was not alive long enough to enjoy the peace, as he was killed in Bulgaria by Krum Khan in 811 CE. However, the new emperor, Michael I, accepted the peace and drew out the boundary lines with Charlemagne, accepting him as emperor of the west, though not emperor of the Romans.

Though awkward, and only centered on Venice, the result was optimal for Charlemagne. By having the Byzantine Empire legitimize his crown, Charlemagne could effectively take his seat for the rest of his life as the emperor of the Romans. By giving up some small plots of land on the far western reaches of his Empire, Charlemagne was able to avoid further conflict with the Byzantines and reach a peace that was needed. Though, with the start of the Byzantine-Arab war and the other military endeavors of Nicephorus I, Charlemagne could have reasonably pushed on and eliminated the Byzantines from Italy, pushing on into Greece and potentially pushing them out of Europe. However, with other wars still pressing on, Charlemagne felt it wise to ensure his legitimacy in the eyes of the Byzantines and try to keep up with positive, fruitful relations before marching through and waging war with one of the most powerful empires in the world at the time.

Chapter 12
Wars with the Northmen

He built a fleet, too, for the war against the Northmen, constructing ships for this purpose near those rivers which flow out of Gaul and Germany into the northern ocean. And because the Northmen laid waste the coasts of Gaul and Germany by their constant attacks he planted forts and garrisons in all harbours and at the mouths of all navigable rivers, and prevented in this way the passage of the enemy.[46]

The Northmen, or Normans, are better known in history as the Vikings. They were a cruel lot, bent on pillaging and piracy while worshipping the Norse Gods, considered to be pagan by Charlemagne. They were tall, messy, and an unkempt people, hailing originally from Scandinavia. They controlled the North and Baltic Seas, as well as the English Channel, using their small, row boats, the Normans were able to move quickly through the water to make it to the mainland and attack the harbors and villages. Also, they would use these small ships to maneuver around the larger vessels, boarding them and plundering their goods. Of note though, is that the Viking's who settled in Denmark, though Norman, were a separate tribe from the rest of the regions. The Normans, who would eventually wage war on France, settled in Denmark but still waged war via the sea.

He conquered the Bretons, too, who dwelt in the extreme west of France by the shores of the ocean. They had been disobedient, and he, therefore, sent against them an

---

[46] Einhard 31

expedition, by which they were compelled to give hostages
and promise that they would henceforth obey his orders.[47]

In 799 CE, the northern coast of Charlemagne's
territory in France was exposed, under constant attack from
the men of the north and their small, fast ships. They ravaged
the territories of Bretain, a territory to the far west of Paris
that Charlemagne had to conquer earlier in his reign, though
in a very uneventful manner. The only real point of note here
is the man who led its siege. Roland, the rear commander who
perished in Spain, and the focal point in the epic work, the
Song of Roland, led the capturing of this territory without
much of a struggle. Because of these attacks on the coast,
Charlemagne instructed his men to build strong, coastal
fortifications to repel any of these invaders and not allow them
to pillage or plunder the coastal cities or their docking ships.
The intention of these fortifications was to protect the rivers
that fed into the English Channel, blocking the path of the
Norman ships into the mainland of France. The majority of
Viking tribes preferred to wage war via the sea, not wanting to
march too far inland, instead targeting cities on the coast.

Following Charlemagne's conquest of Saxony, the four
administrative regions bent to his will, surrendering and
willfully joining his kingdom. Of the four, Nordalbingia,
remained a slight point of contention after the conquest,
though in a sense of having to defend it from foreign invaders
and rival tribes and not from the citizens. Over time, the
Normans crossed the Baltic Sea and invaded Jutland, settling
in Denmark, or Danemark as they called it, while also settling
every island in between on their journey. Many of the original
inhabitants from this region had sense left, splitting off and
migrating across the English Channel to settle on England at

---

[47] Einhard 10

around 400 CE. The region was home to the Angles, Jutes, and Saxons and went all the way down into Nordalibingia. From the edge of Sweden, several large islands sit in the ocean, creating a serviceable bridge that the Normans were able to cross. Though still having to travel from island to island, they did not have to make the trek in one journey, instead spacing it out over the period of decades. Once settled in the European mainland, the Normans were able to start their trek inland, though still staying close to water, traveling down the Elder River and other various water ways. They would raid by land, however, into Nordalbingia and other territories close by, forcing Charlemange to leave several garrisons behind to defend their borders.

The Normans were under the command of Gotfried, King of the Danes, and while this was a foe that Charlemagne was not accustomed to dealing with, his children would be at war with them for many years. With their marauding, pillaging, and warmongering, the Normans would be a threat to the French for hundreds of years. While many of the Saxon leaders sought out the Danes for protection after their defeat from Charlemagne, namely Widukind, a positive relationship could never be established between the two nations.

Now about the same time that the emperor was putting the finishing touch to the war with the Huns, and had received the surrender of the races that I have just mentioned, the Northmen left their homes and disquieted greatly the Gauls and the Franks. Then the unconquered Charles returned and tried to attack them by land in their own homes, by a march through difficult and unknown country. But, whether it was that the providence of God prevented it in order that, as the Scripture says, He might make trial of Israel, or whether it was that our sins stood in the way, all his efforts came to nothing. One night, to the serious discomfort of the whole army, it was calculated that fifty yoke of oxen belonging to one abbey had died of a sudden disease. Afterwards when Charles was making a prolonged journey through his vast empire, Gotefrid, king of the Northmen, encouraged by his absence, invaded the territory of the Frankish kingdom and chose the district of the Moselle for his home. But Gotefrid's own son (whose mother he had just put away and taken to himself a new wife) caught him, while he was pulling off his hawk from a heron, and cut him through the middle with his sword. Then, as happened of old when Holofernes was slain, none of the Northmen dare trust any longer in his courage or his arms; but all sought safety in flight. And thus the Franks were freed without their own effort, that they might not after the fashion of Israel boast themselves against God. Then Charles, the unconquered and the invincible, glorified God for His judgment; but complained bitterly that any of the Northmen had escaped because of his absence. "Ah, woe is me!" he said, "that I was not thought worthy to see my Christian hands dabbling in the blood of those dog-headed fiends."

It happened too that on his wanderings Charles once came unexpectedly to a certain maritime city of Narbonensian Gaul. When he was dining quietly in the harbour of this town, it happened that some Norman scouts made a piratical raid. When the ships came in sight some thought them Jews, some African or British merchants, but the most wise Charles, by the build of the ships and their speed, knew them to be not merchants but enemies, and said to his companions: "These ships are not filled with merchandise, but crowded with our fiercest enemies." When they heard this, in eager rivalry, they hurried in haste to the ships. But all was in vain, for when the Northmen heard that Charles, the Hammer, as they used to call him, was there, fearing lest their fleet should be beaten *back or even smashed in pieces, they withdrew themselves, by a marvellously rapid flight, not only from the swords but even from the eyes of those who followed them. The most religious, just and devout Charles had risen from the table and was standing at an eastern window. For a long time he poured down tears beyond price, and none dared speak a word to him; but at last he explained his actions and his tears to his nobles in these words:—"Do you know why I weep so bitterly, my true servants? I have no fear of those worthless rascals doing any harm to me; but I am sad at heart to think that even during my lifetime they have dared to touch this shore; and I am torn by a great sorrow because I foresee what evil things they will do to my descendants and their subjects."*[48]

The first real encounter between the two, after Charles led in his armies into the area, was centered around Schleswig, an isthmus in Jutland. The Normans, at the time, possessed some of the greatest defensive structures the world had ever seen. While the bulk of civilizations were using vastly high walls with sharp angles, providing flanks for their archers to attack from above, the Normans went a few steps further. The Danes, while at constant warfare with the Slavs and Saxons, began construction of this expansive fortification at around 650 CE. However, Gotfried, under fear that Charlemagne would march his army to the coast of Jutland, hurriedly finished construction of this immense fortification in 808 CE. This structure consists of over thirty kilometers of high walls with deep trenches on both sides to provide the optimal defense for his city. This structure was long, cutting the entire isthmus in half and providing it impossible for Charlemagne and his troops to directly attack the Normans. With this wall, Gotfried was able to send troops out to harass enemies on the

---

[48] Monk of St Gall 138

other side, having them to return without the fear of a direct counter attack. Gotfried was arrogant; at one point inferring that would attack Aachen without facing the wrath of Charlemagne. This, however, would not come to pass, as in 810 CE, Gotfried was assassinated and his nephew, Hemming, would assume the throne as King of the Danes. In 811 CE, Hemming and Charlemagne came to an understanding and created the definite border for their respective countries. The Elder River was now the southern border of Denmark in relation to the French and the two rulers agreed that they would not cross it. Unfortunately, after the death of these two men, skirmishes broke out on the border of the Elder River as the Normans continued to expand, eventually ending up in Northern France and settling in Normandy.

The men from the north were the last real military threat Charlemagne was forced to deal with. His son, Louis, was wrapping up his wars in Spain at the time that Charlemagne was preparing to exit the realm of the living. These men from the north, though, would be the next great threat to Europe, with various tribes settling different areas. The age of the Vikings lasted from the mid 700s all the way until 1066 CE, when the Normans invaded England and captured it. The Normans would lay siege on Paris 845 CE, thirty-one years after the death of Charlemagne. The fortifications constructed on the northern borders of France did not hold, allowing for the Vikings to travel from the English Channel, down the Seine River and into Paris. With their refusal to convert to Christianity, after being exposed to it over the years, one hundred and twenty Danish Vikings ships, carrying upwards of seven thousand men, traveled down the Seine River and laid siege on Paris. Charlemagne's effort to protect the French inland failed, unfortunately, and the Vikings were able to capitalize on it after his death.

Chapter 13
Plots Against Charlemagne's Life

He had by a concubine a son called Pippin—whom I purposely did not mention along with the others—handsome, indeed, but deformed. When Charles, after the beginning of the war against the Huns, was wintering in Bavaria, this Pippin pretended illness, and formed a conspiracy against his father with some of the leaders of the Franks, who had seduced him by a vain promise of the kingdom. When the design had been detected and the conspirators punished Pippin was tonsured and sent to the monastery of Prumia, there to practise the religious life, to which in the end he was of his own will inclined.[49]

Charlemagne's life was not without strife, as noted above. One incident that is not brought up is the relationship he had with one of his children, Pippin, born out of wedlock to a concubine Charlemagne had a brief relationship with. He was disfigured and wrought with illness, though still a son of Charlemagne. Referred to as Pippin the Hunchback, he was forced into life in a monastery before and after the plot against his father.

But, after conquering the external foe, Charles was attacked at the hands of his own people in a remarkable but unavailing plot. For on his return from the Slavs into his own kingdom he was nearly captured and put to death by his son, whom a concubine had borne to him and who had been called by his mother by the ill-omened name of the most glorious Pippin. The plot was found out in the following manner. This son of Charles had been plotting the death of the emperor

---

[49] Einhard 20

108

with a gathering of nobles, in the church of Saint Peter; and when their debate was over, fearful of every shadow, he ordered search to be made, to see whether anyone was hidden in the corners or under the altar. And behold they found, as they feared, a clerk hidden under the altar. They seized him and made him swear that he would not reveal their conspiracy. To save his life, he dared not refuse to take the oath which they dictated: but, when they were gone, he held his wicked oath of small account and at once hurried to the palace. With the greatest difficulty he passed through the seven bolted gates, and coming at length to the emperor's chamber knocked upon the door. The most vigilant Charles fell into a great astonishment, as to who it was that dared to disturb him at that time of night. He however ordered the women (who followed in his train to wait upon the queen and the princesses) to go out and see who was at the door and what he wanted. When they went out and found the wretched creature, they bolted the door in his face and then, bursting with laughter and stuffing their dresses into their mouths, they tried to hide themselves in the corners of the apartments. But that most wise emperor, whose notice nothing under heaven could escape, asked straitly of the women who it was and what he wanted. When he was told that it was a smooth-faced, silly, half-mad knave, dressed only in shirt and drawers, who demanded an audience without delay, Charles ordered him to be admitted. Then he fell at the emperor's feet and showed all that had happened. So all the conspirators, entirely unsuspicious of danger, were seized before the third hour of the day and most deservedly condemned to exile or some other form of punishment. Pippin himself, a dwarf and a hunchback, was cruelly scourged, tonsured, and sent for some time as a punishment to the monastery of Saint Gall; the poorest, it was judged, and the straitest in all the emperor's broad dominions.

A short time afterwards some of the Frankish nobles sought to do violence to their king. Charles was well aware of their intentions, and yet did not wish to destroy them; because, if only they were loyal, they might be a great protection to all Christian men. So he sent messengers to this Pippin and asked him his advice in the matter.

They found him in the monastery garden, in the company of the elder brothers, for the younger ones were detained by their work. He was digging up nettles and other weeds with a hoe, that the useful herbs might grow more vigorously. When they had explained to him the reason of their coming he sighed deeply, from the very bottom of his heart, and said in reply:—"If Charles thought my advice worth having he would not have treated me so harshly. I give him no advice. Go, tell him what you found me doing." They were afraid to go back to the dreaded emperor without a definite answer, and again and again asked him what message they should convey to their lord. Then at last he said in anger:—"I will send him no message except—what I am doing! I am digging up the useless growths in order that the valuable herbs may be able to develop more freely.

So they went away sorrowfully thinking that they were bringing back a foolish answer. When the emperor asked them upon their arrival what answer they were bringing, they answered sorrowfully that after all their labour and long journeying they could get no definite information at all. Then that most wise king asked them carefully where they had found Pippin, what he was doing, and what answer he had given them; and they said: "We found him sitting on a rustic seat turning over the vegetable garden with a hoe. When we told him the cause of our journey we could extract no other reply than this, even by the greatest entreaties: 'I give no message, except—what I am doing! I am digging up the useless growths in order that the valuable herbs may be able to develop more freely." When he heard this the emperor, not lacking in cunning and mighty in wisdom, rubbed his ears and blew out his nostrils and said: "My good vassals, you have brought back a very reasonable answer." So while the messengers were fearing that they might be in peril of their lives, Charles was able to divine the real meaning of the words. He took all those plotters away from the land of the living; and so gave to his loyal subjects room to grow and spread, which had previously been occupied by those unprofitable servants. One of his enemies, who had chosen as his part of the spoil of the empire the highest hill in France and all that could be seen from it, was, by Charles's orders, hanged upon a high gallows on that very hill. But he bade his bastard son Pippin choose the manner of life that most pleased him. Upon this permission being given him, he chose a post in a monastery then most noble but now destroyed. (Who is there that does not know the manner of its destruction! But I will not tell the story of its fall until I see your little Bernard with a sword girt upon his thigh.)"[50]

Charlemagne's love and devotion for the church was not without his faults, because his lust for the flesh is well documented. While he loved his children, the ones he bore out of wedlock were viewed much differently than those who arrived within the sanctity of marriage. With this passion, disdain, and jealousy for his father, Pippin attempted to take his father's life in hopes that he could legitimately take the throne for the nobles who seduced him. This goes to show that not every count, duke, or lord was noble to Charlemagne to the end, and that their own personal ambitions still remained. He was not too far removed from the times when the Frankish kingdoms were all separate, so the bloodlines still existed to

---

[50] Monk of St. Gall

pose a threat from within. Several motives could exist to stir up a revolt, particularly a famine in 792, though it is worth noting that revolts happened for various reasons all over his kingdoms until his death. However, Einhard discusses how many of the plots were stirred up by one of Charlemagne's former queens, Fastrada.

Another dangerous conspiracy had been formed against him in Germany at an earlier date. The plotters were some of them blinded and some of them maimed, and all subsequently transported into exile. Not more than three lost their lives, and these resisted capture with drawn swords, and in defending themselves killed some of their opponents. Hence, as they could not be restrained in any other way, they were cut down.

The cruelty of Queen Fastrada is believed to be the cause and origin of these conspiracies. Both were caused by the belief that, upon the persuasion of his cruel wife, he had swerved widely from his natural kindness and customary leniency. Otherwise his whole life long he so won the love and favour of all men both at home and abroad that never was the slightest charge of unjust severity brought against him by anyone.[51]

In all of history, it is worth noting that by interjecting several foreign cultures into your society, whether through marriage or by force, there will be divisions. By Charlemagne marrying all of the different women that he did, creating and dissolving various diplomatic relationships, he created many enemies that he would, at some point, have to conquer or subjugate. This is not to say that Charlemagne was always magnanimous with his countrymen and citizens, and that he was always pious and humble, but by conquering so many

---

[51] Einhard 20

different cultures and placing Frankish lords in their domain, revolts and plots against him were rather common place, though usually snuffed out quickly and dealt with harshly. He would condemn every plotter to death, removing any land and titles from their family and redistributing to other nobles, rewarding those who remained loyal to him while severely punishing those who were not. It is of note, when Charlemagne conquered a kingdom, he would force all of the existing nobility who he allowed to remain in place to swear an oath of loyalty and give up in claims of autonomy. This did not sit well with many of the men, as they were forced to abide by the laws of Charlemagne instead of ruling over their land themselves.

Chapter 14
The Final Days of Charlemagne

Charlemagne lived an incredibly long, productive life, spanning over seventy years which, for that time, was a feat in of itself. He stayed healthy for a long time, opting to fast when he had a fever and allow his body to fight off the infections, viruses, and other sicknesses on its own. He was a true champion, honing his physical strengths while staying active and healthy. However, Charlemagne knew that his life would eventually come to a close. Because of this, he prepared accordingly. In 813 CE, with his health failing, Charlemagne summoned his only legitimate son, Louis of Aquitaine, to his court. With his own hands, he crowned his son co-emperor, sharing the title with his son as he prepared his kingdom for the next ruler.

At the very end of his life, when already he was feeling the pressure of old age and sickness, he summoned his own son Lewis, King of Aquitania, the only surviving son of Hildigard, and then solemnly called together the Frankish nobles of his whole kingdom; and then, with the consent of all, made Lewis partner in the whole kingdom and heir to the imperial title. After that, putting the diadem on his head, he ordered them to salute him "Imperator" and Augustus. This decision of his was received by all present with the greatest favour, for it seemed to them a divine inspiration for the welfare of the realm. It added to his dignity at home and increased the terror of his name abroad.

He then sent his son back to Aquitania, and himself, though broken with old age, proceeded to hunt, as his custom was, not far from the palace of Aix, and after spending the rest of the autumn in this pursuit he came back to Aix about the beginning of November. Whilst he was spending the winter there he was attacked by a sharp fever, and took to his bed. Then, following his usual habit, he determined to abstain from food, thinking that by such self-discipline he would be able either to cure or alleviate the disease. But the fever was complicated by a pain in the side which the Greeks call pleurisy; and, as Charles still persisted in fasting, and only very rarely drank something to sustain his strength, seven days after he had taken to his bed he received holy communion, and died, in the seventy-second year of his life and in the forty-seventh year of his reign, on the fifth day before the Kalends of February, at the third hour of the day.[52]

Charlemagne stayed active until the end, trying his best to maintain his strength while he stepped away from the day to day affairs. His son, Louis, was marching the army through Spain to finish conquering the lands while also helping to handle the affairs domestically. This was great for his son, as he was able to learn from his father what little he could about running the entire empire. However, Louis was already named the king of Aquitaine and a vassal to his father, so he already possessed a great deal of experience in leading a nation.

In 811 CE, three years prior to his death, Charlemagne opted to make a last will and testament with the idea that he would divide some of his lands and property that would not be passed down to his only legitimate heir to some of his daughters and illegitimate sons. He ensured that his money, robes, and other personal possessions of value and sentiment were given to either the church or his family. Though illegitimate, Charlemagne still loved all of his children, though he understood that the church, or any of the nobility, would not recognize them as a proper heir. Also, through French

---

[52] Einhard 30

tradition, the land is supposed to be divided up by all of the legitimate heirs at the death of the king, just as Charlemagne's father and uncle split the land Charles Martel left and Charlemagne and his brother split the land Pepin the Short left. With only his son Louis as the legitimate heir, these customs were allowed to be passed and the transition proved to be very smooth. He left a great deal of his fortune to several various cities, helping them to honor his life by donating to their treasuries.

He had determined to draw out wills in order to make his daughters and the sons whom his concubines had borne to him heirs to some part of his property; but he took up this design too late, and could not carry it out. But some three years before he died he divided his treasures, his money and his robes, and all his other moveable property, in presence of his friends and ministers, and appealed to them to ratify and maintain by their support this division after his death. He also stated in a document how he wished to have the property which he had divided disposed of. The text and purport of the document ran as follows:—

In the name of the Lord God Almighty, Father, Son, and Holy Ghost. This is the description and division which was made by the most glorious and pious lord Charles, the august Emperor, in the eight hundred and eleventh year from the incarnation of our Lord Jesus Christ; in the forty-third year of his reign in Frankland; in the thirty-sixth year of his reign in Italy; in the eleventh year of his Empire and in the fourth indiction: which division he made for wise and religious reasons of his treasures and of the money which on that day was found in the treasury. Wherein his great aim was: in the first place to ensure that the distribution of alms, which Christians religiously make from their possessions, should be duly and properly made on his account from his wealth; and also that his heirs may clearly know without any possibility of doubt what ought to belong to them, and may therefore (without contest or dissension) divide his goods among themselves in their proper proportion. Therefore with this intention and object he first divided into three parts all his property and moveable goods; which, whether consisting of gold, silver, jewels, or royal apparel, could be found on the afore-mentioned day in his treasury. Then, by a further distribution, he divided two of those three parts into twenty-one parts, and kept the third part undivided.

The distribution of the two parts into twenty-one is to be carried out in the following way. As there are known to be twenty-one metropolitan cities in his realm, one of those twenty-one parts is to be handed over to each metropolitan city by his heirs and friends for the purpose of almsgiving. The Archbishop who at the time of his death is ruling the metropolitan sees shall receive that part for his church and divide it among his suffragans; one-third going to his own church and two-thirds being divided among his suffragans.

Each of these divisions—which, as already mentioned, are made out of the first two-thirds, and are twenty-one in number, according to the number of the metropolitan sees—is separated from the rest and put away by itself in a repository of its own with the title of the city attached to which it is to be given. The names of the metropolitan sees, to which this alms or largess is to be given, are Rome, Ravenna, Milan, Fréjus, Grado, Cologne, Mainz, Juvavum which is also called Salsburg, Trèves, Sens, Besançon, Lyons, Rouen, Rheims, Arles, Vienne, Darantasia, Embrun, Bordeaux, Tours, Bourges.

The following disposition shall be made of the one part hitherto left undivided. When the first two parts have been distributed into the before-mentioned divisions, and have been put away under seal, this third part shall be employed for daily uses, as not being alienated by any bond or promise of the owner; and it shall be so used as long as he himself remains in the flesh or judges its employment to be necessary to him. But after his death or his voluntary retirement from the affairs of the world that part shall be divided into four subdivisions. Of these subdivisions one shall be added to the before-mentioned twenty-one parts; the second shall be taken by his sons and daughters, and by the sons and daughters of his sons, and shall be divided among them in just and reasonable proportion; the third shall be devoted to the use of the poor in the manner usual among Christians; the fourth part shall similarly be divided for alms and go to the support of the servants, both men and women, who attend to the needs of the palaces.[53]

On 21 January 814 CE, Charlemagne took ill at his palace in Aachen, suffering from a lung disease that was making it difficult for him to breathe. Seven days later, on 28 January 814 CE, Charles I of France passed away, leaving behind an incredible legacy and the potentials for an enormous power vacuum in France. He was immediately entombed at the church of Aachen, hastily buried before his corpse would be allowed to rot, though with the winter being terribly cold, was completely unnecessary. He took his final communion prior to his death with the priest reading him his last rites, helping to ensure that his trip into the gates of heaven would be unabated.

---

[53] Einhard 53

His body was washed and treated with the usual ceremonies, and then, amidst the greatest grief of the whole people, taken to the church and buried. At first there was some doubt as to where he should rest, since he had given no instructions during his lifetime. But at length all were agreed that he could be buried nowhere more honourably than in the great church which he had built at his own expense in the same town, for the love of our Lord God Jesus Christ and the honour of His holy and ever-virgin Mother. There he was buried on the same day on which he died. A gilded arch was raised above the tomb, with his statue, and an inscription. The inscription ran as follows:—

"Beneath this tomb lies the body of Charles, the great and orthodox Emperor, who nobly expanded the kingdom of the Franks and reigned prosperously for forty-seven years. He departed this life, more than seventy years of age, in the eight hundred and fourteenth year of our Lord, in the seventh indiction, on the fifth day before the Kalends of February."[54]

His death was mourned across his kingdom with monks, scholars, and nobles all taking time to weep at the passing of their great and beloved leader. His lands, fortunately, did not go into immediate turmoil, as his son as just as gifted with organization as he was. The fear of his father's army was passed down to him, with his successes in Spain telling the stories of his personal success. However, the peace was temporary, as the realm Charlemagne created would be thrust into civil war by 830 CE, sixteen years after his death.

---

[54] Einhard 54

Chapter 15
The Legacy of Charlemagne

As one of the greatest rulers in the history of the world, Charlemagne's legacy is regarded as one filled with achievements both domestically and abroad. While the obvious achievement, his vast expansion of Catholicism and his territory, cannot be stated enough, other things played a significant role regarding his legacy.

Charlemagne is credited with the start of the Carolingian Renaissance, the movement that saw a rebirth in art, music, and language. Through reforming education and importing the best and brightest minds to his kingdom from all over Europe, Charlemagne created the foundation for the culture of Europe through the middle ages and up to the next Renaissance. His achievements in education alone, including the trivium and quadrivium in the common core of his education studies, standardized the method of teaching for the next eight centuries, paving the way for the scientists and great thinkers of the future to be prepared. Without Charlemagne, the world may not have Isaac Newton or Voltaire, two men who drastically shaped their respective disciplines. His educational reforms are one of his greatest achievements and should not be discounted.

The standardization of writing, along with the coding of the laws was another incredible achievement in his legacy. By actually documenting and reforming the laws, it made it simpler to govern the acquired territories and manage the lords and counts that he placed to rule. These would help form the foundation for law, keeping the territories in tact after his death.

The start of the Reconquista is another incredible achievement. By actively fighting the Umayyad Caliphate and the Moors, Charlemagne fought back against the marauding Muslims and kept them in Spain, allowing his son to finish them off and make it to where they never traveled over into France again, creating the Spanish March to act as the buffer state between the two realms. Eventually, over the next six hundred years, the Spanish Christians would fight back against the Moors, driving out the Emirate of Cordoba and establishing a Christian monarchy. Without Charlemagne driving the Caliphate further back, wars with the Moors could have continued for years to come.

His territories would eventually be divided. Upon the death of his son, Louis the Pious, Charlemagne's territories would be split into several of the modern French and German states that are around today. Thus, the vast territory that Charlemagne was able to amass was split up forty years later. The legacy regarding this is how he was able to convert these pagan, Germanic lands into Catholic kingdoms, serving the papacy and standardizing the rule. The early forms of feudalism were crucial to the organization of this empire, especially as land was passed down equally amongst all of the legitimate sons.

To summarize, Charlemagne's legacy cannot be measured by one crowning achievement. Unlike his grandfather, Charles Martel, there is not one outstanding moment in his entire life that stands out as more significant than others. His grandfather drove the Caliphate out at the Battle of Tours, essentially ending the Islamic aggression in France and forcing them back into Aquitaine. Charlemagne's legacy can only be summed up as one of the most complete and total kingdoms in the history of the world.

In conclusion, Charlemagne was a barbarian king who led an army of barbarians to do barbarian things. However, by barbarian king, he was a very noble, pious, and brilliant man who revolutionized many things and inspired positive change in his realm. By an army of barbarians, they were trained, seasoned fighters who were also land holders; many of whom were educated and very wealthy. By doing barbarian things, Charlemagne built one of the greatest empires to ever exist.

Works Cited

The bulk of this work uses primary information; sources credited for being at the event when it occurred and recording the data. Through that information, analysis and conclusions have been drawn from them. All opinions in this work are my own and obtained through the use of these documents, unless otherwise noted.

Einhard and the Vita Karoli

The *following account of that most glorious Emperor Charles was written, as is well known, by Eginhard, who amongst all the palace officials of that time had the highest praise not only for learning but also for his generally high character; and, as he was himself present at nearly all the events that he describes, his account has the further advantage of the strictest accuracy.*

He was born in eastern Frankland, in the district that is called Moingewi, and it was in the monastery of Fulda, in the school of Saint Boniface the Martyr, that his boyhood received its first training. Thence he was sent by Baugolf, the abbot of the monastery, to the palace of Charles, rather on account of his remarkable talents and intelligence, which even then gave bright promise of his wisdom that was to be so famous in later days, than because of any advantage of birth. Now, Charles was beyond all kings most eager in making search for wise men and in giving them such entertainment that they might pursue philosophy in all comfort. Whereby, with the help of God, he rendered his kingdom, which, when God committed it to him, was dark and almost wholly blind (if I may use such an expression), radiant with the blaze of fresh learning, hitherto unknown to our barbarism. But now once more men's interests are turning in an opposite direction, and the light of wisdom is less loved, and in most men is dying out.

And so this little man—for he was mean of stature—gained so much glory at the Court of the wisdom-loving Charles by reason of his knowledge and high character that among all the ministers of his royal Majesty there was scarce anyone at that time with whom that most powerful and wise King discussed his private affairs more willingly. And, indeed, he deserved such favour, for not only in the time of Charles, but even more remarkably in the reign of the Emperor Lewis,[2] when the commonwealth of the Franks was shaken with many and various troubles, and in some parts was falling into ruin, he so wonderfully and providentially balanced his conduct, and, with the protection of God, kept such a watch over himself, that his reputation for cleverness, which many had envied and many had mocked at, did not untimely desert him nor plunge him into irremediable dangers.[55]

Einhard's work is the backbone for any all scholarly works on Charlemagne. His incredible detail, combined with actually taking part in his court, allowed him the ability to transcribe the actual facts regarding his reign and leave historians with a working account of his life. Without the Vita Karoli, historians would struggle to understand why Charlemagne was able to amass such a great empire, as well as understand the great things that he accomplished domestically. His outline of Charlemagne's reforms, including the recruitment of many incredible scholars and religious figures, helps us to understand who Charlemagne actually was, and, furthermore, breaks the stigma of the barbarian ruler. Because of Einhard, we're able to see that the barbarian ruler wasn't what fiction

---

[55] Prologue of Vita Karoli written by Strabo Walafrid

124

writers and Roman historians have depicted them as. They were motivated highly motivated people, though motivated by different things. They were typically organized and had a structure of leadership. The biggest thing about Einhard is that he single handedly broke the stigma associated with barbarians, especially those who fell under the leadership of the Catholic Church. The barbarians who sacked Rome were depicted as murderous thugs who were bent on pillaging and destruction, and it is told that way because the Romans, more specifically the church, kept up with the records of the time; this is one of the few incidents where history was not written by the winners. The Huns were heathens and were bent on conquering and destruction as they were a nomadic race of warriors who eventually settled near the Danube River, so the Roman accounts of them can be viewed as accurate. However, the Visigoths and Vandals, while also told to be violent and ruthless by the Romans, seem to offer a lot more in terms of culture and leadership. They grew from tribes in Germany, assimilating with others and growing into great kingdoms, only to be able to challenge Rome and attack them at their weakest. Both of these groups were not raging hordes of warriors, but organized soldiers who were able to best the Roman legions.

With Einhard discussing, in detail, the people in the German and Slavic states, as well as the Visigothic settlements in southern France, the readers and historians are able to see how the Merovingian and Carolingian rulers came about and how they weren't very different from the Vandals and Visigoths. Charlemagne, however, did reform many of the practices and put the world into motion, bringing Europe out of its "Dark Age," and into a more prosperous time. Without Einhard, we would not know as much as we do about how Europe rebounded after the fall of the Roman Empire.

The Monk of St. Gall

Also known as Notker the Stammerer, he was a beloved Benedictine poet who resided at the monastery of St. Gall. He wrote the story of Charlemagne in late 800s following his death, recanting the tales from many men of the church to preserve the historical accounts. His account is second hand, though regarded as primary in the sense of how close to the time he lived. His personal accounts, combined with the incredibly gifted storytelling, make this work something to be treasured. His playful accounts and anecdotes make Charlemagne appear to be a lot more of a human king, and not just am ambivalent one.

Royal Frankish Annals

These books tell the stories of the kings, wars, conquests, and struggles of the Franks from 741 CE with the death of Charles Martel to 829 CE. They are incredibly detailed and were recorded by a personal scholar at the behest of the king. They were commissioned by the kings, wanting to keep records of their times in office to keep for posterity. Comprised of five different books, many attribute Einhard, the man who compiled the Vito Karoli, as the man who compiled the second book, most closely associated with Charelmagne, as the information overlaps almost identically. However, Volume 1 gives historians the ability to see into the formation of modern France by Pepin the Short taking the territories from his brother and creating a unified line. It's also important because it shows Pepin the Shorts ascension to the monarchy, deposing the former rulers and establishing the Carolingians as the monarchs, and not just the Mayors of the Palace, who were technically the leaders anyway.

The Song of Roland

Regarded as one of the oldest pieces of literature in the world, this work was told orally for many years before finally being written in England in the 1200s. This epic poem follows Roland, one of the commanders of the rear guard of Charlemagne during his Spanish campaign and highlights the treachery that leads to his own death. It glorifies Charlemagne while telling a captivating story for the readers.

Gregory of Tours and the Historia Francorum

In his work, the Historia Francorum, Gregory tells the story of the Merovingian and Carolingian kings, culminating in Clovis's baptism and other highlights. This is one of the few works outlining the period from around 435 CE with the Christianization of Gaul to about 530 CE.

Isidorus Pacensis and the Mozarabic Chronicle of 754

This work covers Islamic rule of Spain, starting with the march of the Umayyad Caliphate through Africa in 610 and ending in 754. This work chronicles the Islamic march through the various European territories, along with the conquests of Bordeaux and the Islamic defeat at the Battle of Tours.

Fear Thy Name

How Genghis Khan's Brutality Created One of
The Most History's Largest Empire

By
<u>Michael Klein</u>

Table of Contents

Introduction

All of the greatest figures throughout history have some sort of reputation attached to them that is regarded as truth by the general population. Julius Caesar is known as a politically corrupt military genius. Napoleon Bonaparte has a reputation of being fiery and irritable. Queen Cleopatra is known for her beauty and charm, and the cunning combination of the two. The issue with these generalizations, however, is that they never paint a full picture of these people. These human beings lived and breathed the same air we do, and felt the same emotions we felt. Every great character in history is more complex than just a one sentence description. All of this is especially true with Genghis Khan.

Genghis Khan was the driving force behind the establishment of the Mongolian Empire. He used his military ingenuity to lead a multitude of successful campaigns across the regions of Asia and Eastern Europe, creating the largest empire the world had ever seen. At the height of his power, Genghis Khan likely controlled more territory than most individuals in history ever have. He used his almighty singular rule to unify a territory of warring tribes, and build a politically and socially united empire that had major implications, such as having the Silk Road, for the first time in its history, existing under one cohesive political landscape. Genghis Khan set out with a goal in his mind that did not just center around global domination, and total control over all people's and territories. His goal was this unification, and uplifting of the people under one dominant rule. He set out to create an empire allied under the same ideologies, cultures, and customs.

As a ruler, Genghis Khan could actually be described as benevolent. He was not the ruthless dictator that his ornery reputation possibly mistakes him to be. He had the interest of the people in mind as he fought valiantly to expand and strengthen his empire. Religious tolerance was a significant practice of Genghis Khan's, encouraging acceptance of varied ways of thinking under Mongolian culture. Genghis Khan's ultimate goal was peace and unity within his empire. Outside of the borders of the empire's territory, however, was a different story.

Genghis Khan's mixed interpretations throughout history stem from his military conquests, and the tactics he used in his sixteen years of conquest. Reports and literature of the military conquests of Genghis Khan are all connected by a thread of brutality and massacre. He was absolutely ruthless in battle, and led with a ferocity that invigorated his followers, and allowed him to enjoy many victories over armies significantly larger than his own. Genghis Khan was a fear monger, striking terror into the hearts of those who opposed him, and he, by most accounts, was very good at it. Some of his bloodiest campaigns were characterized by genocide, and mass murder of the civilian population was a common practice for the Khan.

These conflicting demeanors between Genghis' strategies, an utterly ruthless military strategy combined with a forgiving political and social nature, are what make it so hard to characterize the great and mighty ruler. There are populations across the world who hate him, and many who revere him. Modern day Mongolia even hails him as the founding father of the country, and his birthday is considered a national holiday. The impact he had during his time changed history, and was incredibly influential to the geopolitical makeup of the world today. Regardless of how he is viewed, this impact cannot and is not ignored. It may have been through unsavory tactics, but Genghis Khan most certainly left his mark on the world.

It shouldn't be all too surprising that intense violence characterized the adult exploits of Genghis Khan, considering violence was a part of his life from the beginning. Genghis Khan, born Temujin, came into the world during tumultuous times for Mongolia. It was a divided nation, split amongst warring tribes who all possessed their own petty rivalries. When he was only nine years old, Temujin's father was poisoned and killed by one of these antagonistic tribes, and Temujin found himself thrust to the forefront of his family. He was quickly robbed of a childhood, and survival became his primary concern as an adolescent.

Temujin grew up in a world of political turmoil, and watched and waited until the time was right to exploit these unstable conditions for his own gain. His timing was superb, and Temujin led campaigns to conquer and unite the rival tribes amongst Mongolia, and he formulated the Mongol Empire under his rule. It was here that he claimed the title of Genghis Khan.

Once the nation was unified, expansion became Genghis Khan's only focus. The next sixteen years led from one campaign to the next, with Genghis Khan knowing nothing but victory as his enemies crumbled at his feet. It was one of the quickest surges of power history had ever seen. The Mongol Empire expanded at an unprecedented rate, and began to pose a threat to the entire world. For whatever reputations might be inaccurate about the man, it is safe to say that he was truly unstoppable at the height of his military career.

Unfortunately, we'll never be sure of what Genghis Khan's ultimate goals were. During his final campaign, Genghis Khan was thrown from his horse and suffered severe injuries. Within only a short time he died of these injuries and left the Mongolian Empire to his sons, whom he had divided power amongst years before his death. His sons were able to expand the empire even further, until its eventual fragmentation and collapse years later.

It's astounding that someone who died almost 1000 years ago remains with as much relevancy as Genghis Khan does today. His is a name that is still known all across the world, and many people will at least have some idea of what he did, or what he is known for. Genghis Khan led an extravagant life full of drama and violence, and gave history one of its most astounding stories of human achievement. He may have a reputation rife with blood and brutalism, but the man himself goes much deeper than that. He exists on a very human level, not at all out of touch with his emotions. The details of this man's life provide an intriguing story of someone with clear goals, and a decisive way of obtaining those goals. Genghis Khan's life is one that has earned its place in our history textbooks, and what he accomplished and how he changed the world is something that deserves to be remembered.

Chapter 1
A Tumultuous Childhood

The name we all know this influential historical figure by is, of course, Genghis Khan. However, this namesake isn't actually a real name. Rather, it is a title which roughly translates to "universal ruler." The man who would come to be known as Genghis Khan was not born with this name, but he would certainly come to earn it. Instead, the mighty warlord known as Genghis Khan was born, simply, Temujin.

The name Temujin might not have the same perpetuity and might that Genghis Khan has, but the lineage associated with Temujin was not something to be scoffed at. Temujin's family history is rife with powerful reputation, at least on his father's side. He was born into the House of Borjigin. This clan made up the ruling class of the Mongolian population. Temujin's father, Yesugei, was a major player in Mongolian politics, and was descended from incredibly powerful names in the history of Mongolia. He was the grandson of Khabul Khan, and the nephew of Ambaghai and Hotula Khan as well. These three individuals were all prominent rulers of the Khamag Mongol confederation, which was essentially a loose pact between Mongolian tribes that strived to retain peace and balance in the Mongolian region. Mongolia at this time was comprised of little more than nomadic tribes who had scant need for political constraints. It was the beginnings of political stability in the region, at least in some capacity, and Yesugei would carry on their legacy.

Temujin was also a direct ancestor of Bondochar Munkhag, a Mongolian warlord who, in all of Mongolian history, is only exceeded in reputation by Temujin himself. Bondochar Munkhag was the founder of the Borjigin clan, and had earned his place in Mongolian history as one of their greatest unifiers. He led the most significant Mongolian expansion endeavors in history, until, of course, Temujin came around. Clearly, it was in Temujin's blood to play an active role within the Mongolian Empire, but he of course exceeded all expectations.

Temujin's mother didn't come from a lineage nearly as notable as his father had. Hoelun was nothing more than a captive, and likely did not willingly give Yesugei the four sons he would have by her. She belonged to the Olkhunut tribe, a less prominent nomadic tribe that would still play a role later in Temujin's life.

This was a period of time and in a part of the world where men were the major players in society, and they called all of the shots. Women were more of a commodity, and property available to be traded and married off for nothing more than political gain. Women were used for various purposes, many of which were quite homely. They prepared meals and raised children, primarily, but they were also used to collect bows and arrows after a battle. Sometimes, in keeping with the warlike Mongolian spirit, women were also in charge of finishing off wounded enemies on the battlefield.

In Hoelun's case, she was originally meant to be married to a member of the Merkit confederation, a neighboring coalition of nomadic tribes. On her way to the Merkit camp, however, Yesugei and a band of soldiers attacked her caravan. Hoelun was kidnapped and taken back to Yesugei's encampment. Here, he proclaimed her as his chief wife, an ironically honorable title within Mongolian culture. Polygamy was not an uncommon occurrence amongst these tribes, but the chief wife enjoyed a higher privilege than any of the other wives did. This title made it so only the children

Yesugei had with Hoelun would be heirs to Yesugei's position. Yesugei had two other sons from a previous marriage, but he had four more, one of which being Temujin, with his new captive wife.

Temujin was the second son born from Yesugei and Hoelun. He was born in 1162 and had one older brother, Hasar, and two younger brothers, Hachiun and Temuge. His older half brothers, Belgutei and Behter, were also a part of Temujin's childhood.

Temujin was born with a fighting spirit in his genes, being descended from some of the country's greatest warlords. It may be nothing more than ancient fable, but it is said that Temujin was born clutching onto a blood clot with his fist. This was meant as a sign that he would grow up to one day be a great leader, a prophecy that did indeed fulfill itself.

Ancestry and lineage was an incredibly important aspect of Mongolian social identity at this time, and scrupulous records were kept on family history. This meant that, by reputation alone, Temujin was born with more power than your average child born into a nomadic tribe. Even his name came with its own undeniable power. It is a name derived from two different Mongolian words. The first is *temur*, meaning "of iron," and the second is jin which is indicative of an agency or profession. So, roughly, Temujin translated to blacksmith; a noble, hardworking, and all important title of the time. It also was the name of a chieftain from a rivaling tribe, which Yesugei had captured right before his son's birth. The name brought with it a hardened sense of honor and respect, the likes of which Temujin would soon earn a reputation for in more than just name alone.

. . .

When it comes to the very early life of Temujin, not a whole lot is known. There was a fair amount of record keeping done at this time in history, but when you're talking about record keeping amongst disparate nomadic tribes, it is difficult to keep all of the details intact throughout history. But, while we might not know much of the specifics of the early days of Temujin, we do know the circumstances in which he grew up. Life on the road, living in nomadic conditions, was harsh to say the least. This was a region defined by war, and every sort of cutthroat tactic known to man could be expected in Mongolian conflict. Temujin likely grew up witnessing kidnappings, rape, and bloody conflict all around him. He was a witness of widespread tribal warfare, and had a front row seat to the vile revenge tactics these hotly contesting tribes employed on one another. Growing up in this environment obviously had an impact on the young Temujin. Before he was even old enough to comprehend the more complex political and societal strifes occurring before his eyes, the violence being used to get things done likely made an impression on his young mind.

It is around 1171 that we finally can begin to put concrete details to the life of Temujin. Mongolian society at the time was ruled, more than anything, by tradition. Power had shifted, been passed, and been established in similar ways throughout generations, and the value of namesake was crucial in keeping with Mongolian tradition. Children, much like women, were political commodities. Yesugei didn't have four children by Hoelun because he wanted a big, happy, loving family. He did this to secure his lineage, and spread his name by marrying off his sons to other tribes. This also aided in strengthening political ties between tribes. At the age of only nine years old Temujin found himself to be nothing more than a pawn in the political games of the region. An arranged marriage was set up for him, and he was to be married to Borte, a member of the Onggirat tribe, one of the various tribes comprising the Khamag Mongol confederation.

Temujin was brought to the Onggirats in 1171. He was nine at the time however, and Mongolian tradition stated that he could not marry until the age of twelve. He was to live in service to the head of the clan, Dai Setsen, for the next three years until he was old enough to marry Borte. These plans, however, were quickly squandered by unforeseen circumstances.

While Yesugei made his way back home, after dumping his son off with an allied tribe, he encountered another tribe which he did not hold the title of ally with. The Tatars were another of the five confederations comprising power in the Mongolian peninsula, and a Tatar general held captive by Yesugei is whom Temujin earned his name from. When Yesugei and the Tatars crossed paths, everything seemed friendly at first. Yesugei was invited to dine with the Tatars, with promises of an alliance on the horizon. This was not the case, as the Tatars had ulterior motives up their sleeves. They had poisoned the food which they offered to Yesugei, and he was given a swift, yet dreadful death at the hands of his enemies.

When news of his father's death reached Temujin, he realized he no longer had an obligation to Borte or the Onggirats, and he felt he was more needed with his family. Still just a child, Temujin returned home to take his father's position as head of the tribe. The confidence Temujin possessed as a ten year old was unprecedented, but the other members of the clan wanted nothing to do with him. They were not about to be ruled by a child. As far as they were concerned, with Yesugei dead any influence or control which he and his lineage retained on their tribe was dead with him. A family with which Yesugei had always had tensions with, the Tayichi'ud, usurped power over the Borjigin clan. Probably perceiving Temujin and his family as a threat to the clan's stability, as well as useless and weak additions to the tribe, the Tayichi'ud power banished Temujin and the rest of his family. On the next encampment move, Temujin, his mother, and the rest of his siblings were left behind to fend for themselves. Temujin now had a younger sister as well, Temulin, born just before Yesugei's death.

The family was banished to the woods, and left to depend totally on each other for survival. Hoelun and the children lived in awful poverty for years, barely scraping by on what scarce resources they could find in the woods and plains of Mongolia. Temujin and his brothers would hunt for small game like ox, marmots, or rabbits, while Hoelun would collect wild fruits and vegetables. Before he was even a teenager Temujin had experienced hardship unbeknownst to most of history's greatest leaders.

In 1172 Temujin's resilience was put to the ultimate test when he was forced to do something that would stick with him forever. As he and his family struggled through their abandonment, Behter, one of Temujin's two half-brothers, began to let his arrogance show. He was the oldest male in the family, and began to exercise that power. He made it a point that Hoelun would have to marry him when he became an adult, so that he could assume his power over the tribe. He also made it a point that he would be exploiting his power, and would be unopposed in doing so, given that his siblings were so young and weak, or so he thought.

Temujin wasn't going to stand for this arrogance, and he especially wasn't going to allow the mistreatment of his mother. Women were a discredited proportion of Mongolian society, yet Hoelun did not let this affect her own sense of tenacity. She had an obligation to her children, and she kept this obligation close to her heart as she cared for Temujin and his siblings in their darkest hour of abandonment by their tribe. A fiery anger was building in Temujin towards his half-brother. His overzealous claim to the family name was pompous and obnoxious, but also just false, as Temujin and his full brothers were the true heirs of the late Yesugei, being that Hoelun was Yesugei's chief wife. This resentment towards Behter culminated during a hunting trip one day. Temujin, Behter, and Temujin's full brother Hasar, were out hunting one day, when Behter's arrogance became too much for Temujin and his brother to stomach. They turned their weapons on Behter, and at only ten years old Temujin struck down his own half-brother, and dealt him the killing blow.

Despite not being the oldest of the brothers, Temujin's actions solidified him as head of the family. It was clear that he was going to keep the family safe, and could lead them to safety and remove them from these terrible circumstances.

. . .

Over the next few years Temujin and his family wandered around Mongolia as a family of nomads, constantly scavenging for food day in and day out. Over time their stockpile became greater, and they became a small band capable of fending for themselves. Temujin displayed unprecedented charisma for his age, and could persuade his way out of harrowing situations, and always find a way to come out on top. The family over time managed to secure horses for themselves, as well as supporters who would travel with them for a trade of food, shelter, or security. Temujin found great loyalty in all who chose to be at his side, and at a young age he was already building strength and support around him.

Displays of Temujin's persuasiveness almost sound like tales of legend, yet they paint a very accurate picture of the kind of influence this great figure possessed. There was an incident shortly after the family had secured nine horses for themselves, where eight of those nine steeds were stolen by a band of thieves. Temujin refused to let these thieves enjoy their prize, and he set off in hot pursuit. Along the way he came across a stranger named Bo'orchu. Bo'orchu was busy milking his cow when Temujin rode up on his horse to ask the stranger if he had seen the stolen horses. Bo'orchu must have been completely enamored by the prowess of this young man bravely pursuing a gang of violent marauders just for his horses. His admiration compelled him to abandon his current duties, and instead equip Temujin with a fresh horse, and ride out with him to pursue the thieves. Their pursuit culminated in a success, the horses were stolen back, and Temujin was able to return them to his family. He returned to them with the eight horses, as well as Bo'orchu who, rather than accept a reward for his service, had sworn allegiance to Temujin as a *nokor,* meaning free companion. He clearly saw the makings of incredible things in the eyes of Temujin, as he had abandoned his own family to live and die in servitude to Temujin and his family. Bo'orchu's loyalty would not waver, and he would eventually serve as a general under Temujin, after he came to be known as Genghis Khan.

Temujin's charisma won him loyal friends and close companions, but it also saved his life a time or two. Sometime in 1177, when Temujin was only fifteen, the Tayich'ud family, old rivals of Temujin's father, raided their encampment and captured Temujin. This was done for the gain of resources, obviously, but it was also a chance to humiliate Temujin and his namesake. The Tayich'ud could have easily killed Temujin on the spot, but instead they imprisoned him, and fashioned him with a wooden cangue, a contraption more commonly known in the Western world as stocks. It was a degrading way to be imprisoned, but Temujin knew he was going to use this cockiness against his captors, and only had to wait for a matter of nights before he could do so.

One evening saw the clan distracted with festivities, likely celebrating some recent victory, or perhaps continuing to celebrate their most valuable prisoner. Regardless, the proceedings of the evening left Temujin poorly guarded. Only a single sentry stood in between Temujin and his escape, and so, using the weight of his cangue, he threw himself at the sentry, knocking him to the ground. This bought Temujin the time he needed to flee. His escape became known quickly, obviously, and a search initiated that lasted all night long. Temujin was almost caught when he was seen by one of the Tayich'ud. There was no way to tell what Temujin said or did to this guard to convince him to help him in his escape, rather than turn him in, but that's just what happened. Temujin and his new companion managed to escape the Tayich'ud, and that companion would later serve as a general under Genghis Khan. The Khan was not someone who forgot a face, or its loyalty, and his rule was characterized by rewarding these kinds of actions.

.   .   .

In a few short years of growth, Temujin had earned himself a reputation greater than that of most men double, even triple his age at the time. This reputation spread like wildfire, and it allowed Temujin and his family to regain their prominence amongst the Borgjin clan. Temujin was merely a teenager, but already he was becoming familiar with the feeling of power over both people and territory. He was now faced with political and traditional obligations in order to preserve the integrity of his tribe, and its place within the confederation. Temujin was coming of an age where he could see the power which he could attain if he played his cards right, and so he let his games begin.

Temujin knew he obviously needed as many allies as possible if he was going to begin changing the landscape and writing his own chapter of history. As was so very common with Mongolian tradition, marriage was the best way for him to secure at least one tribe's loyalty. He decided to return to the Onggirat tribe and marry Borte. The marriage occurred when Temujin was still only sixteen, but shortly afterwards, Borte was kidnapped by the Merkits, who themselves already possessed a lot of resentment for Temujin's bloodline. Temujin's own mother was originally a part of this tribal coalition before she was kidnapped by Yesugei, and this wasn't a fact the Merkits hadn't forgotten. They were horribly cruel to Borte, and Temujin knew he was going to rescue her and make her captives pay.

This wasn't something Temujin was going to be able to do alone, though. Lucky for him, between his bloodline and his own charming personality, he had resources available to him. Temujin first sought help from Toghrul, an old ally of his father's. Toghrul was the Khan of Keraites, another of the five confederations of the area. He was known to those at the time as Toghrul, but in 1197 would be granted the Chinese moniker of Wang Khan, bestowed to him by the Jurchen controlled Jin dynasty. Toghrul and Temujin's father had been integral players in establishing relations between the Mongol confederations. Their own personal friendship was very strong, and they had even established an *anda* between them.

Anda's were sworn allies enacting a strong bond, a kind of blood brother relationship that was incredibly valued in Mongolian culture. Toghrul respected this title, and swore to support the bloodline of Yesugei. Thus, he equipped Temujin with an army of 20,000 soldiers.

Temujin sought help from another individual he was sure would come to his aid. This was Jamukha, a childhood friend of Temujin's. The two had grown up together, sharing childhood dreams of conquest and power. Their shared interests created a strong bond between the two, and they would also come to share the title of blood brothers between them. Of course, as they both grew older their desires for power sent them in opposite directions. Temujin was still on his course to holding an impressive title, but Jamukha had already found his own rise. He had risen to become Khan of the Jadaran tribe, and obviously felt the bloodlust driving his desire for conquest. He was reluctant to join Temujin at first, preoccupied with his own endeavors, and likely feeling a bit threatened by the fire in Temujin's eyes. With the help and persuasion of Toghrul, Jamukha was convinced to join forces with Temujin and help lead their cumulative army into battle with the Merkits. He might not have known it at the time, but as Temujin headed north to fight the Merkits and reclaim his captured wife, he was initiating the greatest period of change the Mongolian territories, including most of China and Central Asia, would ever know.

Chapter 2
Mongolia: A Rich History

Temujin, on his way to becoming Genghis Khan, was going to change the political, economic, and geographical landscape of his home territory. But, to fully understand the implications of what Temujin had set out to accomplish by initiating his first attack against a neighboring Mongol tribe, we must understand the history of this tumultuous region which brought it to where it was before 1206, the year Temujin would take his Khan title.

The geographical size and borders of what can be considered Mongolia was in a very liquid state for most of its history. Over the years power had shifted between tribal states and confederations, and the area can be constantly defined by warfare, whether Mongolia was trying to expand, or if it was trying to defend from Chinese invaders. It was not a region established with major cities and significant fortifications. Instead, Mongolia's ancient and medieval history is defined by nomads. The nomadic lifestyle was the only way of life at this time. This was common for the Central Asia reason, but due to geographic limitations, the nomadic lifestyle of Mongolia was different.

Mongolia is a uniquely situated region surrounded by harsh lands completely unsuitable for nomadic living. The region stretches out over the plains beneath the Altai Mountains, with rich rivers flowing through them. The river basins in the region made this area one of the most fertile lands in the world, and an excellent place to settle. Nomads relied on plentiful resources of wild fruits, veggies, and wildlife.

The geographic landscape essentially forced populations to inhabit this area, as opposed to the surrounding areas. To the North of the region was the frozen wasteland of Siberia, a place too deathly cold to even consider living and travelling with nothing more than tents and yurts. To the east was the growing Chinese power, as well as the Indian Ocean. Migration south was not an option either, as the Gobi desert stretched for thousands of miles, making it deathly hot, and equally as uninhabitable as its freezing counterpart in the north. Then of course the Western front was marked by the Altai Mountains, and with such fertile plains at their disposal, living as a nomad in the mountains seemed counterproductive.

These geographical limitations essentially cut off Mongolia from the rest of the world. The majority of its major conflicts before Genghis Khan were with China, as their growing empirical power had the desire to be unstoppable at the time, and Mongolia seemed ripe for the taking. Much of ancient Mongolian history is defined by the power struggle between Mongolia and China.

It was in the third century BC that the first ruling establishment was put into power over the region. The Xiongnu state helped create a sense of shared identity and unity in the Mongolian region, and a national desire for expansion was an enticing idea put into the heads of the tribal leaders. The Xiongnu were the very first people to invade China, and their arrival marked the first significant and consequential emergence of nomadic power in the region. The invasion was repelled, but caused enough of a stir for China to begin building their own fortifications to keep any future invaders, of which there would be plenty, out of their territory. These fortifications were all connected to one another to create a mighty 2,300 kilometer wall, otherwise known as the Great Wall of China.

The very first statehood established in Mongolia made a solid point that they were not part of the Chinese empire, and would exist as their own free region, a power on their own which was totally independent of China. This is one mindset that would remain consistent through pretty much the entirety of Mongolian history, long before and after the great Genghis Khan. The Chinese refuted these claims to power, and continued to wage war against the Mongolians all throughout their ancient history.

The Xiongnu ushered in a new era, bringing BC to AD, but the turn of the century saw their power begin to greatly diminish. By 48 AD the empire was split into norther and southern Xiongnu establishments, both of which left the Mongolian region to seek other prospects. The country was left vacant, and it wasn't long before another statehood had established dominance in the region.

In 93 AD the Xianbei took the place of the Xiongnu. They were up against the Han Dynasty of China, which was filled with national pride, and a desire to continue their campaigns against their nomadic neighbors. The Xianbei continued to fight off their attacks, while also extending their power to the West. The Xianbei marked a period of major growth for Mongolia, as they continued to cause unrest and dissention at the Chinese borders. As the Han Dynasty began to crumble, the Xianbei were able to exploit the internal strife and deterioration of the empire to grab a hold of more power than Mongolia had yet to know.

It was during the Xianbei rule that a faction of nomadic tribes broke off to the north, and established the Tuoba Wei. This clan gave way to the Rouran state, or Rouran Khaganate, which expanded even further north, gaining control of Eastern European territories. The Rouran ruling class was malicious,

147

and massively subjugated the Altai Turkics. They enjoyed growing power to the West, while at the same time China had stopped persisting as such a threat.

It wasn't long before a new threat arose, and it came from what should have been an obvious place. In 552 the Turks revolted against the Rouran Khaganate and earned their own rule over the region, establishing the Turkic Khaganate that same year. Three years later they finished off the Rourans and assumed total dominance of the once Rouran state. It was perfect timing, too, because the Chinese empire was weaker than ever. They surrendered to the Turkic power without a fight.

The Turkic Khaganate remained in existence for nearly two hundred years, subjugating many Chinese populations, and in turn being subjugated by many as well. The power struggle was in full swing at this time, with the Chinese fighting valiantly for their sovereignty. Eventually, the Turkick Khaganate was split into Eastern and Western Turkic Khaganates, and their power quickly disseminated. The final blows were dealt in the seventh century, when the Western Turkics failed in an assault on Chang'an, the capital of China. They were turned away, utterly defeated. The Eastern Turkics continued to fight off subjugation and invasion by the Chinese, but were eventually defeated by a different enemy. The Uyghurs were a subjugated clan to the West that had known great turmoil in the Turkic invasions. In 745 they had had enough, and revolted to establish the Uyghur Khaganate.

Ironically, the takeover of the Uyghur Khaganate marked one of the first peaceful periods of Mongolian history. Trade routes were established between Mongolia and China, and relative prosperity was known across the land. When the Tang Dynasty took power over China, however, they held onto that resentment towards their neighbors to the West. Not wanting to risk dissention, they decided not to directly attack the region themselves. Instead, they encouraged others to do their biddings for them. In secret they convinced the Yenisei Kirghiz and the Karluks, two regions that the influence of Chinese politics and society still had a grip on, to invade the Uyghur Khaganate. An all out invasion by the Kirghiz took place in 840, and the Uyghur were utterly defeated, scattered across the Mongolian plains. Ironically, the Kirghiz had no interest in the region they had just conquered. They were established much further to the West, and control over Mongolia was not in their intentions. Rather, it keeping good relations with the growing power of China that was in their best interest. Thus, the Mongolian region was left relatively empty, with dispersed nomadic tribes living in solidarity and having no influence over global society for the next sixty years or so.

The region knew no sort of statehood until a new leader, Ambagyan, rose up in 907 to establish the Khitan Liao Dynasty. The Liao Dynasty laid claim to most of the Mongolian region, assimilating the scattered peoples left over from the Uyghur Khaganate. This incredibly influential statehood quickly began posing another major threat to China. It grew rapidly, eventually controlling most of Northern China, at least everything north of the Yellow River. They were the first established power in the region to contest the idea of living the nomad life. They actually built cities which they could use as representations of their technical power, and innovative prowess, two things that helped show dominion and might over their subjects.

The Khitan state was, for all intents and purposes, a very successful one, bringing the country forward on a societal level. The Khitan people created their own alphabet, and printing technology also came to fruition in the area thanks to Khitan influence. Peace was known in the area once again until the Song Dynasty rose to power in China, and began to threaten the integrity of the Mongolian state. They did not have the capabilities to defeat the rapidly growing power of the Liao Dynasty, so they called upon the Jurchen, a Tungusic race of people, for assistance in their conquests. The coalition formed between the two powers waged a seven year war on The Liao Dynasty, which unsurprisingly tore the region to shreds.

By 1122 the Liao dynasty had denigrated into a vassal state, and their hold on the region was gone. It had been handed over to the Jurchen, whose leader declared himself the founder of this new era for China in the region. It was with the fall of the Liao dynasty that the Jin dynasty was born, and it came into the world fueled by bloodlust. The Jin wasted no time in spreading their conquests further, dominating the neighboring region of Goryeo, which is where Korea stands today. They even turned against the power which had called upon them in the first place, invading the Song dynasty in order to incite a whole cavalcade of ragged conflict in China. The Jin dynasty waited patiently for the dust to settle so they could lay claim to China, and the wait was worth it. The Jin dynasty would go on to become the ruling class of China for over 100 years, and they would not be challenged again until, you guessed it, Genghis Khan decided their influence needed to come to an end.

The Liao Dynasty marked the last time Mongolia was united under one statehood until Genghis Khan changed everything for the region. Internal struggle kept the country from going anywhere for the next few decades. Warring tribes kept up a consistent bout of anti-progress in the region, and the neighboring confederations trying to inject their own power and influence didn't help either. The beginning of Mongolia's medieval period was a rocky one to say the least. Tribes fended for themselves, and prosperity was nowhere to be found amidst these disparate plains.

The first semblance of a statehood began to reemerge early on in the 12th century. Warring tribes began consolidating, and putting their resources together to become a more unified power capable of fending off the always growing power of China, where the Jin dynasty retained gripping control. By about the halfway point of the century the Mongolian plateau was compromised of five major Mongolic tribal confederations, each with their own agendas, allegiances, and spheres of influence. Perhaps the strongest of these was the Khamag Mongol Khanate, placed in one of the most fertile regions of Mongolia, hidden away in the Khentii mountains at the base of the rivers Onon, Tuul, and Kherlen. This is the confederation of which Temujin was born into, and the one which his lineage had very strong ties to. It was Temujin's great grandfather, Khabul Khan, who became the first Khan of the Khamag Mongols, and it was he who would establish them as a legitimate power in the region.

The Jin obviously felt threatened by any amassment of power occurring in Mongolia, and so they sent an army to stomp out this growing threat, but Khabul Khan successfully repelled them, letting it be known that the Khamag Mongol Confederacy was a force to be reckoned with. Of course, they had other enemies to reconcile with as well.

One of the biggest adversaries of the Khamag Mongol confederacy was a rival confederacy known as the Tatars. The Tatars were a confederation neighboring Khamag Mongol to the East, and sharing a border with China. Before they fell, the Liao dynasty had enacted dominance over the Tatars. Thanks to the Jin invasion, the Tatars were freed from Mongolian subjugation, but this came with an obligation. There was a lot of pressure on the Tatars to throw their allegiance behind the Jin dynasty and, not wanting to face the consequences of denouncing their "saviors," their utmost support was given to their Chinese neighbors.

This period saw a lot of fighting between the Khamag Mongol and the Tatars, and the conflict would last up to Temujin's birth and beyond. When Khabul Khan stepped down from his Khanate duties, he was proceeded by Ambaghai Khan, who wanted to smooth relations with the Tatars. He tried to create an alliance by giving the Tatars his daughter as a bride. This peace seeking gesture was not reciprocated, unfortunately. Ambaghai was captured upon his arrival to the Tatar encampment, and the Tatars handed him straight over to their Jin allies. Upon receiving their prisoner, the Jin made their stance on the Khamag Mongol very clear. Ambaghai was swiftly executed, and then nailed to a wooden donkey for humiliation, and to send a violent message to their opposing forces on the Mongolian plateau.

It was Khabul Khan's son, Hotula Khan, who was elected to succeed Ambaghai and carry on the might of the Khamag Mongol, which refused to bend to the will of opposing forces, especially opposing Chinese forces. Hotula Khan led many an expedition against the Tatars, engaging in a total of thirteen battles with the confederation. The Tatars though, with the backing of the Jin power, were unable to be defeated completely, and retained their power in the East. In the last of these Khamag/Tatar engagements, Hotula Khan was killed, and the Khamag Mongol confederation was left without a Khan. Internal struggles within the confederation halted any political progress, and a new Khan was not elected. Instead, Yesugei, Temujin's father, came on as a supervisor and representative of the confederacy, along with the heads of the other major Khamag Mongol tribes. In 1171 the Tatars revealed that their grudge was still not over when the poisoned and killed Yesugei. This may have been a strategic move for them at the time, but it certainly painted a huge target on their backs for when Temujin decided he was ready to take his revenge and begin his conquests of Mongolia.

.   .   .

Three other confederations existed by the time Temujin was born, yet didn't know quite the power that the Khamag Mongols or the Tatars knew. The first was the Keraite Khanate. The Keraites were a Turco-Mongol tribal confederation who retained a tight grip on their power in Southern Mongolia. They were defined by a deeply loyal army with soldiers who valiantly and unwaveringly served the Khan, and the Khan alone. The Keraites were originally part of the Zubu confederacy, which they comprised the ruling class of. The Zubu confederacy had been a major adversary of the Liao dynasty, and the two had fought tirelessly for control of Mongolia. When the Liao dynasty was forced out by the Jin, the Zubu consolidated to the Keraites, and they reestablished themselves in southern Mongolia. Around the time of Temujin's birth is when the young Toghrul, son of Kurchakus Buyruk Khan, claimed the throne of the Keraites and became Toghrul Khan. His claim was legitimate, as his grandfather, Markus Buyruk Khan, had led the Keraites against the Liao dynasty at the turn of the 12th century. Toghrul became a close ally with the Khamag Mongol confederacy, becoming blood brothers with the late Yesugei.

Another of the five confederacies of the time were the Naimans. This small tribe began their growth in the heart of Mongolia, but had since moved further West. Another confederacy of Turkic origin, the Naimans used this lineage to establish relative peace with other Khanates of the area, such as the Khitan Khanate, also known as Qara Khitai. The Naimans led an existence under the radar, serving powers far greater than theirs to ensure some sort of peace, or at least prolonged survival for their heritage. They proved to be a resilient people who, even after the dissemination of Mongolian confederacies and tribes, continued to have a presence all over the region.

The last of the five confederacies was the Merkit, the confederation that had foolishly kidnapped Temujin's wife, and who would be the first victims of Temujin's unstoppable warfare. The Merkits were comprised of three tribes, otherwise known as the Three Merkits. These were the Uduyid Merkits, who inhabited the lower regions of the Orkhon River, the Uvas Merkits, who lived in between the Orkhon and Selenge Rivers, and the Khaad Merkits, who called the Selenge River bank home. The Merkits operated separately from any of the other powers in the region, but clearly were defined by a grudge against the Khamag Mongols. This certainly had to do with the fact that Yesugei had stolen Hoelun, his wife and Temujin's mother, from their tribe, never to return her. This is what prompted their kidnapping of Borte, an action which they never could have guessed the consequences of.

Chapter 3
Uniting Mongolia

To say that the political stability of Mongolia was shaky during Temujin's adolescence would be an understatement. He grew up surrounded by political turmoil, and spent his childhood learning what did and didn't work in a military campaign. He grew up dangerously smart, and now the time had finally come for him to use his insight directly, and lead a charge that would establish him as a dominant force to be reckoned with, along with displaying the punishments that should be expected for crossing him.

The Merkits knew that Temujin would be coming for Borte, but what they didn't know is the size of the army which he had managed to put behind him. Between the forces of himself, Toghrul, and Jamukha, Temujin was leading a viciously destructive army; one that would be incredibly dangerous to get in the way of.

Temujin and his allies handily defeated the Merkits. They managed to route them, and Temujin was able to practice his strategy of not leaving a single enemy force behind him in his wake. He came in swiftly and destructively, never giving the Merkits a chance for survival. Temujin looked for his conquests to be absolute, and made sure to leave none alive that had the will, the tenacity, or the downright stupidity to oppose him. Merkit nobility were slaughtered, while the common population was assimilated under the Mongolian power which Temujin represented. This would be a very common practice for Temujin, and it was incredibly useful in growing his army, as well as giving him a favorable view in the eyes of the general public. He sought to be more of a liberator for the common people, and a dangerously murderous opposition to the royal class individuals, at least in Mongolia.

Temujin's campaign against the Merkits couldn't have been more successful. He had defeated the first of Khamag Mongol's surrounding enemies, and had also reclaimed his wife. When he and Borte were reunited it was a joyous occasion defined by actual love. Nine months after her rescue Borte had her first child, Jochi. It was assumed that Jochi was the son of Borte and Temujin, but there is no certainty on this. Borte, during her captivity, was likely given away as a wife to one of the Merkit chieftains, or someone in their nobility. Given the timing of Jochi's birth, this will remain as one of history's unsolved mysteries.

.   .   .

Even though Temujin and Jamukha had enjoyed a great victory together, jealously and pettiness would begin to drive their friendship apart. Their childhood bond was shaken by Temujin's prolific military capabilities. Jamukha saw Temujin as a threat to his own want for power, and this is something he openly expressed. The friendship between the two men was on the rocks as they returned from Merkit, and it was completely shattered once they both began pursuing their own rises to power. It became increasingly obvious that their pride wouldn't allow them to reconcile, and only one of them could emerge victorious in retaining power over the growing Mongol state. It wasn't long before they had gone incredibly far away from their friendship, and could now be considered adversaries.

Temujin and Jamukha had drastically different viewpoints on how Mongolia should be governed, and this was likely one of the many reasons their rift developed as they both simultaneously began eyeing power. Jamukha was the traditionalist out of the two men. He believed in the ancient Mongolian power structure, which gave power to a noble class of elitists. These elitists had no merits but their name. Lineage and family name was the basis for the appropriation of power, and Temujin saw this as an incredibly unfit way to divide strength. He believed those with power should possess the personal attributes which make them deserving of that power. He assigned positions based on the talent of the individual, and their loyalty to him. Temujin felt this created a far more dedicated powerhouse to surround himself with. The aristocracy method alienates all of the lower class populations, which Temujin relied on for his growth in power and popularity. His meritocratic policies engaged a much broader collection of supporters, and his popularity amongst the masses posed a major threat to Jamukha.

As it became more and more obvious that Temujin was vying for ultimate power over Mongolia, Jamukha became increasingly worried that he would accomplish this. He had obviously shown his unbridled military might in his campaign against the Merkits, and was seen as a friend of the people, something which the shady and enigmatic Jamukha did not have working in his favor. Even prophecy was acting on behalf of Temujin. A shaman named Kokochu proclaimed that the Eternal Blue Sky, essentially the prevailing God of Mongolia's shamanistic religion, had "set aside the world for Temujin." He was going to barrel towards that power which he knew he could attain, and would be unopposed in doing so if Jamukha didn't step in.

In 1186 the final straw broke Jamukha, and prompted him to take action. This was the year that Temujin was elected Khan of the Khamag Mongol confederation. He had been given the keys to a massive power grab of the entire region, and this worried Jamukha greatly. He acted quickly, and amassed an army containing 30,000 soldiers who had agreed to support his rise to power. Temujin was taken off guard by this sudden hostility from a man he was once able to call friend, and was not prepared in the slightest to deal with an opposing force of this magnitude. Temujin didn't expect his next adversary to come from within, and this was his downfall. He suffered a grave defeat at the Battle of Dalan Balzhut in the year 1187 , and was subsequently exiled by Jamukha, who was now invigorated with ruthless fire.

Jamukha was particularly harsh in his ousting of Temujin, which would not work in his favor in the long run. He took a number of captives in his victory, and selected 70 of these captives to be boiled alive in a cauldron. It was a grotesque and unnecessary act that most certainly turned people against Jamukha. He had every intention to rule by fear, using his power to quell his own insecurities and live the ruling lifestyle he wished to live, which was one that kept himself safe before anyone else. This only drew sympathy for the exiled Temujin, and Jamukha would never know the popularity which he likely longed for.

Temujin had lost his grip on the Khamag Mongols, but this wouldn't stop him from consolidating his forces and looking for other ways to gain power. Toghrul was exiled along with him, so he still had a valuable ally at his side. There exists a ten year period of Temujin's life, stretching between 1187 and 1197, that has scarce historical record verifying anything that happened in this time. It is likely that Temujin was amassing his forces, making sure to lie low during the growing might of Jamukha. Jamukha had been a setback in his plans for taking total control over the Mongol regions, but he knew there were other ways to go about achieving what he set out to do.

This period of time was likely about reputation for Temujin. He was technically nothing more than a low ranking chieftain after his exile, and could easily paint himself to be of no concern to other tribes. He kept his allegiance with Toghrul strong as the two built up their forces and planned their next move into the Mongolian confederations. Temujin had obviously been eyeing the Tatars for a while now. They held strategically important land to the West, and were also the murderers of his father. He wanted to inflict revenge, more than anything, on these people. His opportunity to do so came in 1197.

Temujin had made himself seem totally non-threatening to the Chinese Jin dynasty, all for the purpose of using their prowess for his next move. Temujin and his Mongol forces, along with Toghrul and his Keraite army formed an alliance with the Jin in order to launch a massive assault on the Tatars. Temujin might not have been the primary leader in this attack, but he used his allied resources wisely, and was part of a huge victory over the Tatars. The confederation was all but wiped out, with very few surviving populations being scattered across the region. The Jin showed their great admiration for Temujin and Toghrul by reinstating their power in the region. Toghrul was even bestowed with the highly respected title of Wang Khan. Temujin and Toghrul were now back in a strengthened position to continue their plight of the Mongol confederations. At least for now, they perceived no threat from China, as the Jin obviously didn't see the two of them as much of a substantial force. They could focus all of their attention on their own region, now, and fight back against what the tyrannical Jamukha was trying to do with his harsh rule. In 1201 he had been appointed as Gur Khan, a title which translates to universal ruler most commonly used by the Qara Khitai.

At this point, there were only two confederations which still posed a threat to the power of Temujin and Toghrul, and these were the Merkits to the north and the Naimans to the west. In a series of short yet bloody campaigns, the Merkits were easily defeated, and their namesake was completely scattered. The vast majority of Merkit populations and culture was absorbed by what was coming to be known as Temujin's Mongol confederation. The rest sided with the Naimans.

Jamukha's power had been reduced to nothing more than his control over the Naiman populations, and this was the last great opposition to Temujin within Mongolia. Before he led his campaign into Naiman territory, though, a deteriorating friendship delayed his progress.

There were hardly any signs of this estrangement, but around 1201 Toghrul decided he could not let Temujin continue his unabashed power trip. Toghrul didn't come to this conclusion entirely on his own, but rather was influenced by his son, Senggum. Senggum saw Temujin as the all powerful warlord he would become, and was mighty jealous of how easily Temujin was amassing this power. He was likely frustrated, seeing as his father was aiding Temujin in this great battle for domination, but seeing little reward of his own. Given their rich history, Toghrul had always considered himself an unwavering ally of Temujin and his namesake, and Senggum saw issue with this blind faith. Toghrul was pulled violently in opposing directions, but ultimately had to leave his loyalty with his son. He listened closely to all that Senggum was putting in his ear, leading him to become adversarial towards Temujin, refusing to play the game of political maneuvers that Temujin needed his help with.

Toghrul illustrated this break in friendship concisely when he allowed Senggum to go forward with a plan to assassinate Temujin. Lucky for Temujin, he caught wind of Senggum's plans, and put a quick end to them. Senggum's followers were killed, while Senggum managed to escape, eventually finding refuge with the Xi-Xia to the south. It was now more apparent than ever that the friendship between Toghrul and Temujin had come to an end.

Yet, just in case the message wasn't clear enough, Toghrul let one more action drive home the split in their relationship. Temujin needed a wife for his eldest son, Jochi, and wanted it to be a marriage that solidified an important political partnership. In a last attempt to reconcile their friendship, he requested that Toghrul marry his daughter to Jochi. Toghrul adamantly refused, an act that could be perceived as treasonous in Mongolian culture. The rift was more apparent than ever, and now would begin to take its toll on not just the two men as individuals, but on the world.

Now that they were staunch adversaries, Toghrul sought a way to defeat Temujin, and he found his best option was to seek a former enemy by the name of Jamukha. Toghrul and Jamukha formed a hesitant partnership, and consolidated their forces with the Keraites. Temujin's victories had already given him the reputation he needed to lead any campaign he put his mind to, and as soon as he set out on his campaign to end the alliance between Toghrul and Jamukha, dissention began. Jamukha only knew power by force, and had none of the benevolence of Temujin that had earned him such loyal soldiers. An army without fighting spirit was one that was absolutely terrified by the might of Temujin. Uninspired by the leadership of Jamukha, and the flakiness of Toghrul, many of their allies abandoned them before Temujin and his forces even showed up. As Jamukha's army dwindled, Temujin's only grew. Toghrul, likely aware of his mistake, harshly butted heads with his supposed ally, and their leadership over what army they were left with was practically non-existent. Jamukha's presence led to the crumbling of the Keraite infrastructure long before Temujin's forces would show up. The two arrogant leaders, drowned in their own hubris, didn't stand a chance when Temujin did arrive.

Temujin's campaign against the Keraites in 1203 was another swift and destructive one. It scattered populations and absorbed even more soldiers and civilians. Jamukha managed to flee the fighting, and made his way to Naiman, the last confederacy that could pose as any semblance of safety for him and anyone else who opposed Temujin's rapid rise to power. Toghrul was not so lucky. He managed to flee as well, but when he met up with Naiman soldiers during his escape, they mistook him for a member of the enemy army, and killed him on sight. Just like that, Toghrul, a name that had so much weight and prowess behind it in the early days of the Mongolian confederations, was now dead, due to an embarrassing defeat in an ill-advised, unprepared campaign. Temujin proved himself to be more resilient than any military leader at the time, and showed the world that any who opposed him did so foolishly.

Despite all of the defeats, Jamukha was still not prepared to concede to Temujin. A man he had once valued as a friend and insightful colleague, he was now vowing to oppose till his dying breath. He assumed power in Naiman, and continued to uphold his promise of rejecting Temujin's growing influence over the Mongolian plateau. Temujin was ready to eliminate this issue for good, and formed a coalition of tribes aiming to bring Jamukha to his knees. Jamukha had the strength of his own coalition, the one that elected him Gur Khan in 1201, and was ready to fight against him. Temujin did not want to kill his childhood friend, whose character he still valued, but he was ready to strip the man of every last bit of power he might possibly retain, so as to remove him as a threat once and for all.

It seems that Jamukha is the only person in the entire world at the time that failed to realize he didn't stand a chance against Temujin. He would hear no calls for peace, or even stalemate. He was convinced that Mongolian society could never move forward if both of the men remained alive. His thirst for victory over his former ally was sad, almost desperate, and his forces could see this fact plain as day. Before the campaign got underway, Jamukha was abandoned by a number of his generals, who switched sides to fight for the far more promising Temujin.

Temujin was likely trying to prompt a surrender, but Jamukha wasn't going to give him the satisfaction. He forced more fighting to occur, and a number of battles went underway that eventually led to Jamukha's defeat. Not a defeat on the battlefield, however. Fed up with his arrogant tactics which were sending hundreds of Naiman soldiers to their death, Jamukha's own men mutinied and turned him in to Temujin in 1206.

Temujin displayed clemency once again, and offered Jamukha his life. He had the men who turned in Jamukha killed, as he did not want disloyal men to be a part of his army. He surely hoped this would show Jamukha that he still valued their friendship, and was still willing to reconcile. It was Temujin's final attempt at bringing Jamukha back to his side, but Jamukha once again refused. He told Temujin that there could be only one sun in the sky, affirming Jamukha's stance that there would never be peace or unity amongst the Mongol confederations with both of them still standing. He refused to stand at Temujin's side, and instead requested an honorable death. It was customary that a noble death was one that involved no bloodshed, and rather involved the breaking of one's back. And so, Temujin had his own childhood friend, a close companion who had devolved into a power hungry madman who boiled his enemies alive in cauldrons, put to a noble death, and had his back broken. Jamukha may have died full of resentment towards Temujin, but Temujin respected Jamukha until his dying breath. He even buried Jamukha with the golden belt he had given to him when their blood brother bond was forged. And so ended a tragic saga of two estranged friends.

With this death, Temujin finally found himself unopposed in Mongolia. The last of the Naimans were dealt with swiftly, and any Merkit opposition that had joined forces with them was handled in the same sweep. Temujin was now the unopposed conqueror of the Mongolian steppe, and he had officially established his own Mongol confederation which united all tribes under one unifying association. 1206 would be the last year Temujin answered to that name. His name would now be defined by his title, and that title was of course the mightily ominous moniker of Genghis Khan.

Chapter 4
Mongolia Under Khan

1206 was THE vital turning point in Mongolian history and, in fact, world history. The structure of Mongolian politics was shattered. Tribes and clans were dispersed, and retained no individual power. They were now unified under one code, one ideal, and one ruler. The mass of land that had housed the Khamag Mongol, the Tatars, the Merkits, the Keraites, the Naimans, and various others, would now come to be known only as Mongolia, or the Mongol Empire.

That year, the noble families of the Mongolian tribes met at the kurultai, the council of Mongol chiefs which met to elect new Khans. Temujin was elected unanimously, given that he had more than proven himself worthy. It was the first time in medieval history that Mongolia had been unified. They were now a collective force which possessed the strength in numbers needed to expand, and they had the ruler they would need to make their mark on history. Temujin's military ability had been unmatched, and it was clear he was the only one of them worthy to lead the armies of the consolidated Mongolia into battle. Total power was given to Temujin, and the kurultai overwhelmingly elected him to be their new great Khan, and their universal ruler. They chose him and gave him that legendary title of Genghis Khan.

Genghis Khan sought to completely revolutionize this newly conformed empire he now had universal leadership over. Genghis wasn't only looking for immeasurable power for himself. He also sought peace and prosperity for the empire of Mongolia, and that could only be achieved with a ground-up restructuring of the entire Mongolian political system that had given tribes and clans dispersed power. The social and political hierarchy was a convoluted one, and Genghis in turn consolidated their power to himself, and made sure that he was the only presence which the Mongolian people answered to. He was the sole ruler of the steppe, and knew he could only retain this power if he was treated as such. With the prowess of his stature solidified, he could enact sweeping changes meant to benefit Mongolian people and society, and bring the empire to a more prosperous point of great influence on the world.

The seeds of this sole leadership structure had already been planted during Genghis' campaigns against his rival nomadic tribes. In each of his victories he absorbed the common people under his rule. Members of rival tribes would be guaranteed protection under Genghis' subjugation, and they would be appropriately integrated into his unified society. Genghis even had his mother adopt orphans left behind in his raids, and integrate them into the family.

Genghis pushed a belief on his people that loyalty to him would result in rewards for them, and disloyalty would be reciprocated appropriately. He was a fair conqueror who believed in redemption. Military leaders who opposed him, once defeated, would be given the chance to swear their allegiance to the Khan. Many of those who did were allowed to keep their military ranking, only now they served the Mongol Empire and Genghis Khan first and foremost.

Genghis' system of meritocracy completely went against Mongolian tradition, but Genghis was more focused on building an undyingly loyal support system beneath him, rather than adhere to ancient customs. His strategy was to put the most able bodied individuals in positions of power that they deserved due to their skillset or personality. Social status, heritage, and religion, were not factors in delegating duties, and this made for an incredibly diverse population under Genghis. He also underwent multiple restructurings of his army, so that all cultures were mixed together, and soldiers could be identified by their ranking and their ability, rather than their family history. These major shake-ups of Mongolian tradition marked the beginning of a new era for the country which would continue long after Genghis Khan's death. It was the beginning of Pax Mongolica.

Pax Mongolica translates to "Mongol Peace," and is in reference to Pax Romana, the era of relative peace that the Roman Empire enjoyed just after Emperor Augustus took over. Ironically, Pax Romana was defined by a lack of military expansionism which resulted in the Roman Empire getting back on its feet after the destruction of the Roman Republic. Pax Mongolica is defined by the peace that was spread through Genghis Khan's violent campaigns across the Western world. The idea was an ambition of Genghis' that he wanted to instate across his growing territory, and he would do so by any means necessary.

Before any expansion could take place, Genghis knew it was important that the current state of the Mongolian empire was a prosperous one, but one that was controlled within specific confines that would direct society towards peace. He divided lands and money in a far more fair and balanced manner with much more even distribution between nobles, which included the empresses, princesses, and meritorious servants. He also distributed fairly and evenly to his soldiers, whom he allowed to keep their war spoils.

Mongolia was now under a uniquely new unified rule, and Genghis sought to do away with ancient traditions which used to restrict the territory. He sought to unify his culturally diverse Mongolian population under one code of law, which could be applied universally. Genghis wrote these laws up himself, and called them the Yassa. The Yassa code of law was an intriguing one, given that its exact contents were actually kept secret. The separate provisions covered by the Yassa were decreed when necessary, with very few individuals having access to the whole comprehensive list of laws. This allowed the Yassa to be modified without a single sole knowing, meaning provisions could be altered or added when necessary for the benefit of Genghis. It was also the *de facto* law of the land. *De facto* roughly translates from Latin to "in fact." This meant that the laws were not officially beset by a higher power, but rather they were the universally accepted laws that existed in practice, rather than official documentation. The Yassa was likely written down in one comprehensive text stowed away by Genghis, but no complete list of the Yassa has ever been discovered.

The Yassa may have been put into practice in a shady manner, enforced only by the will of Genghis Khan and his followers, but the laws themselves did in fact have good intentions meant to keep peace and structure social hierarchy in a fair and appropriate way. The Yassa began to be compiled as a series of decrees applying directly to war and Genghis' warfare tactics. His rulings divided his army and created the effective restructuring of his men into groups of tens, hundreds, or thousands, led by trustworthy leaders who swore their loyalty to the Khan.

There were a variety of provisions in the Yassa which aimed to give structure to warfare, and they turned the Mongolian army into a highly respectable one. Soldiers were required to receive their battle equipment from no one other than their commanding officer, and they were personally in charge of keeping their equipment in good condition. Genghis was incredibly serious about his army being properly stocked and prepared, and their weapons and armor would be carefully examined before each campaign. Soldiers that did not take care of their equipment up to the proper standards, or lacked a piece of equipment entirely, were punished.

Soldiers were not allowed to begin a pillage of their enemy unless granted permission by their commanding general. However, once the general had given this permission, soldiers were allowed to keep whatever they pillaged. This was greatly effective in boosting morale, allowing these soldiers to walk away from campaigns with their own personal spoils of war. This provision maintained a happy army, but those who abused their privileges could face severe punishment. Negligence was an offense that could be punished by a severe beating, or even death. Sharing clothing or food with a prisoner of war, unless give permission by the captor, was punishable by death. It was also forbidden for armies to make any kind of peace with an enemy who had not yet submitted to the will of Genghis Khan and the Mongolian Empire.

Genghis developed a multitude of provisions in his Yassa that aimed to harden the loyalty around him, and keep the fires of this loyalty burning strong for his and future generations. One of the ways he did this was by disallowing any subject of the Mongolian Empire to be taken as a slave. Every man in the empire was required to give service, at least for a time, to the Empire. Service to the empire generally meant going to war for them, but those who didn't go off to battle were still required to serve in other capacities. This could have been any number of duties meant to serve and strengthen the army.

Some of the laws decreed by Genghis' Yassa seemed quite strange, yet still must have served some political, religious, or cultural interest for the Khan. For instance, the cutting of an animal's throat to use it for food was banned, and instead it was officiated that animals must be hung by their feet, their stomach's ripped open, and their heart squeezed until death. It also legitimized children born of concubines, meaning these children had entitlement to their father's inheritance, should the father allow it. This decree likely stems from the polygamist attitudes of Mongolian society. Genghis himself had a vast amount of wives in his lifetime, the exact number of which is unknown. Other somewhat strange provisions that likely stemmed from cultural history included the banning of bathing or washing clothes during a thunderstorm, or washing clothes before they were totally worn out. Additionally, subjects were not allowed to dip their hands into water to drink, but rather they were required to use a receptacle. The provisions also forbade individuals to reference each other with a title, and were instead required to acknowledge each other by their given name.

Throughout the Yassa the punishments are notably harsh, and the words, "put to death" can be frequently seen. Any divisiveness within the army was punishable by death, but a number of other practices also came with capital punishment. If you were to find a slave and failed to return that slave to his owner, you could be put to death. If you were found guilty of adultery you could be put to death. Liars, spies, and those that practiced witchcraft or sorcery were also placed under the death penalty. The death penalty seemed to be the most universal form of punishment that was applied to multiple levels of crimes, and discriminated against no one. Even high ranking generals could be put to death if they failed in their duties, or failed to show up when called upon by the Khan. Criminals who kidnapped or sexually assaulted women were given this ultimate punishment, but it was also something applied to liars, cheaters, thieves, and those who disrespected their elders. Even crimes as tame as urinating into water or ashes were punishable by death. The sweeping power of the death penalty shows us what a different and far more ruthless time in history this was. Sodomy was another action punishable by death, which likely means that homosexuality was perceived as a heinous crime.

We may be able to associate a lot of cruelty with the Yassa, but there was one hugely revolutionary aspect to the code which shows the positive progression Genghis hoped to achieve through it. The Yassa was the first code of law which displayed religious tolerance. No leader had ever given such blanket tolerance of such a thing, but Genghis Khan was unlike other leaders. He even gave tax exemptions to places of worship, a custom seen in modernized countries today like the United States. His wasn't complete tolerance, though, as it was still required that all subjects maintained their belief in one God, but that God could be worshiped in whatever way suited the individual. Genghis decreed no singular religion for Mongolia, and allowed subjects to practice essentially any religion they wished. All religions were required to be given respect, and the empire would display no preference towards any of them. Removing religion as one of the pillars of civilized society, and allowing a more or less free range of practice, was unprecedented.

Genghis himself was a tengrist, or one who practices Tengrianism. This ancient religion dominated most of the Central Asian region at the time. It combined principles of shamanism and animism, as well as the worship of ancestors. It was a religion that coincided well with Mongolian lifestyle. The nomadic life required a strong coalition between man, animal, and nature to survive harsh conditions and domesticate wild animals for use. The shamanistic beliefs gave power to the earth, wind, and sky, and animism perpetuated the integrity of animals, and gave way to the idea they each had souls that needed to be respected. This way of thinking had aided Genghis as he grew up Temujin, but as his scope of the world became bigger, his tolerance of the world's diversity became a defining characteristic of his. Genghis always remained curious about other ways of thinking and what they could offer him and society. He was open to learning all he could about various religions, and even consulted great religious leaders. Throughout his life Genghis met with Buddhist monks, Christian missionaries, and Muslims in the Middle East. He also met with Qiu Chuji, the most famous of the Seven True Daoists of the North to discuss life, death, and immortality.

The only religious groups that did seem to receive any sort of subjugation from Genghis were the Muslims and Jews, and this may have been because of some of Islam's practices towards animals and food which went directly against shamanism or animism. For instance, Halal butchering, or the practice of slitting an animals throat, was banned, hence the section of the Yassa which gave far more specific instructions on how to slaughter animals for food. Genghis did take some particularly harsh actions against these groups, calling Muslims and Jews slaves, and forbidding the halal method of eating. Kosher eating was banned, and the Mongol diet was enforced upon these populations. Circumcision was also banned. For all that Genghis did for religious tolerance, he still had his downfalls, but his growing acceptance as he got older reflected a way of thinking quite progressive for the time.

. . .

Now, with the power of the Khan title strengthening his claims, Genghis Khan was ready to expand. Mongolia had enjoyed relatively the same sects of land for the entirety of their existence. Genghis now saw it as time to break past these borders which had been culturally, societally, and geographically imposed on them. He saw the Empire as just that, an Empire. Empires don't just retain control of their relatively small plot of land. They push their borders in all directions, looking to impose the will of their leader everywhere they conquer.

Genghis's ambitions were not born completely from a lust for conquest. Rather, he was fueled by the desire to expand Mongolia's prosperity, creating a unified population in Asia which was diverse in culture, religion, and heritage, but united under a common code of law, and extensive trade routes. Creating a more expansive trade network was going to be a major focus of Khan's during his expansion of the empire. He saw the necessity in having strong networks to trade goods, as the area they currently possessed offered little in the way of viable trading resources. The Silk Road cut through a significant portion of Mongolia, and Genghis made it an intention to expand control over areas the Silk Road also merged with, creating a unified economic network under his empire.

Even before the unification of the Mongol tribes, Genghis was accepting of foreign merchants, and had always been a supporter of international trade. Merchants were also a viable source of information which Genghis used to gather intelligence on his enemies. He saw economic interdependence as a majorly important aspect of society that was necessary for prosperity.

An interconnected society was a very important ideal to Genghis, and he made this clear early on in his takeover of Mongolia. Mongolia can actually be credited for the establishment of one of the earliest postal services in history, referred to in Mongolian history as the Yam. Genghis himself was responsible for one of the most significant expansions of this system, and used it more effectively than most of his predecessors. The Yam was an extensive route system that stretched across the country and was used by messengers to deliver important intel back and forth between cities. It was critical that information move quickly for Genghis, as his armies themselves already moved quickly. The Yam was essentially a series of relay stations, each around 200 kilometers apart, that messengers travelled back and forth from, in a type of relay chain that moved letters, supplies, or horses, from one station to the next. This, along with Genghis's network of spies which operated using the Yam, was one of his greatest assets.

·　　·　　·

One of the most peaceful times Mongolian history had ever known up to that point had been officially established, and Genghis Khan took primary credit for it. He had the unabashed and stalwart support of the people backing his desire to expand. His soldiers were valiant weapons of his that answered to the will of the Khan before anyone else. He had their undying loyalty, and knew this support made his army mightier than any that might oppose him. All of Mongolia now answered to him, and he was going to use this power for the good of the Empire first and foremost. It was time to grow, time to enact dominance of Asia, taking revenge on all those nations and empires which tried to subjugate Mongolia in the past. The region had long standing grudges in every direction, and Genghis Khan sought to put an ultimatum on these grudges. How would he do that? Complete and utter conquest, of course. With the unwavering support of the people behind him, along with one of the most massive armies history had ever seen, Genghis was ready to begin the most significant chapter of his life. He was ready for military conquest.

Chapter 5
Conquest Begins

Genghis Khan possessed incredible ambition for his conquering of the world around him. He had a whole series of campaigns laid out which, if successful, would give him control over more people and land than any single person before him, and probably every single one after him. Through his years of growing military acumen and societal popularity Genghis had managed to surround himself with an incredibly loyal band of generals willing to give their lives for him on the battlefield.

The most obvious choice of where to begin these series of expansion campaigns was the Mongols direct neighbors, the Western Xia, otherwise known as the Tangut Empire or the Xi-Xia, in China. This territory bordered the Mongol Empire's southeast front, and was significantly smaller than the Mongols other neighbor directly to the east, the Jin. They were a territory with enough wealth to make them a worthwhile vassal state which could pay hefty tributes to the Mongols, tributes which would be necessary in the much larger campaigns Genghis had planned. It was also a valuable trade asset, with the Silk Road running right through it. This area had the potential for great revenue for the Mongols, as well as providing a doorway to the Jin.

The Western Xia were a dynasty that had known a long struggle for power. They had been adversaries to the Liao dynasty that controlled the Mongol territory for years, but were never forces to be reckoned with in the eyes of the Liao. It wasn't until the Jin dynasty began their ascension of power that the Western Xia found assistance outside of their borders. They became a vassal state to the Jin, meaning they adhered to the law and customs of the Jin, in exchange for their territory.

The Jin handily defeated the Liao dynasty, and then set their sights on the Song dynasty to the south. For this campaign they employed the help of the Western Xia, and led a crushing campaign against the Song. The Western Xia acquired a significant portion of land from the Song as a result of this campaign, and managed to establish themselves as an influential power in the area. Over time their relationship with the Jin would deteriorate, but they still managed to retain their land and influence. By the time Temujin was being granted the title of Genghis Khan, the Western Xia was a name associated with considerable power. They didn't have the reputation of the timelessly mighty Jin dynasty, but they were an adequate starting point of Genghis' western campaigns.

Temujin had actually already undergone attacks on the Western Xia before he assumed the title of Genghis Khan. In his campaign against the Keraites, fighting against Toghrul, Toghrul's son Senggum had fled the territory. He managed to band together a small force of troops who marched into Western Xia seeking refuge. He would find none, though, and instead his troops took to pillaging border villages. Their time in Western Xia did not last long, and they were quickly expelled.

The time that Senggum spent in the Western Xia territory was just enough time to give Temujin precedence to attack the region for harboring his enemies. In 1205, a year before he would be granted the title of Genghis Khan, Temujin launched a raid near the city of Kara-Khoto. This would lead to a series of additional raids of the border villages. As the Mongol Empire began its rise to power, it let the Western Xia know that their power should not be taken lightly. They were coming in with a vengeance, and any who dare oppose them would know the consequences for such an action. Before the Mongol Empire and before Genghis Khan, Western Xia nobility was already beginning to accept the idea that the Mongols were about to be the world's next unbridled superpower.

Temujin found one of his most loyal generals in this first series of raids when he attacked Ganzhou, a border city known today as Zhangye. The city's commander had a son who was kidnapped by the Mongolian invaders. His son, a small child at the time of his capture, was given the Mongol name of Chagaan, and placed in service to the Mongols. He would be a valued member of the Mongolian army, vowing his loyalty to the Empire from a very young age. Eventually he would climb the ranks and find himself as the commander of the personal guard of Genghis Khan.

The Western Xia obviously knew the threat which was now posed towards them. They knew these raids were preliminary, and the full-fledged campaign was still to come. The Emperor at the time, Emperor Huanzong, had little idea of how he was going to deal with these violent invaders. Huanzong inherited the Western Xia from his father, Emperor Renzong, at the height of its power. His father's policies had established a more or less peaceful time for the dynasty, and he thought these policies would continue to be effective, despite changing times. His weakness as an emperor showed when corruption began destroying the Western Xia economy, and he did little to stop it. Long before the Mongols showed up, he was already becoming unfavorable with the people.

In 1206, Temujin was pronounced Genghis Khan, and Emperor Huanzong still took no action. The threat of the Mongols, now proclaiming themselves as the Mongol Empire, was very real, and everyone knew their sights were set on Western Xia. Furious with his inaction, Huanzong's own cousin, named Li Anquan, led a coup d'etat and overthrew

Huanzong. Li Anquan declared himself Emperor Xiangzong, and sought to reinvigorate the Western Xia people. However, it was too late.

In 1207 the raids on Western Xia began again. Genghis began in the Ordo region, which was the stretch of land looping around the great Yellow River in what is now China. Their campaign along the river saw many Western Xia slain in horribly unfortified encampments and settlements. These raids would continue for the next year, culminating in the sacking of Wuhai, one of the Western Xia's most strategic garrisons along the Yellow River.

Genghis withdrew his forces in 1208 in order to recuperate, assess his enemy, and plan out his full scale invasion of the territory. By 1209 he and his army were ready, and the official campaign against the Western Xia got underway. Li Anquan immediately realized that he did not have the capabilities to withstand this full scale invasion, and requested help from the neighboring Jin. The new Jin emperor, Wanyan Yongji, denied this request. He told Li Anquan that it was to the Jin's benefit to watch their enemies fight and tear each other apart. Li Anquan, underprepared emperor of the Western Xia, was going to be on his own.

Genghis' strategy was to continue his route along the Yellow River, decimating any hostile force in his path. Multiple cities fell under his might, and his progress down the Yellow River was unhalted. Genghis and his army didn't find a serious threat until arriving at the Helan Mountains. The Helan Mountains had only one pass, which led to the Western Xia capital of Yinchuan. This pass was guarded by the fortress Kiemen, a well-fortified garrison which stood proud as Genghis' first real obstacle in this campaign. Genghis marched his army to the plains stretching out before Kiemen, and set up camp outside the walls. Neither side made a move, with each waiting for the other to make the first mistake.

For two months the armies engaged in a relative stand still, with nothing more than small inconsequential skirmishes taking place. Finally, Genghis drew up a plan that would allow them to take the fortress, and it involved a bit of trickery. Genghis launched an attack on the fortress, one that seemed to Western Xia general Wei-ming Ling-kung like a full blown siege, and the beginning of a real battle. Moments after the Western Xia engaged Genghis' forces, he had them retreat away from the garrison, where an ambush lie in wait. Ling-kung took Genghis' bait, and pursued his army outside of the fortress walls. The Western Xia army was now exposed on all sides and Genghis, with a considerably smaller force than Ling-kung, initiated his ambush and made short work of the Western Xia defenders. With this army out of the way Genghis easily took Kiemen, and cleared his path for Yinchuan.

It was obvious that Yinchuan, a fully fortified city, and the most protected in all of Western Xia, was not going to fall for these same tricks. The city housed somewhere around 150,000 soldiers, a force far larger than what the Mongols were working with. For whatever reason, Genghis thought the best strategy was to launch a full on siege of the city. The Mongol army had little to no experience with siege warfare, but it is likely that Genghis considered this his only option, obviously not being able to turn around and end the campaign now.

The siege of Yinchuan began in May of 1209, and drug on all the way to October of that year with little to show for it. The Mongol army simply lacked the equipment and experience to perform a proper siege of such a well guarded city, and their siege efforts made no impact on the campaign. Instead,

Genghis turned to other strategies to break the city. Since he lacked the proper human weapons to win this campaign, he decided to use nature as his weapon instead. Genghis had dikes built to divert the river outside of the city, along with its network of irrigation tunnels. They attempted to divert it into the city, and flood the Western Xia out.

This strategy prolonged the siege a few more months, and by January of 1210 Yinchuan's walls were under considerable stress. It wasn't going to be long before the river would breach the walls and the city would be flooded. However, this didn't happen. The dike eventually broke, and the river flooded before the walls were breached. This flood laid waste to the Mongolian camp, and forced them to relocate to higher ground. It was a dramatic setback for Genghis and his army, yet at this point it didn't even matter. The Mongols had been successful in destroying Yinchuan's system of irrigation tunnels in order to divert the river, and the city's water supply was now cut off. With no irrigation, they had no way of growing crops, and would be starved out within a matter of months. The Jin had already made it apparent at the beginning of the campaign that they would be lending no help to the Western Xia, and so Li Anquan had to reconcile that he truly was on his own. Rather than seeing his people starve within the walls of this crumbling city, he surrendered to the Khan. He submitted to the will of the Mongol Empire, and even illustrated his loyalty to this new vassal status by marrying his daughter, Chaka, to Genghis. He also paid a large tribute of camels, falcons, and textiles. Genghis Khan had officially acquired his first victory outside of Mongolia, and it would be far from his first.

.   .   .

In 1210, after the Western Xia had declare their submission to the Mongol Empire, Genghis and his army returned home to recuperate. He now had the means to build an even stronger army, with great tributes being paid to him by the Western Xia. He was eager to take his newfound power to the West, but there was still one adversary on his eastern front that had to be dealt with.

Shortly after returning home, Genghis Khan was paid a visit by a delegation from the Jin dynasty to the East. The delegation proclaimed Wanyan Yongji's rise to power over the Jin, and they brought word that the new emperor demanded the Mongol empire to submit, and accept the status of vassal state. The Jurchen rulers of the Jin laid claim to sovereignty over the region, due to their defeat of the Mongols so many times throughout history, and their previous partnerships with the Keraites and Tatars. The Jin were arguably one of pre-Genghis Khan Mongolia's most vicious adversaries, and Genghis was most certainly not going to bend to their will now. He vehemently denied these demands of the Jin by spitting on the ground in front of the delegation, mounting his horse, and riding off. This dramatic act stood as an assertion of war, and the adversarial relationship between Mongol and Jurchen was now fully alive once again.

Invading the Jin was not originally part of Genghis' plans, but he found himself under immense pressure to do so. The Western Xia had commenced their own campaign against the Jin, looking to punish them for refusing to give assistance to them during the Mongolian siege. They asked Genghis for help in this campaign, yet he did not provide it immediately. Instead, in the spring of 1211 Genghis organized a kurultai at the base of the Kherlen River. A lengthy conversation commenced about what action to take against the Jin, as it was clear some sort of action had to be taken now that they had so pointedly denied their rule. Genghis decided to look within himself for the final answer to this conundrum, and he took to a nearby mountain to pray alone.

Genghis stripped himself of his armaments, and laid down his weapons so that he could kneel before the Eternal Sky. He spent this time recounting the Mongolian people's long and storied history with the Jin, and was gravely reminded of the horrible atrocities which the Jin had committed against his ancestors. It was a history full of murder, torture, and violent subjugation, and was a history too brutal to ignore.

After four days of prayer and consideration, Genghis emerged with an answer. He proclaimed that the Eternal Blue Sky had promised him both victory and vengeance over the Jurchens, and his campaign against the Jin dynasty could commence. In March of 1211 Genghis mobilized the Mongol army, taking a force of around 90,000 men with him to the east. This was the vast majority of the entire Mongol army, with only about 2,000 soldiers staying back as defense for the empire. This was the first campaign that Genghis brought his sons with him on, and it would be the first time they would campaign independently from their father. With the help of Ala 'Qush, chief of the Ongut tribe which shared its northwestern border with the Jin, Genghis and his army found a quick and clear passage straight into Jin territory, and they wasted no time in beginning an attack.

Genghis and his army were met at the northwestern border by Jin chancellor Duji Sizhong and his horde of 750,000 troops who were posted up along the stretch of the Great Wall which the Jurchens had built to repel Mongolian invaders. Genghis led his army swiftly into battle, in what began the first conflict of the Jin campaign, the Battle of

Yehuling. This eight month battle began with Genghis taking the bulk of the Mongol forces into Wusha forest where he attacked and destroyed the Wuyue camp, the Jin army's primary defensive position. Before mounting this attack, Genghis sent his son Ogedei to lead an attack on Jin's western capital of Xijing. This would ensure a multi-fronted attack on the Jin, and also cut off reinforcements from the west.

Duji Sizhong was killed in the Battle of Wusha Forest, an event that marked the first stage of the Battle of Yehuling. The Mongols took a month off from the fighting, and recuperated their strength to prepare for the next offensive on the Jurchens. Wanyan Chengyu succeeded Duji Sizhong as chancellor, and took it upon himself to retreat the Jin armies in Hengzhou, Fuzhou, and Changzhou, and have them all fall back towards Yehuling. Yehuling was located deeper into the mountains, and Chengyu hoped the terrain here would negatively affect the Mongol cavalry.

The Jin army was admittedly fearful of Genghis, and knew they couldn't hold off his attacks forever. They instead thought peace negotiations would be a viable tactic against the warlord. The imperial court of Jin sent an official named Shimo Ming'an to meet with the Khan. However, in another display of his incredibly power of persuasion, he convinced Shimo Ming'an to surrender to him and defect to his side. He even convinced him to share vital military secrets which the Jin were relying on to stand a chance against the Mongols. Because of this insight, Genghis was able to organize his second offensive on the Jin.

He sent one of his loyal generals, by the name of Muqali to lead a cavalry charge against the Jin through a passage at Huan'erzui. Upon arriving to this mountainous region, Wanyan Chengyu's assumptions were right, and the cavalry had to dismount to fight through the mountain pass. It didn't matter though, because the Mongol army, filled with bloodlust and pride for their country and their Khan, delivered a handy defeat to a massive Jin force of 300,000 soldiers in August of 1211.

Genghis had led his own successful attack at Yehuling, and the Jin forces were completely scattered. Wanyan Chengyu managed to put a small force back together which took refuge at Huihe Fortress. In October of 1211 the Jin forces were discovered and surrounded by the Mongol army. A three day siege of the fortress took place. A cavalry of 3,000, led personally by Genghis, charged on the fortress, and delivered a crushing defeat to the Jin army, wiping out nearly all of their forces. Wanyan Chengyu barely escaped with his life.

With another decisive victory under his belt against the Jin, Genghis and his army took a brief rest. Upon his return to the battlefield in 1212, Genghis took an arrow to the knee and was injured and bedridden for a brief amount of time. It would be another year before Genghis led any more attacks against the Jin himself, but in the meantime he sent Jebe, one of his most trusted generals, to free Manchuria in the east from Jin control. Jebe was successful, and as Genghis recovered his power over the Jin was still known.

In 1213 the Mongol army marched upon the Jin capital of Zhongdu, today known as Beijing. Though they were met with some opposition, no Jin offensive posed much of a threat to the Mongols. They easily broke through the Juyong Pass and the Zijing Gap, laying waste to every Jin army they encountered. As Genghis besieged Zhongdu, his armies continued their pillage of the northern regions of the Jin territory, crushing everything in their path.

The Jin were in hot water, and action needed to be taken. Jin general Hushahu took it upon himself to murder his emperor Wanyan Yongji, and his nephew, Emperor Xuanzong, took his place. Xuanzong quickly appealed to Genghis and agreed to become a vassal state of the Mongol Empire, and even presented Genghis with a Jurchen princess. After receiving hefty tributes, Genghis assumed his campaign against the Jin to be a success, and called his attacks off in 1214. That same year the capital was shifted from Zhongdu to Kaifeng, a city much further south. It was clear that they were still trying to amass some sort of power farther away from Mongol influence, and so Genghis decided to finish his siege of Zhongdu anyways. He was helped by a defecting Jin army, who attacked the city from the south, and an army led by Khitan generals who had surrendered to Genghis in Jebe's taking of Manchuria. Zhongdu obviously didn't stand a chance and, despite reinforcements from the south, the city fell to the Mongols on May 31, 1215.

What followed the sacking of Zhongdu was a series of systematic campaigns aiming to wipe out any and all resistance in the northern provinces of the Jin territory. Genghis would allow the severely decimated Jin nobility to continue operations in their new capital of Kaifeng because, with the Jin no longer posing a threat to Mongol rule, he could turn his attention to the direction he had always wanted to be facing; west.

.   .   .

To the west was the mighty Khwarazmian dynasty, one of this time in history's most powerful empires which controlled a massive amount of land in Central Asia. This was the prize that Genghis' eyes had been set on for decades, but before he could dive into this mighty empire with his armies, he needed to secure safe passage. He found this passage in Qara Khitai, a large region of land to the northwest of Mongolia which shared a border with the Khwarazmian, and had been severely weakened due to their own failed campaign against their western neighbors.

The Qara Khitai was ruled by a man by the name of Kuchlug, who was someone that Genghis himself had a history with. Kuchlug was a prince of the Naiman confederacy, which Genghis had handily defeated in 1204 during his unification campaigns across Mongolia. As Genghis destroyed Kuchlug's homeland, he fled to Qara Khitai. Kuchlug was a welcome member of the Qara Khitai Empire, and was immediately appointed as a military advisor, and even led some of his own military commands. Kuchlug was not in favor of the Qara Khitai's war against the Khwarazmian, and when the campaign got underway he staged a coup d'etat and took control of the confederation by 1213. Kuchlug was fueled by his hate filled grudge against Genghis, and put his back to the Khwarazmian so he could move into Mongolian territory instead. He besieged the Karluks, who were vassals of the Mongols, and Genghis quickly resolved to send them aid, preoccupied with his clean up campaigns across Jin territory.

Genghis' trusted general Jebe was called upon to lead this campaign against the Qara Khitai, and in 1216 he and an army of 20,000 set off to win more territory for the Mongol Empire. Alongside Jebe was another army, led by Subutai, another of Genghis' most faithful generals. Upon reaching the Karluk city of Almaliq and repelling any Khitai forces still besieging the city, Jebe and Subutai split, as Subutai had been ordered to deal with a threat posed by Merkit clans to the south that had scattered and refused to swear allegiance to the Mongol Empire. Jebe led his forces north towards the Khitai capital of Balasagun and began his siege. An army of 30,000

Khitai troops folded to Jebe's army, and Kuchlug was pushed back to the city of Kashgar.

As Kuchlug lost more and more ground to the invading Mongols, his popularity with his people diminished. He was already viewed unfavorably, as his rule of Qara Khitai was defined by religious persecution against the Muslims. He was trying to convert a predominantly Muslim population to his belief in Buddhism, and it was obviously not winning him any support. By the time Jebe and his army reached Kashgar the people revolted against Kuchlug, and he fled the city fearing for his life. Kuchlug made his escape through the Pamir Mountains, where he thought he would be safe but was sorely mistaken. Not long after his escape he was captured by two hunters who promptly gave him up to the Mongols. Kuchlug was beheaded without hesitation and the Qara Khitai was secured as another territory for the Mongol Empire and Genghis Khan to impose rule over.

The Mongol army's first three campaigns had resulted in great successes for Genghis, and before some of the biggest campaigns of his life even got underway, he had already solidified his reputation as a dangerously influential force, and one that threatened the entire Asian continent. The Mongol Empire had already practically tripled in size, and now knew a might far greater than any dynasty in the Chinese regions. But this was only the beginning. Genghis and his army, filled with confidence and high morale, now turned their attention to one of the world's mightiest empires; the Khwarazmia.

Chapter 6
A Violent March West

The Khwarazmian Empire was one of the more substantial superpowers at the time, and their territory encompassed what is most of the Middle East today, along with parts of Eastern Europe. They came to power around the year 1077, but initially only existed as a vassal state to the Seljuq Empire, which they would later defeat. Their existence had been a quiet one until around the time Temujin was unifying Mongolia. The year 1200 is when Shah Ala ad-Din Muhammad came into power and began picking fights with his neighbors, bringing Khwarazmia into the public eye. Muhammad's first attempt at expanding his newly acquired Empire was against the Ghurids, whom he was promptly defeated by. He appealed to the neighboring Qara Khitai for aide in his fight, and with their assistance was able to repel the Ghurid counter attack.

Muhammad's lust for expansion didn't end there. Almost immediately he turned around on the Qara Khitai and initiated conflict with them, a conflict which he got assistance from the Qara Khanids to win. Ala ad-Din Muhammad was not exactly great at keeping friends, though, because he then reversed his opinion on the Qara Khanids and overthrew them as well. He then moved on to stomp out the Ghurids, finishing his earlier campaign, and then surged into the western regions of Persia where he pushed the Khwarazmian Empire as far West as the Zagros Mountains, a massive mountain range cutting through parts of modern day Iran, Iraq, and Turkey.

By the time Genghis Khan turned his attention to the Khwarazmian, it was practically still in its infancy, especially under the very recent rule of Ala ad-Din Muhammad. Muhammad wasn't exactly keeping everything operating smoothly either. Upon taking power as the Shah, Muhammad was adamant about being recognized as the sultan of the empire. He refused to pay his required homage to the caliph An-Nasir unless recognized as such, which was a heinous offense to his people and his religion. Caliphs in this era were representatives of Islam and the Muslim community, and considered to be direct descendants of the prophet Muhammad. Thus, Ala ad-Din Muhammad's refusal to accept any authority from the caliph was inappropriate to say the least, and it put him in hot water with his Muslim neighbors to the South. It was right around this time that Muhammad began his relationship with Genghis Khan.

Genghis' intentions with the Khwarazmian were not warlike in the beginning. His relations with the Empire opened up while Genghis and his armies were still ravaging the Jin. What Genghis saw his western neighbor as was not a threat, but a potential partner in trade. Khwarazmia was a wealthy empire rich with resources, and had substantial control over the Silk Road. They also had a considerably large army, making them a viable ally all around.

The first word that Ala ad-Din Muhammad received from Genghis Khan was a request for a trade agreement to be initiated between the two empires. Muhammad was understandably skeptical of this request, being that it was coming from the man who had his armies slaughter thousands upon thousands of soldiers and civilians in order to instate the dominance of his empire. Muhammad had heard the horror stories from his ambassadors in the Jin capital of Zhongdu about the brutality of the Mongol army, and how they left so few alive who stood in their way.

Genghis even let it be known that he was on Muhammad's side when it came to the dispute between him and the caliph An-Nasir. Genghis refused to ally himself with any other authority which might claim itself to be ultimate and final, which is what Nasir stood for as caliph. He was ready to throw his support behind the Khwarazmian, should any conflict arise between them and their neighbors, but Muhammad was hesitant to agree to any terms quite yet.

Genghis was very serious about opening these trade agreements, and took the initiative to establish them by sending a caravan of 500 Muslim men and women to hammer out an agreement and begin an official trade route between the two empires. Muhammad's distrust of the Mongolians had obviously spread across his empire into the minds of his subordinates, as the Muslim caravan did not make it far before they were stopped. Upon reaching the city of Otrar, the city's governor, Inalchuq, had the entire caravan arrested, claiming their mission was not one of peace, but rather it was conspiratorial.

Genghis was known for using merchants to gather intelligence on his enemies, but this was one of the few times in his life that this might have been a completely legitimate caravan, devoid of any spies. A war with an empire the size of the Khwarazmian was the last thing Genghis wanted while still having most of his army occupied in Jin. He made this stance even clearer when his retaliation to the imprisonment of the caravan did not involve violence. Instead of sending an army, Genghis sent three ambassadors, one of them a Muslim and two of them of Mongolian descent, to speak directly with Muhammad himself. They came to the Shah with the demands that the caravan be freed and governor Inalchuq be handed over to the Mongols to receive punishment.

Muhammad refused to have any positive association with Genghis, and he made this abundantly clear by what he did next. He ordered that the two Mongolian ambassadors have their heads shaved, while the Muslim ambassador received far less gracious punishment. He, along with the entire caravan, were executed. The beheaded Muslim ambassador, along with this shaved Mongolian counterparts, were sent back to Genghis, along with the clear message that Muhammad had no intentions of making peace with the Mongols.

Genghis felt personally offended by this affront from Muhammad, but he took the message to heart. He reconciled that there would be no peace with these neighbors. Now that the Qara Khitai had been annihilated he had a direct route into the empire. He didn't want to use this route for anything other than trade, but the brazenly foolish Ala ad-Din Muhammad had given him no choice. In 1219 Genghis Khan and the Mongol army crossed over the Tien Mountains, and found themselves inside the Khwarazmian Empire's borders, ready to take it for themselves.

.   .   .

Genghis did not march into Khwarazmia unprepared. Like he always did before engaging in a new campaign, Genghis used his extensive spy network along the Silk Road to gather intelligence about his enemy, pinpointing their weaknesses and discerning the most valuable resources for his army to be equipped with. This would also be the first campaign on which all of Genghis Khan's sons, Jochi, Ogedei, Chagatai, and Tolui, would accompany him.

Genghis' army, up to this point, made its reputation through his devastating cavalry. The might of his horsemen could cut through foot soldier armies like butter, and Genghis made sure to fortify his cavalry even further by adding supporting troops within the ranks. He did bring one significant change with him to this new campaign, though, and that was the new addition of siege warfare equipment.

During his campaigns against Western Xia and the Jin, Genghis' army revealed its greatest weakness when it came to sieges. They lacked the proper fortitude to launch substantial sieges which could actually threaten a city. He was now moving into an empire defined by great cities protected by brick and mortar, and he was going to need something stronger than horsemen to bring these establishments to their knees. Siege warfare is what the Chinese excelled in, though, and he was able to take a lot of valuable strategy away from these campaigns. He went into Khwarazmia with an understanding of what a siege meant, and what it required. His war caravan included battering rams, massive siege bows, and copious amounts of gunpowder. Gunpowder was still a young and seemingly mystical weapon which could be as dangerous to the user as it was to the victim. Thankfully, the Mongol army had acquired a number of gunpowder specialists from Western Xia and Jin, making the army equipped and prepared to use the deadly substance to their advantage. Genghis was more than ready for savage, bloody, and explosive warfare.

The Mongol army's first stop was in a region known as Transoxania, and it would be the first place where Genghis would get to test out one of his latest additions to his weaponry. Catapults were rolled out onto the battlefield, loaded with deadly mortar bombs fashioned by the Chinese siege specialists in the army. At the beginning of this conflict

Muhammad found himself in a terrible position to defend. Seeing as his power in Khwarazmia was relatively new, he feared amassing the totality of his forces under one roof, because that kind of power could so easily overthrow his already contested claim to the throne. He also needed to keep his army spread out amongst his newly acquired territories in order to retain them. This would prove devastating to his initial defenses, which fell swiftly to the Mongols.

Genghis had his army split into multiple parts so that his savage spread across Khwarazmia was quick and most definitely painful. He headed the main bulk of the army, which looked to crush everything in its path towards the city of Otrar. He then sent his eldest son, Jochi, to the south to engage Muhammad's army there. This would deal a heavy blow to the Shah on an additional front, and also prevent any reinforcements from stopping his progress.   By the fall of 1219 Genghis Khan and his army reached the city of Otrar, ready to enact revenge on the city which had ruined any hopes of a peaceful alliance between the Mongols and the Khwarazmians. Otrar was the first city that would come under Mongol siege, which was actually to their benefit in a way. The Mongols still weren't completely proficient in siege warfare, and they were unable to make much of a dent in the city's fortifications. Five months of siege went by before the Mongols were able to gain any sort of edge. One of the sally port gates was poorly guarded, and the Mongol forces managed to break through what little defenses stood here, and they quickly filled the city, slaughtering soldiers and civilians alike. They made it very clear that they were out for revenge in this attack, and it became more and more apparent as the bodies stacked higher and higher.

Fighting in the city of Otrar went on for another month, with Inalchuq and his remaining forces holed up in the citadel. Finally, the citadel was breached and Otrar's last defenses were slaughtered within its walls. Inalchuq himself made something that history is hesitant to refer to as a retreat. Rather, in desperation, he climbed onto the roof of the citadel as bloodthirsty Mongols chased him. He began throwing tiles at his invaders, which obviously had no effect, and he was promptly captured, marking the end of the siege of Otrar. Inalchuq was brought to Genghis, who had him beheaded. The remaining population of Otrar was either killed or enslaved, and the Mongol army, fueled by victory, set out to continue the campaign. Genghis left his sons Ogedei and Chagatai behind to lead forces which would clean up any remaining opposition in the Transoxania region, as Genghis and his forces pushed further west.

.   .   .

Three major cities still existed throughout the Khwarazmian Empire that needed to be taken, and they were Bukhara, Samarkand, and Urgench. Samarkand was the closest, but Genghis opted to skirt the city, and head for Bukhara first. As he set out towards the city, he sent his trusted general Jebe to the south where they were to cut off any retreats attempted by Muhammad's forces.

The road to Bukhara was a tumultuous one, as the most direct route was through the Kyzyl Kum desert. This expansive desert region was practically uninhabitable, and dangerous to cross without proper guidance. Genghis' army had taken their fair share of nomadic prisoners associated with the land, though, which came in handy navigating across this deadly expanse. Small oases were at varying intervals across the rolling sand dunes, and hitting these points was vital to prevent the army from drying out in its travels. With the help of their guides, the Mongol army successfully traversed the Kyzyl Kum, and eventually found themselves at the doorstep of Bukhara.

Bukhara, in retrospect, was a horribly ill prepared city when it came to withstanding attacks. Their fortifications consisted of a moat and one wall that went around the city. They were even more poorly prepared considering the Mongols arrived at their door practically unnoticed. The Mongol's attack on the Bukharan garrison is widely considered to be one of the greatest and most successful surprise attacks in history. By catching the city by surprise, they were hardly able to put up a defense. The Mongol siege of the garrison lasted for only three days before, in an act of foolish desperation, the 20,000 garrison troops attempted to break out and take the Mongols in open battle. They must have been blissfully unaware of the most dangerous part of the Mongol army, because this ill-advised move resulted in a quick defeat.

The leaders of Bukhara immediately realized the threat which was posed by the Mongols, and made the wise decision not to instigate that threat with more fighting which they would surely lose. They opened their gates to the Mongols, who stormed in and began their pillage. A small yet brave band of troops remained at the citadel to defend it, which they did for twelve days. At the end of the twelfth day the citadel's defenses were crushed, and all those inside were murdered. The rest of the city was ravaged, with the women and children being placed into slavery, and the young men who had not been a part of the fighting being enlisted into the Mongolian army. Genghis was well aware that the cities he was sacking were part of great artistic and technical innovation, and he by no means wanted to halt this progress. He had trade professionals like artisans, blacksmiths, and carpenters, sent back to Mongolia to diversify his population, and raise his world up high on a pedestal of innovation. For such a brutal man, Genghis Khan still managed to be a lover of the arts, and still respected the intellects of the time, supporting their fight for progressivism.

When the siege ended, looting was rampant, and in the chaos a fire started, which burned the majority of the city to the ground. As Bukhara burned, Genghis assembled the city's political authority in front of their primary mosque. While the fire swept up everything behind him, Genghis exclaimed that he was the flail of God, and had been sent to punish Bukhara and its people for their sins. He then had the leaders executed, and his takeover of Bukhara was final.

. . .

Genghis Khan's next stop was the Khwarazmian capital itself, Samarkand. Being the capitol of the empire, this city was far more fortified to prepare for a Mongol siege, and had a far larger army, reaching as high as 100,000 men, ready to defend it. By March of 1220 the Mongols arrived at Samarkand. Just as they arrived, Ogedei and Chagatai reunited with their father's forces, and the combined might of the Mongol army began their siege. The fighting went on for three days before the Samarkand troops decided to put together a counter attack against the Mongols. Genghis used this counter offensive to his advantage, and feigned a retreat, just as he had done to the Western Xia army at the fortress of Kiemen. A force of 50,000 troops spilled out of the Samarkand garrison, and the Mongols absolutely devastated them. In one fell swoop the Samarkand forces were added to the increasingly long list of foes who had underestimated the ability of the Mongol forces to fight in open combat.

The sacking of Samarkand was marked by a particular viciousness from the Mongol forces. In their initial attacks they had used their prisoners as human shields to protect against Khwarazmian arrows, and now that they were inside the walls of the city there would be no mercy whatsoever. Muhammad, who had clearly put too much faith in his empire's defenses, attempted to relieve Samarkand, but Mongolian forces in the rear of their army easily repelled him.

After five days of fighting all but around 2,000 Samarkand soldiers had been brought to submission. The remaining few, die-hard loyalists to the Shah through and through, took refuge in the city's citadel. These 2,000 dissenters were taken care of quickly, and the rest of the city was taken captive. Genghis wasn't going to let this sacking be the same as his previous ones. With Samarkand, he intended to send a message to the Shah that his country would be broken and tattered at the will of the Mongol army.

Genghis decided that a surrender wasn't good enough for Samarkand. He took back the terms of surrender he had agreed upon with the city's soldiers, and had each and every one of them executed. He then gathered the city's remaining population and brought them out to the plains stretching beyond Samarkand. Out in these fields a horrible slaughtering commenced, and every man, woman, and child who had once tken residence in Samarkand was killed. Their heads were removed from their bodies, and a grotesque pyramid of severed heads was erected outside the city walls. This graphic symbol of Mongol victory sent waves of fear spiking throughout the Khwarazmian Empire. It was clear that the end was nigh.

.   .   .

After Samarkand had fallen, the strength in numbers that the Khwarazmian Empire had relied on was all but broken, and Muhammad knew this. Genghis sent Subutai and Jebe to hunt down the Shah, who had fled with a small band of loyal soldiers to an island in the Caspian Sea. It was on this small island that Ala ad-Din Muhammad met his anticlimactic end, succumbing to disease and dying here in December of 1220. It was now more evident than ever that the power of the Khwarazmian Empire had crumbled beneath the weight of Genghis Khan and his army, and the rest of the war would be a clean-up campaign.

There was one major point still held by the Khwarazmian forces, and this was the city of Urgench. Urgench was a city of great wealth that served as a strategic trading point for whoever retained control of it. Muhammad's mother had presided over the city before the Mongols arrived, but fled upon learning that her son had thrown in the towel and sought refuge. In her attempts at abandonment she was captured and sent to Mongolia.

Filled with morale after such a decisively brutal victory in Samarkand, Genghis expected this next siege to be a cakewalk. He was wrong, though. Urgench still had a fighting spirit, and had been recently taken over by one of Muhammad's generals by the name of Khumar Tegin. Tegin proclaimed himself as the Sultan of Urgench, and vowed to hold the city for as long as he could against the oncoming Mongol forces.

As Genghis, along with Ogedei and Chagatai, approached Urgench from the south, Jochi was coming in from the North after leading successful campaigns across Northern Khwarazmia. Upon reaching the city they were faced with another difficult siege circumstance. Urgench was built right alongside the Amu Darya River, in a marshy delta. The ground here was very soft, causing heavier siege weaponry to sink and become immobile in the mud. There were also very few stones around that were large enough to be impactful with the catapult. The Mongols, already challenged when it came to siege warfare, had to fight a particularly difficult battle against the city's defenders. Regardless, their resilience knew no boundaries, and despite the hearty defense put up by Urgench, the city fell. In typical fashion, Genghis sent the intellectuals and craftsmen back to Mongolia, the women and children were enslaved, and the remaining population was dealt with in one of history's most numerous and bloody massacres.

The Mongol army saw a lot of casualties in this hard fought victory, but Khan lost something far more important to him in this siege than a few thousand troops. He lost the respect of his eldest son, Jochi. For years, the issue of Jochi's parentage had caused tension in his and his father's relationship. Jochi had considerable military acumen, and had earned his place in Genghis Khan's army, yet had never been given the same treatment as his brothers, who were all the unequivocal children of Genghis Khan and Borte. Jochi, due to circumstances out of his control, had always felt like the outcast of the family, and had always been vying for appreciation from his father.

Genghis showed this appreciation finally by promising to give Urgench to Jochi after they sacked it, and so Jochi understandably wanted the city to be left in better shape than that of Bukhara or Samarkand. He initiated talks with the city's defenders to instigate a surrender. When Chagatai found out about this he was furious, and petty sibling rivalry suddenly started to be an issue within Khan's ranks. He quickly nipped this in the bud by anointing Ogedei as the commander of the siege. This act is something Jochi would never forget, and it would permanently drive a wedge between him, his father, and his brothers.

.　　　.　　　.

With Urgench crushed, Genghis was almost done with his campaign. Growing older, he did not have the strength to immediately set off towards the next point of opposition, and so he delegated. In the far western reaches of Khwarazmia was the province of Khorasan, where a significant number of cities were still free from Mongol subjugation, and still harbored significant forces of the late Muhammad. Muhammad had a son though, Jalal ad-Din, who was still keen on retaining his father's empire. His pride for the Khwarazmian Empire gave spirit to other forces scattered across the region, and gave them a reason to rebel against what little Mongol presence existed in the region so far. Genghis knew he needed to stomp this out quickly. He dispatched his youngest son, Tolui, to head an army in charge of ravaging the Khorasan region. This decision was yet another focal point of tension surmounting between Genghis' sons.

Tolui, along with an approximate 50,000 men, 300 catapults, 4000 storming ladders, and 2,500 sacks of dirt to be used for filling moats, set out to begin leveling opposing cities in the Khorasan region. He intended to do so loudly and boisterously, and there was serious a promise of fire. Along with the rest of his siege equipment, Tolui brought with him pots filled with a highly flammable liquid called naptha, which he planned on hurling at his enemies using the catapults. These malicious strategies were highly effective, and the cities of Termez and Balkh quickly fell to Tolui's might. He then moved on to Merv, where an unprepared force of 12,000 men defended the city for six days before Tolui's siege broke through its defenses.

As Tolui launched an unsurprisingly violent attack inside the city walls, the governor quickly surrendered. Tolui accepted this surrender and promised to spare the lives of the city's population. Tolui proved that he was just as good at keeping promises as his father, when as soon the surrender was official, Tolui turned around and slaughtered everyone in the city. It was another unprecedented massacre that brought the death toll of the Khwarazmian campaign into the millions.

The cities of Nishapur and Herat were Tolui's next targets. Nishapur was a quick three day engagement that resulted in the death of one of Genghis' sons-in-law, named Tokuchar. Tolui presumed to blame the whole city for this death, and went about murdering every living thing within its walls, including the animals. When Herat heard about this destruction they immediately surrendered, long before any fighting got underway. They were one of very few cities in the entirety of this campaign to be spared.

By 1221 Tolui made it to the city of Bamiyan, where he began another brutal siege. Bamiyan ended up being one of the more well-fortified cities in the Khorasan region, and they managed to mount a substantial defense against the Mongols. The fighting resulted in heavy casualties on both sides, one of which being Genghis' grandson, and son of Chagatai, Mutukan. As punishment for this death, the citizens and soldiers of Bamiyan were all massacred once it fell, and the city itself was leveled. This absolute destruction would prompt the Mongols to refer to Bamiyan as the "city of screams" referencing the horrible outcries of its inhabitants as they were senselessly slaughtered.

In the next few months, a few more cities fell easily to Tolui, and by the spring of 1221 Khorasan was under total control by the Mongols. After his victory was cemented, Tolui left the region so that he could rejoin his father to the east.

.   .   .

As news of Khorasan's subjugation reached the ears of the new Shah Jalal ad-Din, he decided it was time to consolidate one final defense against the unstoppable Mongols. What little was left of the Khwarazmian army was gathered by Jalal in the failing empire's southern regions, the last remaining safe haven from the Mongols within the Khwarazmian borders. Genghis sent a force down south to deal with this last remaining opposition to his will that existed in the empire. The Mongols met the forces of Jalal ad-Din in front of the city of Parwan, where the Shah had amassed a force of around 60,000, half of which were able bodied Afghan warriors from the region today known as Afghanistan. Somehow, Jalal managed to mount an actual defense, and successfully fought back the Mongol army. After a long day of fighting, the Mongols retreated in embarrassed defeat.

Despite this victory, things were not about to get better for the young Shah. After the fighting had ended, the Afghan warriors abandoned Jalal ad-Din and he had no choice but to leave Parwan and seek refuge closer to India. As he and his forces, many of which were displaced Khwarazmian refugees that had managed to escape the Mongol rampage, headed south, word of the Mongol defeat reached Genghis Khan. He was rightly infuriated, and took it upon himself to lead the army into the final victory they needed to secure in order to complete the Khwarazmian campaign. He quickly set off to the south, in hot pursuit of Jalal ad-Din.

The two armies finally met on the bank of the Indus River. Jalal ad-Din had positioned his forces to take up a wholly defensive stance against the Mongols. On one flank they were protected, or so they thought, by mountains, while the river bend protected their rear. Genghis' initial charge was defended against, and in their retreat Jalal launched a counterattack which nearly broke through the center of the Mongol army. As Genghis held the line against the impassioned Khwarazmian forces, he sent a contingent of 10,000 soldiers around the mountain to take up a flanking position against Jalal. Once the contingent had completed their route, the Mongol army barreled down on the Khwarazmian army, and they were scattered into bloody chaos. It wasn't long before the army fell from both sides, and Jalal ad-Din had no choice but to flee further. He crossed the Indus River, but was pursued by Genghis and his army. They searched for Jalal for a time on the south side of the Indus, but eventually Genghis decided he had other matters to attend to. He left Subutai and Jebe to lead an army to continue the chase, and finalize this dispute with Jalal by the end of a sword. This was more than anything just a matter of principle, as Genghis no longer perceived Jalal ad-Din, and all of the Khwarazmian empire for that matter, to be a threat.

After three years of bloody warfare, the Khwarazmian Empire was no more, and the territory they once presided over now belonged to the Mongols. The Mongol Empire had grown considerably in both size and strength. This campaign had planted the seeds for what was to come to the Islamic world, even after Genghis Khan was gone. For now though, it was time for Genghis and his army to return to the Mongolian steppe and take time off to enjoy the spoils of war, and relish in his greatest victory to date. Obviously, though, his plans of conquest were far from over, and it wouldn't be long before the next wave of Mongolian expansion got underway.

Chapter 7
A Great Rise and A Mighty Fall

The year was 1220. Genghis Khan stood mightily, with yet another victory under his belt. The Khwarazmian Empire had sufficiently fallen, and it was time to return home. Genghis was approaching sixty years old at this time, and had obviously been through quite a lot for his age. It's hard to imagine that Genghis' victories were so much more overwhelming in his elder years. The accomplishments of his youth paled in comparison to what he managed as an adult. He was already in his forties by the time he had conquered and unified the Mongolian tribal confederations, and now, for what seemed like his first time, at the age of fifty nine, Genghis Khan was tired.

Genghis' time in the West, personally, was done, but Mongolian presence in the area was far from over. Under the suggestion of Genghis' most trusted general, and a man he referred to as his "dog of war," Subutai, he split the army into two factions. Genghis himself took the bulk of the Mongolian army with him on his path back to Mongolia. This force would conduct a series of raids in the northern regions of Afghanistan and India, fanning Mongolian influence out just a bit more. Genghis saw expansion in every direction he looked, and gave himself the authority to attack anywhere he felt he could push his borders. He may have been tired, but that wasn't going to stop him from taking military advantage of his route. At the time though, another pressing issue was on Genghis' mind, and that was the still living Jalal ad-Din of Khwarazmia. He sent Subutai and Jebe on a mission to track down the Shah with 20,000 Mongol soldiers at their disposal.

The Shah was in no hurry to rebuild an army, and deemed it best to lie low for a while. He went deep into hiding in India, and wouldn't emerge again until about three years later. With little in the way of leads or hunches, Subutai and Jebe knew they had little chance of tracking down Jalal ad-Din, and called off their search. Of course, they weren't going to squander their time in this new uncharted territory deep into Eastern Europe. They found themselves with a chance to make their Khan proud, and begin to put pressure on the various kingdoms scattered about the region, who were all on edge about what would happen next, due to the fall of one of the area's largest empires, the Khwarazmian. More importantly, it was going to be a type of reconnaissance mission, scouting the area figuring out how to effectively invade, and where to force Mongolian influence first. They sent a request to Khan, asking for permission to spend the next year or two leading a campaign across these territories, and bring great wealth and pride back to the empire. Obviously, messages travelled slow at the time, so it would be a while before the message would reach Genghis' ears. Subutai and Jebe weren't going to sit by idly twiddling their thumbs waiting for a response. Instead, they decided to begin a series of raids, which grew into some significant initial conquests in the Caucasus.

Subutai and Jebe, each leading 10,000 men, began their plight through Persian Iraq and Azerbaijan. What began as small raids on villages quickly grew into full scale attacks on multiple cities. The first to fall was the city of Rey, which was a major establishment in the area until the Mongol army nearly burned it to the ground in their attacks. They then moved on to the cities of Zanjan and Qazvin, both of which put up an impassioned opposition to the Mongol invaders, but still didn't stand a chance. Subutai and Jebe's army was proving to be just as unstoppable as any other Mongol force. They quickly earned the reputation of being a considerable force in the area, and not something to be taken lightly. The city of Hamadan certainly received this message, because they immediately surrendered without putting up any sort of fight. This allowed the city to be spared from too much destruction, but made no guarantee to the citizens, who still saw many casualties in the typically bloody Mongol raids of the city. Ozbeg, the Atabeg of Azerbaijan, managed to keep the Azerbaijani capital of Tabriz out of harm's way by offering up a large tribute of money, clothes, and horses to the Mongols. Subutai and Jebe accepted these gifts, and spared the city.

At this point, the year 1220 was coming to an end and it was getting time for the army to make camp for the harsh winter ahead. After sparing Tabriz, the army continued north and set up their winter camp in the Mugan Steppes. In a few quick months Subutai and Jebe had proven themselves worthy of expanding the borders of the Mongol Empire, and worthy of leading Mongolia's next substantial invasion, which would be in the Caucasus. Azerbaijan was only the beginning. The army regrouped itself and prepared for the next stage of their attacks. During their hiatus from fighting, they were joined by Kurdish and Turcoman freebooters, who swore their service to Subutai and Jebe. With a newly strengthened and invigorated army, the generals set out for their next target early in 1221.

This next victim in the Mongolian sights was the Kingdom of Georgia. This kingdom had already been around for almost 2000 years, and was well established within a stretch of land in between the Caspian Sea and the Black Sea, a geographical region known as the Caucasus. The area is where the country of Georgia currently resides, but the Kingdom had a slightly wide spread at this time, reaching from the southernmost parts of modern day Ukraine, to the northern regions of modern day Iran and Armenia.

One might usually associate a reconnaissance mission with quiet stealth, or careful decisiveness of every move. The decisiveness was plenty present in the Subutai and Jebe led Mongol army, but not so much the stealth. The two fiery generals burst into Georgia with blood in their eyes. Mongol forces always came in hard in order to viciously stake their claim over their new territory, and this surge into Georgia was no exception. A series of violent raids commenced, catching the Georgians completely off guard. Various historical records tell us that the Georgians initially had no idea who these new foreign invaders were, only that they were an issue. Mongolia was still a new influence in these areas so far west from where the empire began. Of course, it was about to be a region where every inhabitant was plenty aware of the strength and brutality of the Mongolian Empire.

The raids eventually motivated the Georgian King, King George IV Lasha, to launch a retaliation. He sent an army of 10,000 to deal with the Mongol invasion, which was successful in pushing the army back. After a quick battle, the Mongols withdrew to the city of Tbilisi. Subutai and Jebe waited here to reconsolidate their forces, but repeatedly launched small counter attacks which were useful in keeping the Georgians on their toes. Once they felt ready and rested, they launched an all out assault against Georgia. King George personally led an army of 60,000 Georgian and Armenia troops to meet the invaders. The Mongols were heartily outnumbered, but this mattered little to their emblazoned spirit. The two armies met on the Kotman River and fought valiantly in the Battle of Khunan. It was a vicious battle fought hard by both sides, but the Mongols, as per usual, were able to take the edge.

After the battle Subutai and Jebe had to retreat and recuperate their forces who, despite the surefire victory over the Georgians, had still taken a beating. Plus, they didn't want to overstep their boundaries and lead the army into an unsuccessful campaign. They reflected the intentions of Genghis Khan in these military actions, and this required careful consideration on their part. Conquering Georgia was not the two men's ultimate goal, but rather they had to send the appropriate message to the country that it did not have the strength to resist their inevitable invaders. Plundering and raising cities to the ground was the most effective way to send this message, and this was set as Subutai and Jebe's intention. They would use a slow burn to drive home this point.

After the battle the Mongols returned to Azerbaijan to take up another strategic point closer to Georgia. They besieged the city of Maragheh for a month, putting their prisoners in the front lines so that they comprised the bulk of Mongolian casualties. At the end of the month, Maragheh fell, and the majority of the city's population met judgement by either sword or arrow. It was yet another brutal massacre to add to Mongolian history. Afterwards, the Mongols chose the city of Hamadan, the city that had surrendered the first time they came around, as their next refuge. The nobility at Hamadan was not as keen to bend to the will of the Mongols this time, which was obviously a huge mistake. The city's defenses were staunch, and caused a decent number of Mongol casualties, but they were certainly not about to become the first city the Mongolian army failed to take. It fell after a time, giving Subutai and Jebe significant power over the territory leading into Georgia. Their forces swelled once again, and by the end of 1221 they were ready to engage the kingdom once more.

Subutai and Jebe re-entered Georgie from the Kura River, the same route they used the first time. The armies of Georgia and Mongolia met again at the Battle of Bardav. King George IV was once again at the head of this army, eager to stomp out this persistent Mongolian invasion. It was near Tbilisi where the armies finally engaged one another, and at first it seemed like the Georgians were going to have the upper hand in repelling their invaders. What they didn't know is that as the fighting commenced, they were only fighting a portion of the Mongolian army. Subutai led this charge full force into the Georgian army, while Jebe led a smaller army, which was lying in wait behind Subutai's forces. It was at this battle that Subutai employed one of his Khan's most viable strategies. He feigned a retreat, which put the Georgian cavalry on his tail in hot pursuit. King George walked right into the Mongolian trap, and had the might of Jebe's ambush brought down upon him. In the ensuing conflict the King was hit in the chest with an arrow, inflicting a wound that would not kill him on the battlefield, but one he would not ultimately survive from.

The Georgians had no choice but to conceded defeat, and repeal their forces before Georgia had nothing left to defend itself with. This gave Subutai and Jebe free range over the country as they continued to lambast the country through violent plunder. Georgia no longer posed a threat to their advancements, but it was still not the generals' main target. They only sought the rewards of plunder, raising everything on their way north. Not being conquered may have felt like a win for the Georgians at the time, but once they became aware that it was the Mongols who were threatening their wellbeing and knocking at the door, an appropriate fear washed over the kingdom. It was a fear that would persist as the kingdom threw itself about in turmoil for the next few years before the Mongols would return.

As Subutai and Jebe continued to advance north, towards the mountainous regions of the Caucasus which would lead to Russian and European territory, a response from Genghis Khan finally made its way back to them. They were given the blessings of their Khan to continue their pursuits in the region, for the glory of their leader and their homeland. The next major obstacle they had to overcome to achieve these goals, however, was not in the form of an army, but rather it was the terrain of the Caucasus itself.

The stretch of mountains that cut through the Caucasus, and led to great mighty northern territories which the Mongols were eager to subjugate, was an incredibly dangerous path for an army to traverse without proper guidance. The bitter cold could be fatal to an ill prepared army, and the rocky mountain passes required careful footing to traverse to say the least. As they approached the Georgian city of Derbent, they struck up a deal. They would leave the city untouched, in exchange for a group of ten guides to lead the army through the Caucasus. Derbent was well aware of the destruction the Mongols had already inflicted on their brethren, and everywhere else on the continent for that matter, and they took this deal without hesitation. To keep things from getting too cozy, Subutai had one of the ten guides executed in front of the others. This most certainly set a precedence, and showed that the Mongols were still in control here, and these guides would be foolish to attempt anything against the Mongols. With what was now nine guides, the Mongol army set off through the mountains in the dead of winter.

Despite the apt guidance, the journey was still harrowing for the Mongols. The rocky terrain was a challenge to traverse on foot, but even more so when you were pulling a siege weapon behind you. Because of this, most of the

Mongolian siege equipment was abandoned, destroyed first so that no one else could use it against them. The biting cold also took a fair share of casualties, and the Mongolian forces took a considerable hit from frostbite. Subutai and Jebe were strong though, and they kept their army pressing forward, knowing that they were making the right move, given they had the support of Genghis Khan fueling their confidence.

After what likely seemed like years, but was only a matter of weeks, the Mongol army found themselves on the other side of the mountain pass. Word of their travels and their intentions had spread, though, and they were met by a strong coalition of forces that had amassed an army for the sole purpose of defending against the Mongol invasion. The Lezigans, Cherkesses, and Alans had put together an army of around 50,000 able bodied men. This coalition also had the support of the Cumans, which were a proud people controlling a vast area of land in Northern Europe. Their kingdom spread from Lake Balkash all the way to the Black Sea, and their opposition to the Mongols was what gave this new coalition a chance.

Khan Koten, leader of the Cuman people had managed to garner the support of the Volga Bulgars as well as the Khazars. He was ready for a conflict with the Mongols, or so he thought. When the two armies had their first meeting, it was fairly inconsequential. Neither side could gain an advantage, and both withdrew. It wasn't a defeat for the Mongols, but Subutai and Jebe were well aware that their army was not equipped for a full scale invasion of Cuman, and they weren't prepared to defend against the combined strength of these armies who had all built considerable resentment towards the unstoppable Mongols. Instead of swords and horses, deceit and craftsmanship would prove the Mongols best weapon against this new foe.

With some persuasion, Khan Koten was convinced to abandon his alliance with the other Caucasus tribes. Subutai cited the Cuman's Turkic heritage as the reasoning for their alliance, as the Mongols had had relatively positive relations with the Turkic regions. They were also promised a worthwhile cut of the Mongol's war spoils which they would acquire from dominating the Caucasian tribes. Once this alliance was cemented, the Mongols made short work of the tribal coalition formed against them, which now lacked one of its most essential wings.

If Khan Koten took one lesson away from this experience, it was never to trust Mongols. After the Caucasian coalition had been dealt with the Mongols almost immediately turned around on the Cumans and broke what was obviously a shaky alliance. The Cuman army was on their way home, feeling safe and secure, when Subutai and Jebe crashed the Mongol force into their rear, splitting the army into two scantily fleeing factions. Both factions were defeated in no time, and the Mongols held back none of their ferocity. They slaughtered all of their prisoners, and used the crushing victory as fuel for the fire as they advanced towards Astrakhan, a Cuman stronghold. This city was sacked with ease, and it sent the remaining Cuman forces to seek refuge out West. The Mongols were eager to put an end to the Cumans, and so they kept up their pursuit. No entity could ever draw arms against the Mongolians, and be left alive to tell the tale.

In the chaos of the Cuman slaughter, Khan Koten managed to escape, and he fled north to Kievan Rus. He sought refuge in Galich, where his son in law Prince Mstislav the Bold was ruler. He came to the city with a grave warning for his son. He told him, with a quiver in his voice, "Today, the Mongols have taken our land and tomorrow they will take yours." He pleaded for help from the Kievan Rus princes to stop the Mongols from advancing any further north. His pleas were ignored though. The Cuman had a long history of raiding their Russian neighbors, and this persistent conflict had built considerable distrust between the kingdoms.

For the next year, Koten would continue to appeal to the Rus for help, while the Cuman people continued to be ravaged by the Mongol army in hot pursuit. They followed them far west, all the way to Crimea, where Jebe dispatched a detachment to plunder the Genoese city of Soldaia. The Mongols had recently made a pact with the Venetians, who occupied territory they were crossing through, that they would keep peace between their armies if the Mongols agreed to destroy any European trading stations they came to. One of these stations was held by the Republic of Genoa in Soldaia, and was dealt with handily.

Eventually, the Mongols rerouted to head back towards the East, and they began following the Dneister River. This river was going to lead them dangerously close to Rus territory, and it is an act that finally spurred some reaction from the princes, much to the chagrin of Koten who had watched his people get slaughtered without anyone else seeming to care. Prince Mstislav, along with Mstislav III of Kiev, Prince Yuri II of Vladimir-Suzdai, and the rest of the Rus princes, formed a coalition and swore to halt the Mongol advancement and end their campaign in Eastern Europe. They combined their armies together to create one powerhouse of an army which would rendezvous with the Cumans and, with the combined forces of the remaining Cumans the Rus reinforcements, they hoped to easily bring the Mongols to their knees.

The Mongols caught wind of the Rus advancement, and began to prepare themselves for an incoming conflict. They made their encampment on the east side of the Dneiper River where they planned to wait on reinforcements. Genghis Khan's oldest son, Jochi, who had been leading campaigns in the north, around the Aral Sea, was expected to send reinforcements. However, before reinforcements could be dispatched Jochi fell ill. Subutai and Jebe received word of this illness, along with the fact that no reinforcements would be coming to their aid, right around the time the Rus armies made their first move. They hoped to pin the Mongols at the river bank, with armies impending from the north, the south, and the main front. Even the Cumans were reinvigorated for the next wave of fighting, and they planned to attack the Mongol's rear front.

The Mongols had never intended to find themselves in conflict with the Rus. These provinces were not part of Subutai or Jebe's invasion plan, and they sent word to Kiev that this was the case. Ten envoys were sent to Prince Mstislav III of Kiev to explain to him that the Cumans were the only concern of the Mongols, and that they had no desire to engage in conflict with the Rus whatsoever. Mstislav was not persuaded by these envoys, and had them executed. The next visitor sent to Kiev was an ambassador for the Mongols, and his message was simple. War.

The Mongols were preparing for major conflict on all fronts, ready for the ensuing conflict which would come to be known as the Battle of the Kalka River. The army set out to the east, attempting to get as far away from Rus as possible before any fighting started. A rearguard of 1000 men was left behind at the river in order to keep tabs on the maneuverings of the Rus armies. Mstislav the Bold was the first to reach the opposite side of the river from the rearguard. He crossed the river and, despite the oncoming barrages of arrows, engaged the Mongolians and quickly defeated this rearguard.

From there, the Rus armies continued onward, and pursued the Mongolians for nine days. It wasn't a retreat on the part of the Mongolians though. They had a plan, and were ready to turn on their pursuers once the time was right. Before they could solidify this feigned retreat, they needed to reach the battle's namesake, the Kalka River. Upon reaching the river they marched alongside it for a time, until they were ready to reverse their direction and lead a vicious counterattack against the armies pursuing them.

The military acumen of Subutai and Jebe let them know exactly when it was time to strike, and when they did their enemies fell apart almost instantly. A decimating cavalry charge sent the Cuman army into utter chaos, and they began their retreat before their entire army had even engaged in the fighting. A gap was made in the Rus ranks so that the Cumans could flee, but the Mongol cavalry quickly took advantage of this gap. They charged through and wiped the floor with the quickly crumbling Rus armies. It was an ill prepared engagement all around, as another army bringing up the rear wasn't even aware that the battle had started before they ran into the fleeing Cumans. A cluster of confusion erupted between various broken armies and the Mongols were quick to capitalize on this. They commenced their decimation of the Cumans and the other Rus armies, and even managed to cut off the Rus retreat. Very few Rus escaped that decisive battlefield, and the ones that did were subsequently hunted down by Subutai and Jebe.

Rus' involvement in this conflict with the Mongols, that really should have only involved the Cumans, was one of their greatest downfalls. They were now left virtually defenseless, with the vast majority of their armies being at the receiving end of Mongol blades. A good amount of their nobility had also been either killed or captured, throwing the region into political turmoil as well. The nobles that had been captured, including Mstislav of Kiev, were given a particularly brutal punishment, and were crushed beneath the Mongol victory platform on which they enjoyed their victory feast, literally over the Russians.

With the region in utter turmoil, the Mongols likely could have subdued any opposition there with ease, and Subutai and Jebe could have been responsible for expanding the empire even further west than they did, but despite their overwhelming victory Rus was still not in the playbook. They headed back East, gathering up a few more small victories on their way back towards Mongolia. After a long and fruitful campaign, Subutai and Jebe were finally going to reunite their armies with Khan and return as a collective to the homeland. Sadly, Jebe died at the end of this campaign from historically uncertain causes, but would forever be remembered by Genghis Khan and the rest of the Mongolians as an incredible general, and a valiant leader of the Mongolian army. He had been a part of one of history's longest cavalry campaigns, which stretched over 5,500 miles. With the return of Subutai and the late Jebe from their Western campaigns, Mongol expansion westward under Genghis Khan would come to an end.

.   .   .

Genghis Khan, Subutai, and the rest of the Mongolian army finally returned home in 1223. There were still threats to the empire in all directions, but the army took the time it needed to recuperate, and the aging Khan got himself well rested before heading out on what would be his final campaign.

The most immediate threat to the Mongol Empire was now a foe they had already faced once before; the Western Xia dynasty. Genghis had been planning his return to the territory ever since he was denied aid from the Western Xia, who were supposed to be a vassal state to the Mongols, in his Khwarazmian campaign. They told Khan that if he did not have enough troops to carry out his invasion, then he had no claim to the supreme power which he used as the platform for his expansion. Genghis would obviously be preoccupied with the Khwarazmian for the next few years, but he never forgot what the Western Xia had done. Western Xia realized the gravity of their actions, as well, and attempted to unite themselves with both the Jin and the Song dynasties, knowing another Mongol invasion was inevitable.

By 1225, Genghis was once again ready for battle. He amassed a staggering force of 180,000 soldiers to march on Western Xia, which had only acquired a new emperor two years prior, after Emperor Shengzong abdicated the throne. The Mongols first stop was Khara-Khoto, which fell quickly and opened up the Mongols swift path to the south. Expecting opposition, the Mongols were surprised when they were met with no army marching on them. The bulk of the Western Xia army, led by Asha, were unable to march west from Yinchuan, as it would have meant enduring an exhausting 500 mile march across the desert.

Western Xia was ripe for the taking, and Genghis took full advantage of the open playing field he had before him. He fanned out his armies, systematically sweeping the countryside, leveling any city or garrison they came across. It was a merciless campaign that saw your typical Mongol death and destruction. Once the army reached the Qilian Mountains, Genghis split them in two, taking the bulk of the forces east towards the Western Xia capital, while Subutai marched in the opposite direction to deal with Western Xia's westernmost cities.

The Mongol bloodlust was alive and well, once again, and this time they were far more prepared for siege warfare than the last time they had engaged the province. Cities fell with ease, with some of the longest sieges only lasting up to five weeks, like Genghis' siege of Suzhou. When Genghis reached the city of Ganzhou, he found the father of one of his generals, Chagaan, in command of the city. Chagaan, who was born and raised in Ganzhou, attempted peace talks with his father. These didn't last long though, because the city's second in command staged a coup, and murdered Chagaan's father. He then promptly refused to surrender the city, giving Genghis no choice but to lay siege. This was a far more challenging siege than its predecessors, and one that took five months to win. Upon breaching the city, Genghis was ready to burn it to the ground, but Chagaan convinced him to let it be, and execute just the organizers of the coup instead.

After yet another long but successful siege, Genghis had to give himself a rest. He took refuge in the Qilian Mountains while his army took the city of Wuwei. By August of 1226 Genghis and his army were ready to move on Yinchuan, the Western Xia capital. The timing couldn't have been worse for the Western Xia, as their Emperor Xianzong died just as the Mongols began their next march. The state was falling into disarray as the world's most powerful army descended upon them. By November the Mongols had reached Lingwu, which wasn't more than 20 miles from Yinchuan. They began their siege, and utter defeat seemed to be on the horizon for the Western Xia.

With a massive army of 300,000 troops, the Western Xia thought they still stood a chance in one final counter attack, their last hurrah against their Mongol invaders. Clearly, though, they hadn't learned much from their previous encounters with these vehemently unstoppable forces. The 300,000 soldiers became 300,000 dead bodies, and the Western Xia's chances of defeating the Mongols on the battlefield were done. Their defenses in Yinchuan were their last hope.

At the beginning of 1227 the Mongols reached the gates of Yinchuan and immediately began their siege. Yinchuan was still an incredibly fortified city, and they were able to hold their own against the Mongols, using at least some of the insight their previous encounters had enlightened them to. Regardless, it was clear that the Western Xia campaign was going to end in success, and Genghis could turn his attention elsewhere. One more Chinese province still resisted him more than any other, and that was the Jin. Genghis left the siege at Yinchuan in the hands of his soldiers, while he led most of the army along the Wei River, beginning to impede on Jin territory. He made it clear that the Jin were his next target, even going as far as to send soldiers over the Qin Mountains to impose on Kaifeng, the Jin capital. He also had Subutai regroup in the east, and their two armies began a sweeping campaign across the Lilupan Mountains, the Tao River valley, and the Lanzhou region. City after city continued to fall to the Mongols, and Genghis was eager to begin stomping out the Jin for good, as soon as he had wrapped up things in Western Xia.

While he was laying siege to the city of Longde, Genghis sent Chagaan to Yinchuan to negotiate a Western Xia surrender. The siege had been persisting for six months now, but it was clear that no matter what the result of that siege, Western Xia had still lost, so Genghis thought it best to end it sooner rather than later. Chagaan put together terms of surrender with Emperor Mozhu, who requested a month to prepare appropriate gifts for his Mongol rulers. Genghis agreed to these terms, despite the fact he had every intention of killing the emperor as soon as he surrendered.

Knowing that the negotiations were bringing the conflict with Western Xia to a definitive end, Genghis turned his full attention back towards the Jin. They had attempted to make peace with their invaders, but Genghis angrily denied these requests. He set him and his army up at the Jin border which they shared with the Song dynasty, and began to prepare for a full scale invasion of the Jin. However, Genghis himself would never get the chance to partake in this invasion.

In August of 1227, Genghis Khan was dead. His death is one of the most widely disputed in medieval history, and a variety of theories persist about what happened. Many attest that he was killed in action while running his final campaigns against the Western Xia. Other theories suggest he died of wounds inflicted from being thrown from his horse months earlier, or that he succumbed to illness. Given that he was in his sixties, any of these theories has validity, but the true cause will forever remain a mystery. Regardless, the great Khan was gone, and it was right in the middle of a campaign.

The death of Genghis Khan was kept heavily under wraps while the Western Xia campaign was still in operation. A month after his death Emperor Mozhu made good on his surrender promises, and turned himself and the city into the Mongols. Fulfilling the wishes of their Khan, Mozhu was executed, and Yinchuan was ravaged by the Mongol soldiers, filled with grief for their Khan and furious anger towards his enemies. The entire city was pillaged, and the entirety of the population was slaughtered. Even the imperial tombs to the west of the city were ransacked. This marked a very brutal and very final end to the Western Xia. The dynasty was then nearly removed from history, as it was Genghis Khan's intention to wipe their population from the face of the earth in what might have been history's first attempt at genocide.

With Genghis dead, Mongolia now found itself in a strange position. The empire still had enemies, and the army still had plans for great conquest, some of which was already underway in Jin at the time of Genghis' death. There was a legacy now to be fulfilled in Genghis Khan's succession, as his accomplishments had to be followed by something substantial if the might of the Mongol Empire was to persist. It was now up to the sons of Genghis Khan to keep the empire strong and alive, and continue to push its borders in every direction. They obviously had a tough act to follow, and sibling rivalry would usher the Mongol Empire into a new era full of harrowing and unexpected change.

Chapter 8
A Matter of Succession

It is hard to believe that a man of such stature and prowess as Genghis Khan was still, in fact, mortal. August 18, 1227 proved this, though. News of the Khan's death truly sent the Empire into a state of disbelief. The mighty Genghis Khan, whose accomplishments made him seem nothing short of invincible, was gone.

When the campaign in Western Xia was officially concluded, the Mongol army returned home, bringing Genghis Khan's body with them. He was to be buried on his own soil, yet according to Mongolian custom, he was not to be buried with any distinct markings to denote his gravesite. Genghis specifically reinforced this point years before his death. He was not to be commemorated in one specific spot, but rather have his memory live on in the entirety of Mongolian soil.

Genghis' burial place was kept a closely guarded secret, and it is a secret that died with the men who did the deed. To this day, it is unknown where the body of Genghis Khan was laid to rest. It is assumed it was in the vicinity of his birthplace in Khentii Aimag, likely near the Onon River, and in the shadow of the Burkhan Khaldun Mountain. The Burkhan Khaldun held particular significance to Genghis, as it is where he hid after failing to overtake the Merkits in his first campaign across Mongolia. The mountain was considered a sacred place of great spiritual notoriety, and Genghis himself had given his submission to the Gods while taking quiet refuge within. It was a mountain of truly great power that would watch over the body and spirit of Genghis Khan.

There is a lot of rumor and mystery surrounding Genghis' burial site, much of which is likely exaggerated legend, but interesting nonetheless. It is said that the funeral envoy was so serious about keeping the burial place a secret that they murdered anyone in their path on the way to the burial site. They also allegedly diverted a river over the grave, which would have made recovering it impossible. There are also rumors that they had horses stampede over the gravesite, and that trees were planted over his body, all for the sake of concealment. Valid stories or not, it still stands to reason that we will never know the exact burial place of Genghis Khan, but instead we have the Genghis Khan Mausoleum, an elaborate temple constructed years after his death, as an homage to his memory, but not a marking of his gravesite.

.   .   .

The Mongolian people may have been convinced of Genghis Khan's immortality, but Genghis himself knew this was not the case. He could feel himself growing older and wearier, his endless campaigning taking its toll on his body, mind, and spirit. He began to pick up on his deterioration years before his death, and made moves early on to guarantee the continuation of his empire after his passing. As was customary for the culture, his succession would be left in the hands of his sons. Of course, sibling rivalry was not uncommon amongst his children, and he made a point to make sure this wouldn't happen after he was gone.

His biggest concern was the tension between his sons Jochi and Chagatai. His relationship with Jochi had always been on the rocks, with the issue of parentage clouding Jochi's trust of his own father. Chagatai had always been the hot headed son who could fly off the handle at a moment's notice. He had repeatedly brought Jochi's parentage into question, and Genghis was well aware of the power struggle that could erupt between the two. In order to combat this, Genghis decided that his empire would be split amongst his sons, who would each have control over Khanates. When he returned home from the west, before setting out on his Western Xia campaign, he wanted to officiate his succession, and called for his sons to return to him in the Mongolian heartland. Ogedei, Chagatai, and Tolui obeyed, but Jochi, who was still far off to the northwest, refused his father's request.

Jochi was to be left with the westernmost reaches of the Mongol Empire, allowed to control the land that reached as far west as Mongol horses had trod upon. However, now that he was being difficult, his inheritance was in question. Genghis had Ogedei and Chagatai march out to meet Jochi, prepared to potentially draw arms against him if he continued to refuse his father's wishes. Before they met their brother, however, news reached them that Jochi passed away in February of 1226.

The circumstances of Jochi's death are another considerable mystery. It is perfectly reasonable that he was killed in battle, as he was still in the midst of campaigning around the Aral Sea, or that he succumbed to an illness during his march across the bitterly dangerous northern tundra. However, there is another theory that suggests something far darker.

Ever since the events at Urgench, where Jochi lost the city he was promised, along with his father's respect, he had held a major grudge. This grudge contributed to his refusal to ever return home to look his father in the eyes again. He was totally estranged by the end of his life. His estrangement might have been taken a step further, though, as some historical records suggest he may have been conspiring against Genghis, with plans to assassinate him. If we choose to believe this, we can also choose to believe that Genghis got word of Jochi's secret plans, and retaliated. There is a troubling rumor floating around the life of Genghis Khan that claims he poisoned his own son, so as to prevent him from dissenting and causing any disarray in the empire. We will never know the answer to this question for sure, but given the fact that Genghis generally put the sanctity of his empire above everything else, including his own family, it is a rumor that stands to reason.

With Jochi unable to receive his inheritance in life, the land was passed down to his sons, Batu and Orda, who became Khans of their own respective territories. Jochi had established his territory as the Golden Horde, and Batu and Orda split the horde into two wings, the Blue Horde and the White Horde, which they controlled respectively. These two factions eventually combined to form the Kipchak Khanate, or Khanate of the Golden Horde. This province was the window to the Russian territories, which the Mongols still had their eyes on after their initial campaigns there under Subutai and Jebe.

Chagatai was left with a considerably larger track of land, as he was betrothed rule over Central Asia and northern Iran, mostly territory that had been conquered in the Khwarazmian campaign. He would transform this region into the Chagatai Khanate. Genghis' youngest son, Tolui, had specific stipulations on his inheritance, given that customs were different when it came to the youngest son. He was given the smallest amount of land compared to his brothers, receiving only a section of the Mongolian heartland, a still honorable land to control given that it is where the reign of Genghis Khan began, and where it spread immensely from. However, Tolui was given something arguably better than land. As the youngest son, he was entitled to the bulk of Genghis' army. Jochi, Chagatai, and Ogedei were each bestowed around 4,000 men, leaving Tolui with control over an army of over 100,000 able bodied soldiers, which contained the majority of the Mongol cavalry forces, the most valuable sect of the entire army.

Finally, it was Ogedei who would receive the most from his father's inheritance. Ogedei had consistently proven himself to be the most level headed of his brothers. He was likeable and charismatic, and put the Mongolian empire before himself, following in the practices of his father. Out of the four sons, he was the most trusted by Genghis, especially on a military level. Ogedei was a valuable player in many of Genghis' campaigns, and he is who took over the siege of Urgench when Jochi and Chagatai fell into dispute. Because of this undying loyalty and his reasonable nature, Ogedei was given the title of successor to Genghis Khan. Genghis split the empire into Khanates in order to diffuse sibling tension, and spread his sons out and away from one another. However, the Khanates were still to be wholly united under one rule, and that rule was Ogedei Khan's. He was named the Great Khan, and given the territories of Eastern Asia, which included China. Genghis also likely saw Ogedei as the most competent in continuing the Mongol campaigns against the Jin, and other Chinese dynasties.

In 1229, two years after Genghis Khan's death, an official kurultai was held, which made the borders of the Khanates, and the division of power official. Chagatai, Tolui, and Jochi's sons all assumed their power, while Ogedei prepared to lead the Mongol Empire into its next era. He took this mission incredibly seriously, following in the footsteps of his father, and honoring the legacy which he left behind. Ogedei's first actions were to stamp out small opposition on both the western and eastern borders of the empire.

Ogedei sent a small faction of troops to the Kipchack steppes out west, near where Jochi's sons had assumed authority. Here, they squashed rebellions from the Bashkirs and the Bulgars, and subjugated their populations. Out to the east, the Eastern Xia and Water Tatars had taken back Manchuria from the Mongols, and Ogedei sought to put a quick end to this. They were defeated easily, and by 1230 Ogedei was ready to begin his first real campaign as ruler of the entire empire. He would kick off his legacy of Mongol expansionism by finishing what his father started with the consistently problematic Jin.

Ogedei, being the reasonable leader he was, made an attempt at peace before engaging in the campaign which he probably knew was inevitable. Nevertheless, he sent an envoy to the Jin court to discuss peace. Emperor Aizong was not in the mood for negotiations, though, and slaughtered the whole envoy, making it plenty obvious that peace was not an option. Ogedei then personally led the Mongols into this campaign, with his father's trusted general Subutai at his side. The Jin had clearly learned a lot from their last encounter with the Mongols, and came prepared to do extensive and exhausting battle with them. Their army, led by Wanyan Heda, was one of considerable might, fueled by a long winded hatred of the Mongols. Wanyan Heda was able to put up a substantial defense, and actually claimed victory in the first conflict of the campaign.

Subutai's first push against the Jin was unsuccessful, and he had no choice but to withdraw. The Mongols spent a few months recuperating and planning their strategy to take down this unexpectedly considerable foe. In 1231 Ogedei led the next push, which resulted in the taking of Fengxiang and Cheng'an. They were then immediately able to turn their attention to Kaifeng, the Jin capital. Their plan for taking this well fortified city was to use a three pronged attack. Ogedei and Subutai would lead forces from the east and north, while Tolui would come in from the west. Tolui was also meant to cut through Song territory to the south, and launch a surprise assault of Kaifeng's southern front as well.

Wanyan Heda was alerted to this surprise maneuver, and personally led 200,000 soldiers to meet Tolui and cut off his advancement. He prepared an ambush near the city of Dengzhou, a city that sat at the bottom of a great mountain range. He hid two separate cavalry forces behind the crest of the mountains, ready to ambush and pin Tolui's army. The Mongol spy network came in handy once more, though, because Tolui learned of the ambush before he arrived at Dengzhou. Knowing that the element of surprise was squandered, Wanyan Heda gathered the entirety of his troops to prepare for a direct engagement with the Mongols. In the shadow of Mount Yu, the two armies met in heated battle. Wanyan Heda came considerably over prepared, and Tolui was greatly outnumbered. After realizing the futility of the battle, Tolui pulled his army back. He left only a small force of troops at Mount Yu to keep Wanyan Heda occupied, while the majority of his forces diverted north towards Kaifeng.

Tolui and his army paved the road to Kaifeng with blood and ash, taking every city or village they came across, and burning everything of value in their path, so that it could not be utilized by Wanyan Heda if he were to pursue. Eventually, Tolui's army caused enough of a stir that Wanyan Heda had no choice but to direct his attention towards them, knowing exactly where they were headed. The Jin troops stationed near the Yellow River were forced out of their position to head south to deal with Tolui's oncoming might. Ogedei seized this opportunity to cross the river, which allowed him to meet up with his brother.

At Three-peaked Hill near the city of Junzhou, Tolui and Ogedei reunited their armies and prepared to face off against Wanyan Heda, whose army still outnumbered that of the combined Mongol forces. At this point, though, the numbers didn't matter. Wanyan Heda may have still had as many as 100,000 men, but they were 100,000 cold, hungry, exhausted, and downright broken men. By burning supplies as they went, Tolui's army was effective in starving out the Jin troops. This gave the Mongols a dangerous advantage over the Jin, who were hardly able to stage much of an opposition with little in the way of morale to lift their spirits.

It was a devastating defeat for the Jin, as they were slaughtered in their retreat. Even Wanyan Heda was killed in the fighting, bringing the Jin army to its weakest point of the entire campaign. Once the Battle of Three-peaked Hill was over, it was clear that Kaifeng didn't stand a chance, with the Jin having little remaining in the way of an army. Emperor Aizong hastily fled the city, retreating to the city of Guide.

Emperor Aizong attempted to rebuild an army to stop the Mongols, but his attempts were all in vain. Internal strife within the authority of the Jin dynasty made it difficult to gather any sort of unified strength against their attackers. The found a hint of success in one counterattack launched against the Mongol camp near Guide, which resulted in many Mongol casualties. However, Emperor Aizong knew he couldn't stay in Guide, as its defenses would not be able to hold out forever against a horde of angry Mongols. He reluctantly decided to move out, and give his army refuge at Caizhou. It was on the way to this city that the Jin dynasty's fate would be sealed for good.

The Mongols took Guide, and began a quick pursuit of Emperor Aizong. Ironically though, it was not the Mongols who would take complete credit for ending the Jin dynasty. The Southern Song dynasty decided that they wanted in on the conquest as well, and dispatched a massive army to meet the Jin troops in a field outside of Caizhou. The Jin army barely pushed past this obstacle, and the survivors holed themselves up in the city. The Song army began besieging the city on one side, and when the Mongols arrived they began a siege on the other side. The Jin army was pinned in its final soul crushing holdout against the combined strength of their enemies. Emperor Aizong knew this was the end, and took his own life, rather than letting the Mongols do it for him. He committed suicide, and the following day Caizhou fell. The year was 1234, and the Jin dynasty was officially no more.

.   .   .

The Mongols next focus was on a place they were also quite familiar with. The Kingdom of Georgia, far out to the West, was in shambles and ripe for the taking. After fleeing the Khwarazmian Empire with little more than his own life, the Shah Jalal ad-Din Muhammad had been hard at work amassing an army to fight back against the Mongols with and take back the territory lost by his father. He had demanded that Georgia assist him in this fight, but they refused. Jalal retaliated violently, and sacked the Georgia capital of Tbilisi in 1226. Jalal ad-Din continued to build his army over the next few years but was assassinated in 1231, leaving his territory practically defenseless, and Georgia in pieces.

By 1236 the Mongol army stepped foot in Georgia once again, and this time the kingdom put up little resistance, knowing the consequences of such actions were grave. The vast majority of cities laid down their arms without a fight, while others evacuated and fled further west. Queen Rusudan was one of the many who fled, showing the rest of the kingdom that there was no need for opposition. They had sufficiently lost. The Mongols systematically acquired every city in the kingdom, being met with little resistance. By 1243 Georgia had officially submitted to Mongolia, and accepted Ogedei Khan as the Great Khan, and ruler of their people.

.   .   .

Another campaign took place simultaneously to the Georgian campaign, and this was the conquest of Kievan Rus, another familiar ground to the Mongols. Subutai, along with Batu Khan, grandson of Genghis Khan and son of Jochi, led an army into Volga Bulgaria in the later months of 1236. The next year was spent destroying the last of the resistance that the Volga Bulgarians, the Alani, and the now aligned Cuman-Kipchaks, could muster up.

With these northern territories submitted to Mongol rule, the pressure was turned up drastically on Kievan Rus and its prince Yuri II of Vladimir. Yuri attempted to uphold his country's honor by refusing to submit, and the Mongols promptly showed him why that was a horrible idea. They ravaged the city of Ryazan, and defeated an army of Yuri's shortly after. From there they made haste for the capital city of Vladimir-Suzdai, ransacking cities on their way. On February 4, 1238 a three day siege on the city commenced. At the end of the third day the walls were breached and the Mongols set the city ablaze. Prince Yuri II was the only member of the royal family to escape the blaze, and he fled across the Volga where he hoped to gather a new army. This new army was indeed gathered, but it was flattened almost as soon as it was raised.

Batu Khan proceeded to raise hell in the rest of the region, never failing to take a city he wished to destroy. Cities burned and villages saw their entire populations destroyed as the Mongols continued their vicious assault across Kievan Rus, which now had no strength of its own, and was just prolonging its own demise. It wasn't long before the Mongols could stake a confident and surefire claim over the entire region.

The Mongol Empire now stretched all the way from the Pacific Ocean on its eastern border, to the west, where it now bordered central Europe. Batu Khan wasted no time in continuing his assault of the European countryside. He promptly invaded both Poland and Hungary, who were ill prepared to say the least. Polish cities began dropping like flies to the Mongol invaders, and it prompted them to form an impromptu alliance with the Moravians, as well as the Christian military orders of the Teutonic Knights, the Hospitallers, and the Templars. This allied army was sizeable enough to slow the Mongol advancement at Legnica, but the pushback was only for a time. On April 11, 1241 the two armies met again on the banks of the Sajo River, where the Europeans, now allied with the Croatians as well, were crushed by the Mongols.

The momentum of Batu Khan and his army was building at an alarming rate. For every small victory the Europeans might have enjoyed, the Mongols celebrated two large victories that saw far more damage to their enemies than themselves. The army pillaged their way through Bohemia, Serbia, Babenberg Austria, and even began making small advancements into the Holy Roman Empire. The great threat to the east was no longer just in the east. They stretched far into the reaches of what would be considered the western world, and who knows how much farther Batu Khan would have taken his unstoppable forces if not for what occurred at the end of 1241.

December of 1241 saw the death of Ogedei Khan. It was imperative now that a new Khan be chosen by a kurultai, in order to maintain the stability of the rapidly growing empire. In the wake of Ogedei's death, it was his wife, Toregene, who obtained interim power before the kurultai could be assembled. Toregene was responsible for a significant number of changes in the Mongol political and social structure. She did away with many of her late husband's officials, mainly the Khitan and Muslim ones, and surrounded herself with her own allies instead. Rather than an attempt at full power, Toregene was just instating new ideals for her son Guyuk to build upon, as she had garnered support for him amongst the Mongol elites to become the next Great Khan. However, for the kurultai to take place, all of the Khanate rulers were required to be present. In an attempt to stall the processions, Batu Khan refused to attend, claiming the Mongolian climate didn't agree with his health. This delayed the process for four years, as the rift in Mongolian politics became wider and wider.

Eventually, Batu Khan conceded and sent some of his brothers and generals to attend the kurultai on his behalf. Guyuk was elected as Khan, and he immediately set out to begin stabilizing the chipped nation. He reversed the majority of what his mother had put into place, and restored the policies of his father, reinstating his officials. The rule that followed under Guyuk saw more expansion, this time into the Song dynasty to the south, and further into the Islamic world, driving campaigns into Iran and Iraq.

Guyuk's rule was short lived though, as he died of an illness while marching west towards Russia for historically debated reasons. At the request of Batu Khan, the next kurultai to decide on Guyuk's successor was held in his own territory in 1250. This further illustrated the growing divide between the eastern and western reaches of the empire. The successor which this kurultai elected was Mongke Khan, the son of Tolui, Genghis Khan's youngest son. This was yet another affront to the Ogedei lineage in the east, as it was customary that only his lineage would have a right to the title of Khan.

Mongke Khan's rule further divided the empire, while expanding it at the same time. He put the country through a series of administrative reforms that allowed for more religious tolerance, as well as a reformed taxing system. He also put a particular focus on making sure his power was secured across the empire, putting his allies in positions of power around him. He made his own brothers, Hulagu and Kublai, rulers of Persia and the Mongol-controlled regions of China, respectively.

The Mongol border continued to be pushed south under the command of Mongke Khan, as they worked further into China and the Middle East. Mongke Khan dealt one of the most definitive blows to the Islamic world when his conquests culminated in the siege of Baghdad in 1258. A year after the successful siege, however, Mongke Khan died and his succession was a major point of conflict across the empire.

The empire erupted into civil war following the death of their Great Khan. Mongke had failed to name a successor, and so the title was up for grabs between his brothers Hulagu, Kublai, and Ariqboke. Kublai was interested in the throne, but more interested in his personal conquest of China. This was until he heard that Ariqboke was going to attempt to claim the throne for himself. Hulagu was forever faithful to his brother Kublai and his claim, but died in 1264, leaving his territory vulnerable to their cousin Berke who was stirring up dissention in the northwest region of the empire. The entirety of the empire was on shaky ground as more and more factions emerged which shook the once unified stability of the region.

Eventually, it was Kublai Khan who would claim control over at least the eastern regions of Mongolia, after leading successfully ravaging campaigns in China, and establishing the Yuan dynasty. Kublai had a firm grip on his eastern territories, but the same could not be said about the regions further out west. Competing factions were tearing that region apart, and the collapse of the Mongolian Empire began to reveal itself on the horizon. In 1294 Kublai Khan died, and the four way split in the empire was cemented. Kublai had left behind the Yuan dynasty, which encompassed all of eastern Mongolia territory, while the west was split between the Golden Horde, the Ilkhanate, and the Chagatai Khanate.

The last 100 years of Mongolian history before 1294 were defined by nothing but conquest and civil war, with violence characterizing every single one of those years. However, with this divide in the empire, the region was ironically approaching its first peaceful era in a century. The four Khanates agreed on a peace treaty in 1304, which established the nominal rule of Temur Khan of the Yuan dynasty. This rule meant little more than a title, though, as the four khanates operated virtually independently, seeking little in the way of conquest.

With this disintegration of the empire as a collective force, the work started by Genghis Khan had essentially come to an end. Mongolia would never engage in a collaborative military effort again, and over time their borders began fighting back, and the four khanates began growing smaller and smaller. To call the territory of Mongolia an empire anymore at this point would simply not be fitting. The rest of the medieval period saw power shifting hands from khan to khan in Mongolia, with the khanates slowly dissolving one by one. Varying cultures and religions gradually crafted borders which began to reflect what we see in this region today.

Today, Mongolia inhabits a region scarcely bigger than what Genghis Khan started with in 1206. But who is to say it would be this way if Genghis Khan hadn't done what he did all those centuries ago. It stands to reason that Mongolia could have just fallen off the map in those early medieval periods, dissolving into nothing more than its warring nomadic clans, which could have so easily been absorbed by Chinese advancements if not for the incredible consolidation of power that took place there. Genghis Khan quite literally put his country on the map, and gave birth to what was nearly the largest empire in all of human history.

Chapter 9
Remembrance of Genghis Khan

When you look back at this legacy, it is easy to see why we remember Genghis Khan. In his lifetime, he made sure that he would be remembered forever, by setting a new precedence and forging a new path for a newly united country. His vision of the world gave him an unmatched desire for expansion. Many men could not do what Genghis Khan did in his lifetime if they had 1,000 lifetimes of their own. But Genghis Khan was not many men. He truly changed the landscape of the world, crafting it how he saw fit by the use of force and militaristic violence.

The Mongol Empire under Genghis Khan will forever be mostly remembered for its utter brutality, which solidified their incredible expansion. However, we must remember that with this growth of power also came a growth of influence on society. The Mongol way of life stretched across nearly the entire continent of Asia at one point in history, meaning Mongol society, and particularly the values which Genghis Khan spread through his conquering, was the most prominent way of life for this period.

The greatest empires in history seem to all have had their power transferred by bloodline and lineage, with a collection of noble families having control of nearly every aspect of politics and economics. Genghis Khan pushed this status quo, and instead spread meritocracy throughout his empire, a practice which put loyalists in positions of power, and giving titles to men who were right for the job, rather than ones who possessed the right last name.

The vast Mongol Empire also was able to unite their territory under a shared economy, much of which included tributes and vassal payments to the Mongol overlords, that created a strengthened sense of financial unity. Trade flourished because of what Genghis Khan did for the Asian continent. The Silk Road was almost entirely within the Mongol Empire's borders at their height. The intricate relay system, or Yam routes, that Khan established also continued to be highly influential innovations long after his death. They were essentially the basis of the postal system that exists today.

Genghis Khan is also responsible for kicking off one of the most intriguing economical innovations in history. A few years before his death, he authorized the use of paper money to be used as legal currency in the empire. He had already unified the empire under one currency, which was nominally thought to be the Chinese silver ingot coin. Upon this approval though, paper money began to circulate throughout the empire, and it was backed by silver and other precious metals. This concept of paper currency took off rather quickly, and was kept in effect after Khan's death in 1227. Ogedei was responsible for creating a department of the government responsible for the destruction of old bills, and issuing more paper currency backed by silk reserves. When Mongke Khan took power in 1253, he created an entire department for monetary affairs, which regulated all issuance of paper currency. When the great explorer Marco Polo came to Mongolia, the paper currency was one of the most fascinating things which he saw. He called it a marvel of   the world, and was amazed by the uniqueness of the Mongolian monetary system, which was still able to operate effectively within such a large empire, most of which was still using the Chinese ingot. Genghis Khan might not be able to take full credit for these innovations, but he most certainly lit the fire that turned into the most commonly accepted currency material in existence today.

Khan also set himself apart from other notable leaders by not assuming complete and utter control over his entire empire. All of his legions and subjects most certainly answered to their Great Khan first and foremost, but the authority was spread plentifully amongst family members and close companions. If not authority, then Khan was spreading financial gain, entitling his family members and allies to large issues of land. Shares of war spoils and tributes were spread even further, with the rewards trickling down to empresses, princesses, meritorious servants, and even the children of concubines. This system, known as the Appenage system, was unprecedented for its time, but it was a staple of Mongolian culture, and it is a hugely influential factor in the respect and loyalty which Genghis Khan was able to earn from everyone who served under him. He was a man who believed in incentive, and used it as a tool to gain undying support from everyone in his ranks.

.   .   .

Despite all of these hugely positive influences which Genghis Khan gave to the world, we cannot forget how he dug in that sway over the world. He did so through hellish violence, with an army bred for bloody warfare that were willing to die 1,000 times over for their Khan and their country. The loyalty of Mongol soldiers was absolutely unprecedented, and Khan made this so through reward systems, and promoting those who deserved it most because of their skill and personality, rather than family name. Genghis Khan did choose many of his closest supporters because of his own family ties with them, but he would always give the job to the man more able to do it. One of his most trusted and infamous generals, General Subutai, had no royal blood ties whatsoever, yet was one of the highest ranking officials in Khan's army. He allegedly came from a family of farmers, yet became the leader of the Mongol campaigns in Eastern Europe.

Mongol forces were divided into ranks in tens. A division in the tens was an Arban, in the hundreds was a Zuun, thousands was a Mingghan, and tens of thousands denoted a Tumen. Splitting forces up this way gave generals more direct command, as they were in charge of their Tumen, or their Mingghan, and nothing else. Soldiers were not allowed to switch between units, and the general could lead his unit as he saw fit, using his best judgement. This goes to show how much Khan trusted those he put in charge. It was also a way to devise more intricate attack strategies, pulling units away from battles to set up ambushes, and things of that nature. The system could also be utilized to draw attacks on multiple flanks, which was a consistently successful tactic of the Mongol army.

Perhaps the most significant aspect of the Mongol army which allowed them to be as destructive as they were, was their cavalry. The use of horses by the Mongol army was unprecedented, and the hooved beasts truly were used as their most viable weapon of war. Every Mongol soldier was in charge of three to four horses, meaning that there was never a shortage of the animal. It also allowed soldiers to rotate horses, which made it so they could travel unbelievably long distances. The Mongol marches were longer and more exhaustive than most in history, but with the cavalry they could cross lands in half the time their rivals could. The cavalry made fleeing from the Mongols a terrible option, and many an army learned what turning your backs on the Mongol cavalry meant. Spoiler alert, it was always death.

Genghis Khan was arguably one of the greatest military strategists of all time, or at least the combined efforts of his generals made it so. He used unprecedented tactics against his enemies, such as the feigned retreat which tricked so many of his foes into pursuing him, only to be turned upon and slaughtered by an ambush. It was a brutal lesson to learn time and time again. They were also masters of psychological warfare. The Mongol army understandably struck a gut wrenching fear within anyone who knew they were being targeted by the horde. They fought with a particular ferocity that was unknown to other armies at the time. Their knack for pillaging and ransacking, raping and murdering, was unprecedented. Everywhere they went they left behind blood, ash, and horror stories. The few who survived a Mongol attack would spread fear throughout the land, telling of the malicious tenacity of the Mongol soldiers who brutalize and decimate the country side without batting an eye.

The Mongols especially used their psychological warfare tactics when it came to taking cities. Cities were always offered the chance to surrender and agree to pay a tribute to the Mongol army, in exchange for being spared. The Mongols almost always made good on these promises if the city submitted, showing their dominance sometimes without swinging a single sword. However, when cities refused they unleashed the beast, and often were put to the flame, and punished through ransacking and burning for their refusal to bend to the Mongol will. The Mongols left a trail of burned cities in their wake, and it spread a message to the entire world that they were an unstoppable force of nature.

.   .   .

There is no doubt about Genghis Khan's incredible influence on the world, and how that influence made its impression on our modern world. It is obvious why he is a name that is remembered and recognized all across the world. The more intriguing factor is how he is remembered, though. History has painted Genghis Khan in a variety of lights, all of which have their validity. His actions against certain parts of the world were so divisive and so irreversible that it has given him a multitude of reputations across the globe.

In Mongolia, Genghis Khan is still, and probably forever will be, a revered figure. He is considered the father of Mongolia, and is credited with the creation of the country as it is today. If not for Genghis Khan, Mongolia could have fizzled out and the region could be a part of China or Russia today, rather than its own independent nation. Genghis Khan was never officially deified, but he receives an essentially legendary status in Mongolia today. Khan refused any images of him to be created in his lifetime, but today his image, or what we assume his likeness resembles, can be seen all over the country. There are many temples and institutions dedicated to the Great Khan, and his image is even imprinted on the 100 Tenge coin, a part of Khazakstani currency.

In the latter half of the 20th century, there was a push back against the recognition of Genghis Khan during Soviet rule of Mongolia. The Soviets regarded Khan as a reactionary, and attempted to defame him and remove his name from history. Russia understandably holds a grudge against the great leader, as he was responsible for considerable destruction and bloodshed in Russian territories. When the Mongolian People's Revolutionary Party went under the influence of the Soviets, there was a major purge against Genghis Khan. The secretary of the party's Central Committee erected a monument to Genghis Khan in 1962, and the Soviets promptly had him removed from this position.

When the Soviet Union fell in the late 1980's, Mongolia underwent a huge political revolution, and Genghis Khan was revived tenfold. Today, his likeness can be seen all over Mongolia, almost to the point of oversaturation. His name and image is plastered across streets and buildings, and his face appears on everyday products like candy and alcohol bottles. His birthday has become a national holiday, and the international airport in Mongolia is even named after him. Located in Ulaanbaatar, the Chinggis Khan International Airport sees hundreds of planes fly in and out every day. A grandiose statue of Genghis Khan in all his might also stands outside the Mongolian parliament building.

There is certainly some bias in the country of Mongolia, because the brutality of Genghis Khan is something that is essentially glossed over in his reputation amongst the population. Instead of the massacres of civilians and the burning of ancient cities, Genghis Khan is remembered in Mongolia for unifying its people under one ethnic and political identity. The warring tribes all had conflicting values which Genghis Khan wiped clean and reestablished with consistency. His code of law is also revered today, and the Mongolian president Tsakhiagiin Elbegdorj hails Genghis' political policies as ones that promoted the defeat of corruption, and encouraged prosperity for the middle class and equality for all citizens under a unified law.

When it comes to the rest of the world, the perception of Genghis Khan is a bit different. The Middle Eastern countries, which saw a particularly vicious level of destruction inflicted upon the Muslim people by Genghis Khan and his Mongol hordes, don't hold him to a very high standard today.

In fact, he is widely considered a rampaging warlord who promoted genocide. This view of the man is quite understandable, considering he is estimated to have killed as much as three fourths of the population of the Iranian Plateau. This means Genghis Khan and the Mongol army were responsible for the murder of ten to fifteen million people in just those campaigns alone.

Genghis most definitely used his bloodiest and most destructive tactics against the Muslims, primarily in his campaign across Khwarazmia. His successors continued what he started, pushing even further into Iran and the rest of the Middle East. If you ask an Iranian today what he thinks of Genghis Khan, Hulagu, or Timur Khan, you will most likely be met with disgust. This is the general reaction in many of the Eastern and Central European countries who knew subjugation under Mongol rule at one point in their history, whether it was from Genghis Khan or those who continued to expand after him. They care little for what unity Genghis Khan might have brought to the region in the long term, and tend to focus more on the pyramids of severed heads which his armies constructed outside the walls of Samarkand, and elements of that nature.

In China, the relationship to Genghis Khan is more of a love-hate situation. Genghis Khan was responsible for unprecedented destruction and murder in China, and his conquests saw the Chinese population drop drastically. He didn't reserve his killings to just enemy soldiers, either. Plenty of civilians were slaughtered as well, making it difficult to remember him for anything else. However, since the Chinese dynasties were such close neighbors to the Mongols, their conquest also brought about new innovations. They were able to enjoy the benefit of the Mongol trade and financial systems that more decimated populations to the west were not. The

Mongols also shared a respect for Chinese culture, and Genghis made a point to learn from it, particularly their military culture. They inherited much of their siege technology from Chinese armies, and were some of the first to bring the advent of gunpowder to western cultures. Unlike other territories, Genghis Khan did not scorch the earth of the Chinese dynasties and leave them for dead. It was a much more symbiotic relationship, despite the obvious bloodshed. Kublai Khan, grandson of Genghis Khan, was also responsible for establishing the Yuan dynasty, which provided one of the greatest periods of unification in Chinese history.

This relationship has resulted in Genghis Khan continuing to be a revered name in China. The country has a population of 5 million ethnic Mongolians, which is ironically twice the size of the Mongolian country's population. Statues and other works of art depicting Genghis Khan can be found all over China and, while his likeness may not be as prevalent as in Mongolia, his is not a name immediately met with a vile reaction.

Regardless of his depictions and perceptions, Genghis Khan is not a name that history is ever going to forget. He made an indelible imprint on the world in his lifetime, and his reach stretched to more populations, more ethnicities, and more cultures, than any conqueror before him. He stands as a poster child for the time period, characterized by brutality and rancorous ambition. He saw society as it was, and changed what he saw fit, in order to make the perfect empire for himself and his loyal followers. He did things most men of the time could only dream of. Through sheer will he built an empire, and in his entire life saw nothing but growth and success for that empire. He gave birth to a country, and an identity. He is the father of the Mongols. He is Genghis Khan.

Bibliography

History.com Staff. (2009). Genghis Khan. Retrieved June 30, 2016, from http://www.history.com/topics/genghis-khan

Andrews, E. (2014). 10 Things You May Not Know About Genghis Khan. Retrieved June 29, 2016, from http://www.history.com/news/history-lists/10-things-you-may-not-know-about-genghis-khan

Genghis Khan, Founder of Mongol Empire: Facts & Biography. (n.d.). Retrieved June 29, 2016, from http://www.livescience.com/43260-genghis-khan.html

Weatherford, J. M. (2004). *Genghis Khan and the making of the modern world.* New York: Crown.

Cleaves, F. W. (1982). *The Secret History of the Mongols.* Cambridge, MA: Published for the Harvard-Yenching Institute by Harvard University Press.

Scipio Africanus

The Roman Military Genius

By
<u>Michael Klein</u>

Table of Contents

Foreword

Publius Scipio Africanus the Elder and Hannibal Barca were major players in the Second Punic War – known to Romans of the day as "Hannibal's War. However, neither the conflict or the family histories began with the Second Punic War. In fact, the Punic wars grew out of territorial disputes between the two leading powers of the day, the Phoenicians and the Romans. The Greeks, Egyptians and Syrians were also players in these events, but they were the supporting cast, so to speak, in these episodes.

Carthage, the great Phoenician city (the word "Punic" derives from the Roman word for Phoenician) was founded around 814 BC. Settlers from Tyre claimed the land, and constructed the sea port. The area was fertile, and many of the settlers farmed the land surrounding Carthage. Others continued to carry out the ocean voyaging and sea trade for which the Phoenicians were famous. It should also be noted here that the Phoenicians are the same people as the Biblical Canaanites.

Meanwhile, elsewhere in the world, the people who would become Romans were having their fair share of difficulties. There are a variety of stories about the founding of Rome, including the familiar story about Romulus and Remus, the twins were reared by wolves and who founded Rome on two hillsides. Archeologists and anthropologists are by no means in absolute agreement on the origins of the Roman people, but there are some stories that are fairly consistently mentioned.

One of these stories is that the Romans were actually Etruscans, and that the Etruscans came from Asia. One legend has it that in a certain kingdom, the people were starving. There was so little food that they drew lots, and people ate on alternate days. At last the situation became so bad, that this no long sufficed, so the Etruscan king used the lots to divide his people into two groups: those who would remain with him, and those who would sail away with his son to find more hospitable lands.

The son, who was named Tyrrhennus, helped to found cities on the coast of the area that is now Italy. At first the Etruscans were mostly in scattered villages, but as time went on, they clustered together more closely, forming larger settlements. They were agrarian, and they herded sheep. But they also developed a reputation as pirates. Of course, "piracy" was one of those words that rival cultures threw around at random, right along with "immoral" and "indecent." The Greek city states were also developing alongside the Roman culture.

There is a high probability that there were already people living in Italy at the time that the Etruscans landed and began founding their settlements. Mention is made of other tribal inhabitants who might very well have been there before the Etruscans. In all probability, they intermarried and the cultures blended.

The village of Rome was founded around 753 BC. For several hundred years there was no conflict between Rome and Carthage. In fact, they made several treaties and did a bustling bit of trade. (We won't mention piracy here – but there was probably some of that going on, as well.)

The Romans developed a society that had distinct social classes. At the top of the society were the Patricians, the founders who were the primary governing body. There was also a class called the Clients who were free, but took no part in the government. They were usually attached to one of the Patricians, or a Patron. At the bottom of the pecking order were the slaves, who had minimal rights (none) other than if they could come up with their purchase price they could buy their freedom. Also layered into this many textured society were the trades people – free men who were not clients or patrons, who ran small shops or created items that were beautiful or necessary. They might also take care of certain jobs that required more decision making than could be expected of a slave. Although, many masters took the long view, and put effort and expense into educating slaves for a variety of positions, including keeping accounts, writing, and fulfilling certain positions of responsibility.

To add to this mosaic of inhabitants, there were also resident foreigners, people who had come to Rome for trade or for other reasons. And there was the multitude of general residents, often referred to as plebian. After a time, a governing body called the Assembly provided representation for the plebeians – some of whom had become quite wealthy.

Each year two consuls were elected to run the city. In times of emergency, they might appoint a dictator, whose term in office was only six months. Perhaps such a person governed Rome while the consuls were in the field with the military.

Two quaestores were appointed each year to manage finances, under direction of the senate. Aediles were elected by the plebians in a section or quarter of the city and fulfilled a position roughly analogous to a policeman.

At first, many of the regulations of Rome were dictated from the top down by the Patrician, but as the centuries slid buy, the plebians gained more power and the ability to be voted into almost any office – including that of Dictator.

The problems with the neighbors did not arise in noticeable form until around 265 BC, when Rome had finished conquering the Roman peninsula.

Meanwhile, Carthage had also been growing in power and influence. Its territory had grown to include the island of Sicily. It was said that the lights of the cities of Sicily could be seen from the cities that were on the banks of the Italian peninsula.

The problem switched into high gear when one of the cities on Sicily appealed to Rome for help. Of course, that was music to the ears of the Roman senate – they were being invited to a conflict and they were more than happy to oblige. The only problem was that, even though the Etruscans had sailed to Rome, the current Romans were primarily land dwellers and farmers. In order to get their armies across to Sicily, they needed ships. At first they hired vessels to carry their armies across, but that proved to be less than satisfactory. The hired ships were not particularly interested in being drawn into a conflict with the Carthaginians, who were developing a growing reputation as able seamen. The Romans could fight on land, but that proved to be less than satisfactory when it came to taking over Sicily because the Carthaginians just kept landing shiploads of men and supplies from the seaward side.

Eventually the Romans did what they did best: they captured a Phoenician ship and copied it. The full story of how that all turned out is told in the second chapter of this book as a fireside tale.

In an imaginary setting, we look in on a world that might have been: Publius Cornelius telling his two young sons the story of how their Grandfather Gnaeus was captured by the Carthaginians, but was also instrumental in allowing the newly constructed Roman fleet to unload men and supplies in Sicily with scarcely a scratch.

That was the beginning of the First Punic War, and it belonged to the era of Publius Scipio Africanus' grandfather. Although Grandfather Gnaeus (not to be confused with Uncle Gnaeus) was censured for his error in judgement, he was again elected consul six years later. Nor was he the first of the Cornelius family to serve Rome. They had a distinguished record as upright Roman citizens and staunch supporters of the empire.

Indeed, the Cornelius family was one of the First Families of Rome. They knew their duty to city and country, and they willingly did it. In exchange, they expected honor, respect and – yes, indeed – a relative degree of wealth.

These were all to be had in Rome, in those days. These were the heyday of Rome's expansion. They built roads – wonderful roads. Indeed, there are Roman roads that still exist today. They conquered, and they incorporated the conquered into their society.

At the same time, the Carthaginians were trading, conquering and making their presence known. The two scruffy little nations had become big, grown-up political entities that were flexing their muscles and pushing hard against each other.

Our story begins with the Second Punic War. In fact, you could almost say that the story of the Punic Wars is the story of the family of Publius Scipio Cornelius Africanus. Not only did his grandfather, his father and his uncle – as well as himself – serve in the battles between Rome and Carthage, but so did his adopted grandson, Scipio Cornelius Africanus the Younger.

Finding the truth about Publius Scipio Cornelius Africanus is a challenge. Not only is there the difficulty of lost records – always a problem when trying to trace information that is more than two centuries old – but there is also the custom of telling outrageous stories for their intimidating effect on the other side.

Among the other things that Publius claimed, there was the story of how he was born by being cut from his mother's womb, and the enormous whopper he told of how his father was not the late Publius Cornelius who was cut down by enemies in Spain, but that daddy was really Poseidon, the powerful god of the sea. Apparently, he was completely indifferent to the light in which this cast his mother – women were not greatly considered at that time.

Publius Scipio Africanus and his brother Lucius Scipio took part in the Macedonian wars, as well. These involved Macedonia's having waited until it felt that Rome was worn down by its conflict with Carthage before starting to make aggressive moves toward Greece. Greece was far too close to Rome to ignore Phillip the Fifth quiet snabbling up of small Grecian villages.

The Macedonian War was not a popular one in Rome, and it was the beginning of the downfall of the brothers Scipio. But enough of that. Perhaps it is time to plunge into our story. As much as is possible, this book follows established cannon where Publius Scipio and the events that governed his adult life. But there are many areas where so little is known, that the author has relied upon snippets of information from a variety of sources to create plausible scenarios. These are inserted as background and for the amusement of the reader. They are plainly labeled, but it is the writer's hope that readers will enjoy these departures from strict historical fact. Perhaps one day you, the reader, will try your hand at writing a story or two about shadowy historical figures.

Certainly, Publius Scipio was not above embroidering upon the truth, so we are in good historical company when it comes to the weaving of tall tales.

Moreover, could it just be possible that in trying to slip into those historical shoes that we can begin to understand the continued struggle that seems to be woven around this fertile area, the lands around the Mediterranean Sea. It almost seems as if this area where three continents meet, where the spice trade, the silk trade and now oil exacerbate the struggle to survive, is almost like the umbilical of the world. Oh, to be sure there are other areas that are rich with resources, but it is possible that there are few places in the world that are so exceptionally rich in tradition or that have hosted so much interaction between cultures.

Perhaps if we reach back in time, if we try to understand the emotions, the drives and the circumstances that powered the conflicts between Rome and Carthage, and between Rome and Macedonia, we can begin to understand the workings of our modern world. Publius Scipio Africanus was but one man – but he was a man who stood tall amongst other historical giants, and whose actions were interwoven with major historical events of his time.

In the end, we find him -- but no, wait. That is getting ahead of our story. It is indeed time to focus on his tale. Indeed, you have no doubt, gentle reader, skipped over this foreword and headed on into the central theme of this narration.

Chapter 1
A Roman Childhood

Publius Cornelius Scipio, born around 236 BC, was the son of Consul Publius Scipio and Pomponi. Publius Scipio the elder was a patrician, and the third generation to serve as consul. Pomponi was the daughter of the plebian consul, Manius Pomponius Matho. Young Scipio was their first child, according to some accounts. According to others, he was the younger son. Although it would mean little to the Cornelii at the time, Hannibal Barca would have been about ten years old at the time of Scipio's birth. In the company of his father, Hamilcar (who would have been known to the household as a rival general), his brothers and brother-in-law, Hannibal was already in Spain as part of the Carthaginian efforts to take over that part of the country.

Not a lot is known about Scipio's childhood. Keeping records of the events surrounding children was not the fashion of the day, and although Scipio is said to have kept a diary it has long been lost. Gone also is Plutarch's account of his life. What remains are Livy's accounts of the man's military life, and mention of him in The Histories of Polybius plus various commentaries on his military prowess and his silver-tongued oratory.

Some accounts suggest that he was born by Caesarian, just as was the famous emperor, but this scarcely seems logical, since other accounts mention a younger brother, Lucius Cornelius Scipio Asiaticus. On the other hand, if Lucius was actually the eldest, this would pose no logistical problem. Since sources indicate that Publius and Lucius had the same mother, if Publius Scipio was the elder, the birth by surgery is somewhat problematical. Still, it is just possible that from somewhere there was an exceptionally skilled physician capable of preserving both mother and child in good health. Perhaps the boys were twins, and Scipio the elder by minutes instead of years. The past is full of Mystery – and evidence is scant.

Medical science was certainly in its infancy in those days. Surgical births were usually reserved as a last resort, when it was clear that the mother would not survive the birth. In truth, in such cases, it was rare for the baby to survive, either. With the scarcity of accounts, even the exact year of Scipio's birth is in question; the date is usually calculated from military accounts that record the year of the event and his age at the time of the event. With such a paucity of records, we are left to speculate what his life might have been like rather than to be able to say with certainty the kind of childhood that he might have had.

With mother and son or sons possibly in danger, Publius senior would probably have either engaged a wet nurse or have purchased a slave that had recently given birth so that young Publius would have a source of sustenance. Animal milk, at that time, was not always safe to drink; and as medical science has discovered, the best food for a human infant is human milk. Even if Pomponi was capable of nursing her own child, he would no doubt have gotten a serving woman for her, to help with the children and with needful personal care.

As soon as he could toddle, Publius would have begun learning how to behave as an adult. Although there was some recognition of childhood, for the most part children were treated like short adults. Since the family was patrician, they would probably have lived in a nice home in the city when Publius was serving his term in office; the rest of the time, they probably lived on their country estates, some distance outside of Rome.

It is likely that the family had slaves to work the farmland, and almost certain that Publius would have had a tutor who would have taken up looking after him as soon as he was old enough not to need his nurse – even though she might have continued to look after practical matters such as seeing to his clothing or making sure he washed his feet before going to bed.

Since the Cornelii were a military family, it is likely that Publius and Lucius began learning combat skills at an early age, as well as how to read, write and calculate. They would also have learned oration and possibly argumentation, since serving in the government would be expected of them. They would also have been encouraged to study famous battles, and would probably have played tabletop games of strategy.

Wealthy children did have toys, and it is probable that the boys had toy carts, perhaps a set of carved animals, and maybe even a set of carved toy soldiers. Toys of the day were made from wood, leather, and cloth scrap. Some of the little animals might have had wheels and a string by which they could be pulled. Dolls could be made with joints, and with costumes that could be put on and taken off. Perhaps the lads had one or two that could be dressed up as soldiers.

Even though Publius and Lucius would have been kept busy, it is probable that they found time to play. Even if toys were in short supply, sticks, stones and other naturally occurring objects could easily have been converted in a child's imagination into weapons, or made into small forts. The young of all sorts engage in play as part of their training for adulthood. We sometimes lose sight of that in our modern age;

yet the toys that are provided for our children still reflect that principle.

Although we can only imagine what it might have been like in a Roman household, thanks to stories and legends we can gain some idea of what it might have been like to spend an ordinary day in a Roman household. Let's imagine a time when Publius was a gawky adolescent, just short of his twelfth year, and Lucius was a promising lad who would have been only a year or two younger. This is a process that is called "fictionalizing" and it used to be common in biographical works for elementary school children. So, turn back, pages of time and let us look in on the Cornellii on a morning when they were not going to war.

The hour was early, but Pomponi was already at her loom. She had finished spinning the season's wool the week before, and was determined to create a new tunic for Publius, Senior before the council season. Once that was done, she would use some of the remaining wool for herself. The boys would get tunics made from her husband's discarded tunics – suitably cut down to size. No point in wasting good fabric on youthful bodies that would heedlessly haul the fabric through muck and briar, giving the washer women cause to cluck their tongues and complain.

If there was enough wool, she might make Publius Scipio, Junior, a new tunic, however. He had been promised a trip to Rome with his father next council season. It was, quite clearly, time to begin thinking of him as a young man. He was already taller than Pomponi, and would soon be catching up with his father. Perhaps some of Publius's outgrown tunics could be made to last another season or two for Lucius, who was also growing up far too rapidly.

As if thoughts of them called them forth, the boys came racketing into her solar, shouting and playing at being invading Moors and Roman defenders. "I have you!" Publius shouted.

"Nay," cried Lucius, "You'll not take me alive! I am of solid Roman stock, and I'll stand fast to the end."

"So be it!" said Publius, drawing back a hand holding a stick from the wood supply as if to stab his brother.

But the hand is caught by a larger, stronger hand. "Hold, enough. Have a care with your younger brother, Publius. One day you may need him on a real battlefield. Wife, what is this unseemly racketing about? Where is that worthless Grammaticus? I paid good coin for him – 4,500 to be exact. If he does not prove worth his keep, I'll demote him to the field, so I will. A few days harvesting the grain will sharpen his attention."

"I am here, Master Publius, I am here!" A slender man with blond hair and blue eyes who resembled the statues one sometimes sees of winged Mercury hurried after the boys. "We were reviewing the late war in Hispania, and the reenactment grew a bit intense."

A tiny serving girl appeared at that moment. "Cook seths dat beckfust is weady," she lisped in her childish voice, "If it pwease you, sir and madam."

"Thank you, Blossom," Pomponi said. "We will be there directly." Then she addressed her husband and sons, "It will not go well this day if we keep Cook waiting. You know how temperamental he is. If we hope for an edible noonday meal, we had best attend his efforts."

"Of course," the elder Publius said. "Boys, go wash those grubby hands then join us hence at table. Grammaticus, see to it! These lads will be consuls one day; they need to learn manners as well as battle moves. M'lady wife?"

Publius offered his arm to his frail wife, who had never quite fully recovered from the difficult births of their two sons. She placed her hand upon his arm, and managed to rise gracefully from her seat at the loom, even though he could feel the strain in her as she rose. "With pleasure, m'lord husband."

They adjourned to the serving room, passing through the main room to get to it from Pomponi's solar. Breakfast was a rich barley porridge, laden with cream and honey. There was a fluffy mound of scrambled eggs, delicately spiced, a huge round of cheese, and a bowl of fresh figs. There was no meat with this meal; it was summer, and not yet the season of butchering. There was no practical reason to kill an animal for a simple family breakfast.

The boys came in from the courtyard, hands and faces conspicuously clean and the edges of their hair damp from their recent ablutions. They both looked a bit chastened, and approached the table with sober decorum, so it was relatively certain that the Grammaticus had given them both a good dressing down. Pomponi carefully did not notice the grass stains on Lucius's tunic or the mud on Publius's knees. Clearly, the morning lessons had been lively.

Little Blossom, the cook's baby daughter, waited upon the table with grave care – even though she could barely reach the tabletop. Publius deftly caught his cup, and did not chastise the little one for her efforts to wait table. Their household was a gracious one, rarely marred by internal strife.

There was more than enough of war and conflict away from home.

The eggs were superb, and indeed would not have been edible had they delayed their meal. The cheese was new, and squeaked between their teeth as they ate it, but it was still good. The barley porridge was hot and deliciously sweet and rich. The boys dug into it with relish, while Publius savored the spicy eggs. Then he turned his attention to his wife, who was nibbling delicately at a fig.

"You are not eating much, my wife," he said gravely, "Are you unwell?"

"Just a touch of the old troubles," she said. They had both hoped for a large family, but her health had put an end to that dream. Still, he could not ask for a better helpmate, and although he could have put her aside for a more fertile woman, Publius valued her steady hand upon the estate during his inevitable absences.

"Try just a little of the egg, and a bit of the barley," he urged. "they are both quite good."

"Perhaps a bit of the barley porridge, but only a taste of the eggs. The spice upsets my stomach, you know."

Publius nodded. He did know, and had no desire to walk the halls that night with a woman groaning in pain. So, with his own hands, he dished a generous serving of the barley porridge and a small taste of the egg, and watched approvingly as she made the effort to eat. "The new cook is worth every penny we paid for him," he noted approvingly. "And it was worth the added cost to bring his family with him." Publius patted little Blossom on the head as she brought around a heaping tray of bread and butter. "Ah, that is very nice, little one," he approved. He then noticed that Lucius had one foot stuck out, just where it could trip the small girl. He fixed the boy with a glare, and Lucius looked properly ashamed and drew in his foot. Some masters would have encouraged such behavior and laughed uproariously at when the little one fell and even have punished her for clumsiness. Publius congratulated himself that he was not that sort of person. One never knows, he thought to himself, what fortunes might befall us tomorrow.

"He is, indeed," Pomponi replied, discovering that the porridge was just to her liking and beginning to eat it with some appetite. She did not miss the little by-play between father and son. Publius Junior did not seem to notice it at all, but she was fairly certain that he did for he made sure to keep his own feet tucked in and gravely assisted their small waitress. Blossom was very much the household darling, and quite spoiled even with her new duties at table.

After breakfast, Publius decided that the Grammaticus deserved some time off after the lively morning study session, and took his two sons to the new fields at the edge of the estate. There, he put them to work at that perennial farmer's task of picking rocks and piling them at the edge of the field where they would be used to make walls. When the lads were well at work, he walked on over to one of the older fields to view the harvesting going on there. The slaves were hard at work under the supervision of Agrarius, a recently freed slave who continued to work on the estate for a small wage. In many ways, the man's lot was harder than it had been before, but he seemed to take pride in his condition as freedman and was a symbol of a possible future for all the slaves, if they worked hard and saved their earnings. Publius allowed each of them to keep a portion of any money earned by hiring out to the neighbors. These could be sturdy, loyal clients, as attached freedmen were called, in time.

Near the house, two clusters of workers were threshing the grain and separating the grain from the chaff. One group was flailing the ripe grain on the threshing floor, while another group was tossing the grain into the air and catching it is a basket. Just a little farther away, a small donkey was walking in an interminable circle while the clean kernels were poured onto the bowl of the stone grinder. There would be fresh bread and perhaps even sweet cakes. Publius savored the thought. In the far fields, he could see a man plowing, using an ard-type plow, drawn by one of his prize oxen. It was good to be home for a time – even if it turned out to be only a short while.

The work was going along well, and Publius picked a few ears of grain from the field to chew as he walked along to the sheep pasture. Here, the shepherd boy was tootling mournfully on a set of pipes while gazing off down the valley. He was mooning after one of the serving girls, but that was no excuse for not noticing the half-grown lambs that had just blundered into a thicket of briars. Publius cuffed the lad soundly, and then helped extract the foolish sheep.

By then, it was time for the midday meal. Publius walked back down the mountain, and shared a lunch of bread, cheese and cold spring water with his sons. One of the reasons he had chosen this land was for the cold water that bubbled up from a spring that ran the year around. It was one reason, he felt, that the workers and family who lived on the farm seemed to have better health than those who lived in the city.

When lunch was over, he showed his sons how to stack the stones, dry, into a wall and left them again to their task. His next stop was a lower field that was being plowed for a winter grain crop. He followed that up with checking on the new plantation of olive trees and grapes. He then returned to the boys, checked their work, praising them and correcting a couple of errors.

The three of them then returned to the house. Their evening meal was a frugal one by patrician standards. They had a freshly slain chicken, roasted and stuffed with savory grain. There were figs, of course, some new wine which was not bad, a crusty loaf of bread from the estate's bakery oven, along with more of the new cheese. There was a trifle made of almond paste, shaped into the form of a swan for dessert. This would have been Pomponi's contribution.

In addition to the sweet, Pomponi had a surprise for her menfolk. She had completed the tunics for Publius Senior and Junior, and had discovered that she even had a breadth left to make one tunic for Lucius. They declared the new garments very fine, and Publius said that when he took young Publius to visit the city, they would certainly wear them. He also made a mental note that he would take a full complement of the new guardsmen who were training; the city was a dangerous place, and the new garments would mark them out as being prosperous.

Rome in those days was a rabbit warren of alleyways, shops, and open air market places as well as the fine avenues with their rows of statues and elegant buildings. It would not do to relax his vigilance and lose his sons to some lowly footpad now that they were growing tall. Publius the elder smiled to himself. It would be a pleasure to take his two fine sons and show them off in the capital city, to watch their eyes grow round with wonder at all the sights and to share their excitement at the spectacles in the Forum.

Fictionalized? Absolutely, because we have almost no records at all of the Publius Cornelius household. Complete fiction? Not quite. We know that the records show a Caesarian birth for son Publius, yet the family tree shows that both boys are sons of Pomponi. There are a number of possible answers for this: the records are simply exaggerated; there was a second wife, of whom there is no record; the boys might have been twins; or Lucius might have been the elder son. Since there is no recorded birthdate for either, Lucius might have been the younger son by minutes instead of years. We simply do not know the answers to these questions. Whatever records might have explained the mystery are long turned to dust.

What do we have left that show records of Roman life? We have inscriptions on tombstones and graphitti scratched on walls. We have mosaics showing scenes from domestic life. We have the hideous tragedy of Pompeii that left ready-made molds of volcanic ash for plaster casts of the people who died there, creating models that are so realistic we can see the agony etched on their faces. And we have the terrain, the foods that are still grown in the region and the knowledge that farming works pretty much the same way anywhere it is practiced. Oh, there are variations on themes – some areas are lucky enough not to have rocks to pick, but the Roman fields are not among them.

These things tell us of possible activities on a typical day in a patrician family setting. Some of the families became so obsessed with a display of status that they had a separate slave for every household function; but the Cornelii don't seem to be cut of that sort of cloth. They were military men, men who focused on duty to country and a degree of honor. I have chosen to think that Publius the father was capable of affection, that he cared for his estate, and that he acted as a father figure, not only to his two sons, but also the many people who lived and worked on his farm. Shall we say, feudalism at its finest rather than at its worst. History tends to bear this out, for subsequent events – which we will examine at greater length – indicate that Publius Scipio, someday to become Africanus, had a deep and abiding affection for his father.

We also know that creating fabric was the primary preoccupation of women in Rome and in similar societies. This was a practical need, not some sort of vanity occupation. For example, in feudal England, each lordly household was obligated to provide two sets of clothing to each and every man and woman on the estate. Since spinning and weaving was all done by hand, the woman of the house and her ladies in waiting – often daughters of neighboring estates who were being fostered out – would spend many hours every day spinning and weaving. With the advent of weavers' guilds, this changed, and it became more of a display of a refined skill. But in the days of early Rome, the women's handiwork would still be needed.

Many of the serving people on an estate such as the one described here would have been slaves. Rome carried on a thriving slave trade. It was not limited to any one color or race, and its saving grace was that a slave could save up funds and buy his or her freedom. Theoretically, that is. Someone like the Grammaticus, whose purchase price was extremely high, might never manage his own purchase price.

Still, it was a busy, bustling world and flawed though it was, it laid the foundations for the formation of a democratic form of government. Publius had privilege, but he also had duties. He was obligated to be part of the governing body, and he was obligated to military service to his country. He would have been gravely concerned about the education of his sons, and he would have expected them to learn every aspect of life on the estate so that they could run it wisely when it became their turn to do so. And while he had the opportunity to do so, he would have wanted to look over his fields and farmlands, making sure that his people were all doing their jobs.

Rome was, at the time, a giant melting pot of cultures as her armies brought in new slaves, new prizes and new goods. It made no difference that the slaves were ripped from their homes, that the goods and gold had once belonged to someone else; this was the way that many nations operated at the time. It made Rome wealthy, bustling, and the Place to Be.

There were many other things going on in the world at the same time, but the Romans were oblivious to places and events that were beyond their very well-built roads and out of marching distance of their armies. Perhaps this is a good thing; who knows what might have happened if the Pax Romana had owned tanks and automatic weapons, airplanes and trains. Those things were left for a later war and a different conquering race.

As it was, they made their way as far southeast as Arabia and Northern Africa and as far northwest as the southern border of Scotland. For a culture that traveled on foot or horseback, that was an extensive amount of territory, essentially defining the area of the "known world." Spain, Gaul and Britain – that is, Wales and England, were gathered in, as were Syria and Israel. Carthage was one of the holdouts, and thereby will hang the rest of this tale because the military commander of Carthage and the military commander of Rome would make this conflict personal. Young Publius and young Hannibal would inherit their fathers' war, along with the charges from their fathers to each son to fight the other's culture for as long as they would live.

This enmity would drive Publius Cornelius Africanus's activities for most of the rest of his life, and would earn for him the last part of his name. But on this summer day, picking rocks or whatever other chores that a Roman place in the country required of a young patrician lad, he was a boy and would have been enjoying the activities of a lad of rank and privilege. He would be educated in the classical manner as well as in arms and armor, learning strategy, rhetoric and oration. Compared to hundreds of youngsters who lived in Rome itself and in the surrounding countryside, young Publius had it good.

With no birth control, babies proliferated. Unwanted infants were often exposed, frequently with a distinctive little necklace that would identify the child if he or she somehow managed to survive. In fact, it was a major theme of dramatic entertainment – the child that was exposed at birth, then turns up later just in time to inherit an estate or to save the family, identified by the baby necklace. Modern moms might wonder how any mother could possibly give up her baby, but the real truth is that women had no more rights than a prize mare. If the father did not approve the babe, out it went – usually before the mother was up and around and able to even arrange alternative custody for the infant. That has come up as a theme for legends as well – the Arthurian cycle, Moses, Osiris; that business of disposing of unwanted babies or hiding them has a lengthy history. New born humans are pretty short on self-defense.

But being exposed wasn't the only thing that could happen to infants in the days of the early Roman Empire. Sanitation was limited, even in the elegant homes of the rich. Fleas, lice, and vermin of all kinds abounded, as they do anywhere that large numbers of humans gather together, right along all the diseases that they spread. Those who could afford the trip would go to the country in the summer when disease was at its most rampant. But hundreds of migrants, slaves and other ordinary people would have to live through the Roman summer inside the city.

Other things could happen to children, as well. Rome might not have had automobiles, but it did have chariots, horses, ox carts, venders and sometimes panicked crowds. In the narrow, twisting streets of Rome a mob could and sometimes did lead to people being killed in the crush.

Children were expected to work and no allowance was made for their age or fragility. And some of those jobs would have had any modern Family Services department on the doorstep of the establishment with warrants and custody papers for the kids. Rome was exciting, but it wasn't safe.

It was a place where people could make futures or lose them, develop a wonderful life or wind up dead in an alley. It wasn't even all that safe for those who were in in the upper echelons. Power shifts, poisoning, assassination and more – Rome was a city of intrigue. Hollywood only publicized the most famous ones – as can be attested by the many gravestones with left-handed compliments to the deceased.

This was the city where Publius Cornelius planned to bring his oldest son for a visit. His father and grandfather had both been consuls there, and he had every expectation that he, himself, would one day hold office, and so would young Publius and perhaps Lucius also. It was the way it had been, and it was the way that it would always be. Publius Cornelius could envision no other possible course for his son and heir, or for his second son.

Chapter 2
Fireside Tales

Let us fast forward a few years. Publius and Lucius are both taller, their father has gone a bit gray and has picked up a few scars from battle. Their mother, although a little more fragile, still manages the estate. These days she is assisted by the Grammaticus who proved to be adept at record keeping and numbers – a skill he was teaching his young charges. Again, we are creating a fiction born of imagination, because there are no accounts of this time. However, story-telling has long been a favorite pastime of many cultures, and stories of famous ancestors always makes good telling. The setting here is fictional, but the story about the grandfather is drawn from history.

The family is gathered around the fireside. Little Blossom, now grown into a slender preteen, gracefully places apples on the hearth to bake, brings drinks and takes away the used cups and dishes.

"Tell us a story," Lucius begs his father.

"Yes, please tell us a story," Publius adds his voice to the plea.

"Well, I don't know," their father mused, "I hear that the Grammaticus had to wrest you from the dairy to attend your lessons this day."

Publius colored up like a girl. His father kept a straight face, and their mother bent her head over her sewing. Neither commented, but the father was sure that the mother was aware that the new dairy maid he had brought home as part of his spoils of war was a comely lass. "Please father," Publius's voice cracked and broke, and he cleared his throat and tried again. "Please, tell us a story. You are not home often now, and your stories are the best."

"Very well, that is a good point. What story would you like to hear?"

"Tell us about Grandfather Gnaeus and the first Roman navy," Lucius suggested.

"Ah, yes. Grandfather Gnaeus." Publius, the father, seemed to ponder for a moment. "Yes, I suppose that would be a good story." He settled himself back in his chair, and took up the pose that he always assumed before starting to tell a story.

This was the story that he told:

In your grandfather's time, you could stand on the shore near Reggio in the late evening, and if you looked across the waters, you could see the lights of Messina on the Island of Sicilia. Now, that would have been no great thing, but the other end of Sicilia stretched out toward Numidia. On that shore stands Carthage.

Now, the Carthaginians were great sailors in those days, and they had no trouble sailing over the waters to Sicilia, where they were rapidly claiming territory. Much alarmed, the citizens of Messina felt they had a choice of appealing to Syracuse or to Rome. Syracuse was already showing signs of waxing fat with power, so they called out to Rome as the lesser of two evils.

Rome hesitated. To come to Messina's aid, since she was not a Roman province, would constitute an act of war against Carthage. Carthage was not and is not a small power.

Rome has fought its wars, but this one would not be on land – it would be on the sea. But after a time, Messina signed a treaty making it a Roman province. After that, there was no hesitation.

Appius Claudius, at the Ides of March at the beginning of his term of office (264 BC, for modern listeners to this tale) marched his men, double-time to the edge of the sea where allied ships were waiting. Before you could shout, "Cast off!" it seemed, they were across the strait and marching into Messina. Appius Claudius consolidated Messina's status as a province and his soldiers settled in to fortify the city and surrounding country side.

You may rest assured that Syracuse and Carthage certainly noticed this action. Although they had long been enemies, they at once made an alliance against Rome. Appius Claudius appealed to Hiero, the tyrant of Syracuse, to make a peace treaty. But Hiero would have none of it. Claudius was not one to sit about when there was an enemy to rout or work to be done, so he left a little housekeeping force in Messina and marched toward Syracuse. He made short work of them and then he tore into the Carthageans, routing their forces as well.

But then winter fell, and it was the season of Council. So nothing more was done at that time. In the spring, however, two consuls and their forces were dispatched – and Sicilia fell to the marching boots of Roman soldiers.

"But what about Grandfather?" Lucius piped up, his voice still a childish treble.

"I'm coming to that," Publius the father said. And the story went on.

Now, the combined forces of Manius Valerius and Octacilius Crassus marched across Sicilia, having no trouble at all subduing the villages and settlements to the interior of that island. But the towns that lay on the seacoast were a different matter. No sooner did they think they had subdued one, but the Carthaginians supplied it from the sea, dashing in with their tall ships with five banks of oars, and leaving both supplies and men hauled from what seemed to be an endless supply from Carthage and Numidia.

Hiero of Syracuse, however, grew worried that while he was battling Rome, Carthage would nip in and steal victory from them both. So, like Messina, he decided that the Republic of Rome was a better choice as an ally than the Carthaginians, who were well known to be sharp traders and not above a little larceny on the side. So he sent a peace envoy to Valerius and Crassus, and they gladly drew up an agreement. Syracuse would have to pay an indemnity to Rome, but they would also have a staunch ally against Carthage.

Carthage did not like this alliance one little bit. They gathered mercenary forces and launched a vast navy and army which would land at Agrigento, an independent city-state that had been a protectorate of Carthage for some time. When 40,000 Carthaginian troops landed on Sicily, Rome – whose assembly had hoped their troubles were over – sat up and took notice.

"Was that when Grandfather ruled the navy?" Lucius asked. Publius, the son, covered his lower face with one hand, but gravely answered his brother, "Not quite yet. Stop interrupting or we'll never get there before bedtime."

Publius, the father, ignored this byplay, and went on with the story. By now, he had collected quite an audience, for this was a favorite tale and he was a good story teller.

The Roman armies descended upon Agrigento, but then things started to go wrong. Valerius and Crassus were not the best of generals, and they allowed the Carthageans to gather up all the food. Had not Hiero intervened, the Roman army would have starved to death before the city they were besieging gave up for lack of food. But Hiero was an honest tyrant; once he made a bargain, he kept it.

"Is that when..." Lucius started, but his brother put one hand on his arm, and he subsided.

Now, it just so happened – as I think I mentioned before – that many of the Carthaginian forces were mercenaries. When the provisions grew too thin, one night they all sneaked out to the ships and sailed away, leaving Agrigento undefended. With no army left, Agrigento surrendered. The Romans enslaved and sold most of the population – but they were purchased by the people of Syracuse with the understanding that the money would be paid back later. But that action did not make the other small cities love Rome. It was a bad decision on the part of Valerius and Crassus.

For the next few years, Sicily became the chew-bone in a tug-of-war between Rome and Carthage. Rome was superb on land, but Carthage had a masterful command of the sea. A Carthaginian saying was that Rome could not wash its hands in the Mediterranean without Carthage's permission. But that was about to change.

In all of these battles, a Roman force managed to capture a quinquereme – one of the tall ships used by the Carthaginians and the Phoenicians – that being the name for the people of the greater area around Carthage.

Carthage had 120 quinqueremes. With them, they ruled the seas. Rome had never made ships before, but they had captured a quinquereme in Messina. They carefully took it apart, piece by piece, copied the parts and made ships. They built a model on land, and hired instructors from neighboring lands to teach their land bound people how to row. By spring, Rome had a navy of 100 quinqueremes and two hundred triremes.

"Now it is time for Grandfather!" Lucius burst out, unable to contain himself.

Publius, the father, hid a smile. "Yes, my son. Now it is time for Grandfather."

Gnaeus Cornelius Scipio had a solid reputation as a general on land, but he had never commanded a force at sea. He took his army overland to Reggio, and crossed safely into Messina. However, the navy had to travel by sea, and with such a rabble of inexperienced sailors mixed with a few experienced hands, some of the ships made better time than others. Grandfather Gnaeus didn't want to sit around and do nothing while he waited for the rest of the fleet to catch up.

So he took the seventeen ships that he had, and headed out to Lipari, thinking that if he captured that island he would secure a shipping lane for Rome. He didn't have a bit of trouble taking Lipari, which is a tiny island after all, but he forgot one small detail.

Publius, the father, paused dramatically for his audience to fully appreciate the moment.

With only twenty warships, the Carthaginian navy swooped down in the night and blocked the entrance to the harbor. When morning came, there was nothing to do but surrender the ships. The crews fled into the hills, but Gnaeus Cornelius Scipio and most of his army were captured.

"Oh, poor Grandfather!" Lucius breathed.

"Not one of his finer moments, for sure," Publius the father smiled. "But all was not lost, and a lesson learned. Carthage was so intent on capturing your grandfather and his seventeen ships that while they were distracted the other 283 ships with their cargo of sailors and soldiers sailed into Messina without losing a single one. As for your grandfather, he was traded to Rome in a prisoner exchange, and six years later was elected consul again."

The audience clapped in enthusiastic approval.

"But what happened, then, Father?" young Publius asked. "Surely those ships and men did not just sit there in dock."

"You are quite right, young Publius," his father replied. "They certainly did not. With your grandfather captured, Gaius Duilius was left not only in charge of the army, but of the navy also. He reasoned that since the Carthaginians were so agile at sea, that it was best to slow them down a bit. So he invented a thing called "the raven."

Now the Raven was an interesting contraption. It fastened onto the mast of the ship, near the prow of the boat. The ship could then be aimed at another ship, head on, and when it got close enough for ramming the Raven would drop its beak onto the other ship. This would hold it fast so that it could not get away allowing the army to get on board and take over the ship. As you all well know, the Roman army is very good in close quarter combat; this would give the Romans an advantage over the troops from Carthage who might be good at sailing, but were out of practice in real battle.

Gaius Duilius equipped all of his ships with a raven. He sailed out of Messina, looking for trouble – hopefully in the form of the Navy from Carthage. His hopes were answered, for he soon met a wide line of 100 quinqueremes. The Carthaginian troops shouted with derision as they saw the awkward line of Roman ships advancing toward them. But soon their shouts turned to dismay, for the Roman ships came faster and faster, not caring if they broke their prows by ramming into the ships from Carthage. Worse yet for the Carthaginians, when a Roman ship came within ramming distance, it dropped a raven on the opposing ships deck. As soon as the raven held the ship secure, battle hardened fighters boiled over the railings onto the deck, dealing death and mayhem to those aboard. Three thousand Carthaginians died and seven thousand were taken prisoner. Better yet, thirty of the Carthagean ships were captured, including the flagship, and fifteen of them were sunk.

Now, the applause burst out full of enthusiasm, for none of this household – save the new milkmaid – had come from regions that supported the Phoenicians or their primary city, Carthage.

When the applause had died down, young Publius, eyes shining with patriotic fervor said, "But that wasn't the end of it, was it father."

"No," his father said, "There is still plenty of opportunity for brave deeds and marvels of generalship. Rome immediately set about making more ships, for if there is one thing we do well it is making things. When Carthage heard of this, they swore that no Roman soldier would set foot on African soil.

The next spring, Rome set out with 230 galleys; Carthage met them, already in battle formation, with 250 ships. The superior force bore down on the Roman ships in an arc-shaped line divided into thirds. The center would take out the main force of the ships, and the sides would then wrap around the flanks and surround the opposing ships.

But, oh, did they ever get a surprise! The Romans met them with a wedge formation, the supply ships and the slower moving vessels at the rear, positioned in the wide part of the V shape. But also back there was a third of the military vessels to protect the transport craft. The Carthageans expected to quickly subdue the inexperienced sailors, but they were met with such ferocity that the center of their line could not hold and began to retreat. But instead of chasing them, the two forward lines of the V wrapped back around, and attacked the flanking ships that were launching an offensive against the transport ships!

The ships from Carthage that were nearest the open sea were able to get away, but the ones that were nearest the Sicilian shore were cut off.

The Romans lost twenty-four ships that day, but the thirty of the Carthagean ships were sunk and sixty-three of them captured.

Again there was applause. Even their mother, who was often quiet at such times clapped her hands together in praise of the event and of the story-teller, upon whom she looked with quiet pride.

Then she said, "It is time for me to retire. Do not stay up too late, my sons. Tomorrow is another day, with many things to do." She did not say it, but it hung there in the air: the knowledge that one day, before too long, these two sons would follow their father into battle for the honor of Rome.

Thus, we spin another fictionalized tale of an event that could have happened in the household of Publius Cornelius Scipio. The story of the naval battles are a matter of history – it seems that keeping record of such things was more important than records of fashion of the day, or the scandals that might have surrounded the rich and famous. Did such an evening occur? We will never know. But it might have. Publius, the father, was trained in oration as were all patricians of the day. Story-telling is an art found in many cultures, and a way of instructing the young. With no television, winter evenings could become long – story telling was a favorite event in many cultures until the boxed vacuum tube brought a different kind of story telling into our living rooms.

But now you, as well as the boys and servants of that long ago household (even if we see it in our imagination) know of the events that began the Punic Wars and that would become a driving force in two military households.

Indeed, all households of Rome with men between the ages of 18 and 46 could be said to be military households. Military service was expected of all able-bodies men, and there could be no social or political advancement without it.

If a young man entered as a cavalryman, he could expect his service to be only two years long. The reason for this was because of the financial cost. A cavalryman would be expected to provide his own horse, and to bring a slave or servant to help care for the horse. This expense also effectively kept those of lower ranks from entering the cavalry.

An infantryman, on the other hand, would be expected to serve for 20 years. They would be organized into legions. Each legion would be composed of 4,000 infantry – except in times of war when they would number 5,000. Each legion was divided into 10 cohorts, numbered according to their length of service. The commander in charge of the highest numbered cohort would be in charge of the legion. The troops were of mixed ages; an arrangement designed to allow the older, more experienced soldiers to assist the newer ones and keep up their moral. They were also there to step into gaps in the ranks should a soldier fall. Keeping the phalanx even and moving was an important part of infantry combat.

Weapons included short swords, and a pair of javelins. By way of defense, they had body armor and shields. When compared to the foot soldiers, the cavalry were lightly armed and armored. Their best defense was speed.

The Roman army was motivated by civic duty and patriotism. They knew that great or small, they would be honored for their service when they returned home. The sons of first families knew that they would be expected to serve Rome in the Senate and possibly in some civil duty between their bouts of service in the army itself.

Chapter 3
The Young Soldier

Indeed, it would not be long before young Publius would be setting out on his own military ventures. But before we take a good look at his adventures, we need to visit Carthage for a short while.

The Barca family was the Carthaginian counterpart to the Cornelius family. Hamilcar Barca took command of the military forces of Carthage in Sicily at around age 30, in the year 247 BC – nearly 17 years after Grandfather Gnaeus' ignominious defeat. Hamilcar also fathered a son that year, and named him Hannibal.

Hamilcar was an able general, and had he been provided the support he deserved, that might well have ended this tale before it began. But like many other nations before that time and since, Carthage was divided politically. On the one hand, Phoenician ships traded all across the known world. They ventured as far north as Denmark, and far down the western coast of Africa. But on the other hand, they were able farmers and had learned the best ways to take advantage of their local environment. The two factions were – as one might readily suppose – in opposition. The farmers preferred to keep the armies at home, isolating the country. The traders wanted expansion. After all, the farther the reach of Carthaginian borders, the greater their trading area. The Hanno clan was isolationist being composed primarily of those with agrarian interests, and the Barca clan expansionist and interested in trading. With all of the opposition at home, Hamilcar Barca was given only two legions with which to manage Sicily.

With such a small force, Hamilcar elected to establish his military base atop Monte Pellegrino, where he could see all of Palermo. From this vantage point, he could view Roman maneuvers, including any approaching ships from the sea. The location gave the defenders the advantage, and from time to time Hamilcar's forces would sally forth to conduct guerilla raids on the rearguard of the Roman army as they lay siege to Marsala. When the Romans attacked his position on Monte Pellegrino, he handily defeated them.

For four years, this stalemate continued. Hamilcar expected the Romans to sue for peace. But they used a different strategy. Having observed that Hamilcar's position was unassailable by force, they decided to cut his supply lines. However, this involved preventing ships from sailing in with supplies, and that meant that Rome would have to reconstitute its navy. By now, their current ships were in bad shape and that meant that they would need to build at least 200 new quinqueremes. The Roman treasury was all but empty, and they did not want to levy a new general tax or ask their allies to help defray the cost. Instead, they issued war bonds and required land owners, members of the Senate and public officials to purchase them. After the conflict was ended (hopefully with lots of booty) those who had purchased bonds would be able to redeem them.

In the spring, Carthaginian ships sailed toward Sicily. But this was not a fighting force – they had grown contemptuous of Roman seamanship. It was essentially a supply convoy, intended to bring troops and supplies to Hamilcar.

The wind had favored the Carthaginian ships. As the Romans sailed out from some small islands, the wind drove the ships from Carthage straight into the Roman fleet. The fighting was fierce, but as had happened before, once the situation moved from being maneuvers at sea into hand-to-hand combat, the Romans excelled. The ships from Carthage were saved by a shift in the wind that enabled flight back to Carthage. Once there, the commander in charge of the ships was crucified for his defeat.   At this point, Carthage ordered Hamilcar to petition Rome for peace. The terms of the treaty called for complete withdrawal of all Carthaginian forces from Sicily, and for Carthage to pay 2,200 talents to Rome in installments over ten years. In return, Rome would allow Carthage to remain independent. However, the Roman Senate was not pleased with this battlefield decision. They dispatched a committee of ten to further assess the situation. However, upon arrival, the committee concurred that Catulus, the Roman general who had drafted the treaty, was correct in his assessment of the situation. The only change they made was to raise the yearly payment to 3,200 talents, with the added 10,000 talents to be paid in a lump sum as soon as the treaty took effect. In addition, the small islands around Sicily would also come under Roman control.

Thus ended the First Punic War, in 241 BC, a conflict that had lasted for twenty-three years – time enough for a lad to grow into a man. One might have expected some years of peace to follow. Such was not the case.

Carthage refused to pay the mercenaries that had made up a great part of its army. Instead, its officials argued that they had fought only half a year, and would therefore be paid only half that sum. To make a fairly long story short, Hamilcar was given the task of defeating the rebellious mercenaries. At first he was lenient with them; but when they cut the hands, feet, ears and nose off an emissary and buried him alive, Hamilcar proved his efficiency as a military commander. He drove them up onto a little hill, fenced them in and held them there until they resorted to cannibalism, eating their prisoners and slaves. They sent out a party to request peace, but Hamilcar killed them.

The besieged rebels took this to mean that the diplomatic party had defected, and they attacked. That was all that Hamilcar needed. He sent in the elephants, drove the rebel army into a little depression, and they were trampled to death. That went a long way to restoring order at home for Carthage.

With Sicily and its surrounding islands in Roman hands, the expansionist Barcas turned their eyes toward Spain. Spain was a rich prize, with natural resources, gold mines and more. Legend has it, that as Hamilcar was preparing for departure, Hannibal – who would have been around nine years old at the time – begged to go with his father, brothers, brother-in-law, and uncles. Hamilcar, apparently spotting an opportunity, is said to have placed his son's hand upon the animal being sacrificed to Baal in preparation for the trip, and said to him: "Swear, my son, that you will never be amicus to Rome." Now some translations say that this meant that he swore his son to eternal enmity toward Rome, while Livy wrote that Hannibal was never to be a friend to Rome. But "amicus" also meant ally or subject of Rome. Since Rome's habits of acquisition were well known around the Mediterranean, it is entirely possible that Hamilcar's primary purpose would have been to keep Carthage out of the hands of the ever-spreading Roman empire. How did Polybius and Livy learn of this? Well, it seems that many years later, Hannibal was in exile at the court of Antiochus III. He was age 54, and needed some sort of proof that he was a reliable ally against Rome, and told the story of his oath at that time.

In the year 229, Hamilcar died in battle, and Hasdrubal took over the invasion of the Iberian (Spanish) peninsula. Hannibal, who was by now a young man aged somewhere between 18 and 25 years, ably aided his brother-in-law, Hasdrubal, in the conquest. Hannibal's brothers, Hasdrubal and Mago also were in command of portions of the Carthaginian forces in Spain. They establish a strong presence in Spain.

Meanwhile, Rome was not idle. It annexed Sardinia and Corsica, further consolidating its own presence in the Iberian Peninsula. In 226, the Ebo or Ibrus river was established as a boundary between the territory gained by these two warring superpowers. In 221, Hasdrubal fell in battle, and command of the Carthaginian forces was taken up by Hannibal.

In 220, the people of Spain appealed to Rome for assistance against this brash young general. According to treaty, the river Ebo divided Spain into Carthaginian territory and Roman territory. But the city Seguntum, located on the Ebo, was essentially a Roman city.

In spring 219, Hannibal attacked Seguntum, and laid siege to it for eight months. In November, it fell to the armies from Carthage. This had Rome's attention. The conflict broke the treaty made at the end of the First Punic War, and also violated the agreement that the Ebo would be the boundary. Rome declared war.

Unfortunately, the lack of help from Rome and the punitive sacking by the Carthage armies had the Iberian people's attention also. Raw and angry, they whipsawed back and forth between supporting one side or the other. Meanwhile, other subjugated states noticed how little and how late the support from Rome, and added their own restiveness to the situation. In fact, when asked to support Rome by resisting Hannibal's armies, the Gauls laughed so uproariously, wrote Livy, that the elders and the marshals had a hard time quieting them.

When lots were drawn for the various areas needing Roman legions sent out with consuls, Publius Scipio Cornelius and his brother Gnaeus drew Spain. Publius was diverted to Northern Italy where the Gauls were staging an uprising, and Gnaeus went on to Spain. This was in 218, after the fall of Seguntum. It was also in 218 that Hannibal would take his elephants, which had proven to be a supreme tactical asset, over the Alps, thus allowing him to attack the Romans on Italian soil, in an area where they had always thought that the geography would protect them.

No one is quite sure exactly where he crossed the Alps. It is known that on the way up, the mountain dwellers rolled rocks down on his army, and generally harassed them. But once they entered the pass, and started down the other side, they were left alone. On the Italian side, their greatest challenges were the weather and rockslides. Two major avalanches had blocked the way, and it took several days to build a space wide enough for horses and elephants to traverse. By the time Hannibal's army reached the more hospitable plain, his elephants were in sad shape.

In 218 BC, Publius Scipio Cornelius, the father of Publius Scipio Africanis the Elder, and his brother Gnaeus were sent to Spain with the Roman armies to put a stop to the advance of Hasdrubal and Mago, Hannibal's brothers. However, there was a Gallic uprising in northern Italy, and Publius delayed to help put it down while Gnaeus went on to Spain.

The Battle of Ticinus

Seventeen-year-old Publius Scipio (someday to be Africanis) was with his father's army. Publius Scipio Cornelius left his son in the company of a seasoned cavalry unit – possibly for the lad's safety. But seeing his father and uncle about to be killed, young Scipio rallied his cavalry unit and led a charge to rescue them both. This story was told to Polybius by Laelius. Laelius was said to be a close friend and comrade to Publius Scipio, as well as his able lieutenant.

As we have in earlier chapters, let us imagine what it might have been like at that battle.

In the early dawn hours, near the banks of the Ticinus, Publius Scipio watched his father and uncle organize the troops, giving them instruction. All about him, men were gearing up – as were he and his friend, Laelius. First they donned their regular tunics. Then, they added a wool tunic – in Publius Scipio's case, woven by his mother's handmaiden, little Blossom who had grown up to be a lovely woman. His mother had in recent years become too frail to manage the big loom, and confined her work to fine linens woven on a much smaller loom. The wool tunic would absorb perspiration and cushion their bodies from chafing. They draped a scarf around their necks – again to protect their skin from the metal cuirass. Publius and Laelius helped each other into their cuirasses, checking to make sure that the lacings and buckles were secure. About their waists they fastened the baltea, a leather belt which would hold up the balteus – a weighted leather apron intended to protect the groin – as well as the sheath for their short swords. Their sandals had nails embedded in the outer sole, intended to dig into the earth for better traction. Shin guards helped to protect their legs. They checked the inner sole of each shoe carefully to see if an added layer of leather was needed. Those nails hurt if they wore through, even if it was the flat blunt end of them.

Because they would be on horseback, Publius and Laelius carried small, round shields and short spears.

As dawn broke, and after a bit of shouting, the armies clashed. As the day wore on, the lads could see from their vantage point in the rear guard that fewer and fewer men were standing on either side. Although the Cornelii brothers had started out in two separate units, as the fighting wore on, they drew closer and closer until their units were side by side, and then back to back. Suddenly, their standard bearer went down, and the fighting grew intense. Publius Scipio saw his father fall, and he could bear it no longer!

With a shout, he alerted his unit and they plunged boldly into the fray, jabbing with their wicked little spears and blocking blows with their small, round shields. Publius and Laelius rode to the center of the knot of fighting men and took up the older Publius and Gnaeus on their horses. The men were sorely wounded and bleeding, as were many of the soldiers with them. The fighters, both foot soldiers and cavalry, formed up around the leaders. Step by step they worked their way out of the center of the fighting.

And now, a return to recorded history.

With their leaders severely wounded, the Roman army began a strategic retreat back across the Po river to Placentia. Hannibal taunted them, inviting further combat, but the senior Publius refused to engage. The Gallic unrest was too great. Nearly 2,000 Gallic and Celtic conscripts deserted and joined the Carthaginians.

Perhaps it was at this point that, wounded, weary and disheartened, the older Publius begged an oath from the younger one, an oath that said he would always fight against Carthage, even unto death, and that he would forever defend Rome. Or perhaps that is the story the son told later, to explain his enmity toward the Barcas. It is said that, years later, when Publius Scipio heard that his father and uncle had, fallen in battle that he wept, screamed at the gods, and swore vengeance.

Legend is somewhat unclear on this point, but it is fairly certain that the encounter at Ticinus was Publius Scipio's, someday to become Africanis, first encounter with Hannibal. It would certainly not be his last.

Over the next four or five years, it is certain that he, his father and his uncle were deeply involved in the Roman endeavors to hold back this aggressive young military genius. At the time of the **Battle of Trebia,** since Scipio Cornelius had been wounded in the battle at Ticinus, Sempronius had been sent to take his place and was the general in charge. This was music to Hannibal's ears because he felt more confident of his ability to trick Sempronius.

Hannibal had his younger brother Mago hide his troops in the thick brush along the Trebia River. There was a clear plain behind the brush, which at first glance would appear to be empty. At dawn, the Hannibal's Numidian cavalry attacked the Roman encampment. The Romans, roused from sleep, hastily formed up and turned the defense into an offense. The Numidians rode across the Trebia, and the Romans followed in hot pursuit. Sempronius ordered the men to wade river to pursue the fleeing cavalry.

Wet, cold, and hungry, the Roman soldiers were also engaged in an uphill battle, coming up from the river as they were. Now, Hannibal brought up the rest of his troops, with his elephants positioned in front of his cavalry where they could do the most good. This was one of the Roman's first encounters with Hannibal's elephants. The elephants rendered the unaccustomed horses in the Roman cavalry useless. The terrified animals broke from the control of their riders, dashing about and creating almost as much carnage as the elephants themselves. The Romans were at a supreme disadvantage. They would either have to retreat into the freezing cold waters of the Trebia or they would have to meet Hannibal's warm, dry and well-fed troops head on. Sempronius urged his troops forward, pushing at the center of Hannibal's line as was the custom of Roman troops of the day – a tactic Hannibal would use against them over and over.

As soon as they were well engaged, Mago's troops rose up from the bushes where they had been concealed, trapping the unfortunate men between two battle ready forces. Sempronius had taken nearly 40,000 men into the fray, but only about 10,000 survived to return to their camp at Placentia.

This debacle caused the Romans to have to raise a new level of 30,000 men to replace those lost to Hannibal's trickery. It almost seemed as if he had an endless supply of men, even though he was actually out of touch with Carthage. The reality was that Hannibal had lost scarcely any men at Trebia, although he had lost most of his elephants.

Tricking the Roman army seemed so easy to him. Soon, he discovered another place where he could set up an ambush.

The battle of Lake Trasimene

This one he set up based on what he knew about the opposing Roman general, Flaminius. Flaminius was known to be impulsive and to plunge in without thinking – particularly if he was angry. Hannibal knew just the way to do it. He also hoped to show the natives that Rome could not protect its allies. To do this, he rampaged around the countryside burning buildings and killing the livestock. He did not succeed in winning the people to his side, but he certainly enraged Flaminius.

On a misty May morning, Hannibal lured Flaminius into pursuing his army down a narrow path that lead onto a small plain beside the lake. Previously, Hannibal had stationed more troops in the corners of the plain, where they could not be readily seen. Once Flaminius forces were committed, Hannibal made short work of them, slaying nearly 15,000 of them – including the commander, Flaminius. Only 6000 Romans escaped.

Emboldened by his successes, Hannibal set up for what would be his greatest triumph on Roman soil: **The Battle of Cannae.**

The Roman troops at Cannae had been under the generalship of Lucius Amelius Paulus and Caius Terentius Varro. General Paulus fell in battle and it was under Varro that the armies made their retreat.

There are many accounts of the Battle of Cannae – with conflicting tales, and varied numbers. But on some things those accounts do agree. Hannibal had swelled the numbers of his troops by recruiting Spaniards, Gauls and Celts who had reason to detest the invading Romans. He was not relying on mercenary troops who would desert if they were not paid, or if the profits were exceeded by losses. But there were two things working against him. First, he had taken considerable losses in his journey over the Alps – his surviving elephants were sick and weak. Then he had lost more elephants at Trebia. Men and horses had also fallen on that journey, and at each battle – although his losses were small compared to those of Rome – he did lose men at each battle. Second, when he sent to Carthage for reinforcements and supplies, his request was refused. He was, therefore, unable to muster the men or supplies to lay siege to large cities. Instead, he had to rely on harrying tactics to wear down the Roman forces.

At Cannae, he filled the center ranks with Gauls – whom he fully expected to give way when confronted with the well-trained Roman legions. When they did, Hannibal's seasoned troops emerged from the bushes on both sides of the committed force. Perhaps if Paulus had been a more astute general or if the Roman army had not been riddled by desertions, the outcome might have been different. But as it was, the forces commanded by Paulus and Varro were caught between the jaws of the Carthaginian army, and only a few were fortunate enough to survive.

Who knows how history might have changed had Hannibal been adequately supplied and supported. In spite of his requests, Carthage sent only small amounts of supplies and few reinforcements. In spite of the victory at Cannae, Hannibal continued to make small sorties, keeping the Roman consuls busy putting out small brush fires, as it were.

At the Battle of Cannae – a dreadful loss for the Romans and a triumph for Hannibal – in 216, young Scipio served as a military tribune. At the end of the disaster, he escaped to Canusium with 4,000 other survivors. Legend has it – as told by Laelius to Polybius – that after the battle he came upon a group of young noblemen who were planning to defect.

Now, it had come to be said that young Publius Scipio was an orator of some extreme talent, as well as being well trained in the martial arts. He first held this group of would-be deserters at sword point. One does wonder how he was able to do that since the sword is hardly a distance weapon and can only target one man at a time. Perhaps he collared the leader of the group, and in that manner held sway. Or perhaps he cornered them in a room, and held the doorway against their leaving.

But however he did that, he managed to gain the group's attention, and then he began to orate. He threatened, he cajoled, he appealed to their pride. By the end of his speech, he not only made them all swear never to desert Rome, but to slay any man they might find who was similarly inclined. It should be noted that this was standard policy for Roman troops, but in the desperate moments at the end of the Battle of Cannae, it might have been understandable that some would turn faint of heart. It is said that the Romans lost some 44,000 troops in that battle, downed by the military prowess of Hannibal.

The real significance of Cannae was the lesson that Scipio learned from post-battle examination of Hannibal's tactics. Rome had entered the field of battle at Cannae with the superior force – 50,000 men to Hannibal's 40,000. Hannibal had become quite a thorn in Rome's side, and Rome was responding in its usual way – by sending in an overwhelming number of troops.

Hannibal had combined force with sweet-talk and promises, and had taken over a large portion of northern Italy following his daring foray over the Alps. By the time of the battle of Cannae, the Romans were truly worried that the daring young general would march on Rome itself. They did not know that he was limiting himself to wearing them down because he was receiving very little support from home. Hannibal knew very well that he did not have the forces needed to either take the city or hold onto it afterward should he have succeeded. But that didn't keep him from entertaining the Roman's attention with his antics.

His battle plan at Cannae took full advantage of Roman hubris and the general's need for a big win. By positioning his weakest troops in the middle, Hannibal drew in the Roman troops which were arranged in traditional fashion which was to place the light infantry in front, then to follow it up with the heavier infantry, with the cavalry on the flanks where they were more maneuverable.

By placing his weakest troops in the center of his forward line, Hannibal cozened the Roman commanders into thinking that they were winning, and they pressed forward. By the time they realized that it was a trap, their men were already deeply committed, and because of the traditional arrangement, they were unable to pull back. Thus, they were trapped by the pincers of the reserves that Hannibal had positioned on both sides of the field.

Scipio learned his lesson from this knavish tactic. Hannibal's combined approach of espionage and trickery were serving him very well, despite having to swell the ranks of his army by converting the Gauls. These were maneuvers that Scipio would use in Spain and then take with him to Africa, where he would turn the tables on the Carthaginians.

In many ways, Hannibal, ten years Scipio's senior, was very much his instructor in tactics. Scipio talked with soldiers, read reports and in all ways studied the methods that Hannibal was using to wear down the Romans.

However, not all the Romans were as easy to take in as Sempronius, Flaminius and Aemilius. Fabius, who had been observing Hannibal's tactics now began what might best be described as a war of attrition. He harried Hannibal with small battles, cut off his supplies, and refused to give him rest. Following the Battle of Cannae and well into the latter years that Hannibal was in Italy, Fabius kept up these tactics, earning him the title of Cunctator or Delayer. Fabius kept up these tactics for twelve years. It was only toward the end that he became impatient, and that proved to be his undoing. But more of that later.

A small side note, which has little to do with the main theme concerns a siege of a major city in Sicily. Hiero, the ruler of Syracuse, had long been an ally of Rome. But upon his death, he was succeed by his grandson, Hieronymus. Hieronymus allied himself with Carthage. Marcellus, the governor of Sicily became alarmed by the pro-Carthaginian faction. When Hieronymus tried to rouse the neighboring city of Leontini, Marcellus immediately took notice. Syracuse closed its doors to him, and he laid siege there.

Now, here is the truly interesting bit. Many of the siege engines invented in Syracuse during 214-212 were designed by Archimedes, the mathematician who said, "Give me a fulcrum, a lever and a place to stand and I will move the world." When the siege ended, Archimedes was killed because he was too busy with a mathematical problem to follow the directions given to him for surrender.

Whether that was truly why he did not give himself up or whether there was some other reason, it still makes an interesting story.

Chapter 4
The Quaestorship

Publius Scipio returned to Rome after Cannae. Somehow, in spite of the dreadful defeat, Scipio was now considered a hero. The records are sparse for his civilian life, and like much of our quest into his history, must rely on small clues and general knowledge about the times. It is known that he was wed to Aemilia, daughter of Aemilius Paulus, the consul who fell at Cannae. Precisely when they were wed is not known, although it is a matter of record that they had two sons and two daughters.

Scipio organized games in honor of his father and uncle, and threw himself into them with gusto. Perhaps he met Aemilia there, and the two were drawn together in their mutual grief; or, perhaps they had been betrothed by their fathers before the battle. In any event, they were wed, and for a year or two Scipio led a civilian life.

When he was only twenty-four, he was elected curule aedile. There were two curule aedile in Rome. They oversaw other officials, such as the ones in charge of weights and measures. The lesser aediles kept order in the streets, looked after the market and in general functioned much like the police of today. The two curule aediles functioned somewhat like chiefs of police. The senate was not particularly happy about his election. They pointed out his youth, saying he was too young for the position. To this he pertly replied, "If all of Rome has voted for me, then I am old enough."

It is likely that it was during these years that he began his family. Apparently, he did quite well for himself in those days, and during the years when he returned to military life.

Certain accounts say that when the lady Ameilia Tertia (she was the third child of Amelius) went to the temple to make sacrifices that she carried fine vessels for the sacrifice, such as gold rimmed crystal goblets. She would bear four children to Scipio – two sons and two daughters.

Let us again turn in imagination to what it must have been like for her, this Amelia Tertia. Women in Rome were so little valued that they were given a family name and a number. Ameilia was the third daughter of the Amelius who fell at Cannae – Tertia means three. Marriage to Publius Scipio, who was quite the rising young star in Rome at that time, would have meant both status and security.

As a military daughter, having recently lost both father and the man who would have been her father-in-law, she certainly would have been aware of the fragility of human life. At the same time, as a young woman with little family support, she would have been aware of the need to support her husband's position in the city. By dressing in her very best, and having a fine retinue of servants carrying fine vessels to the temple not only indicated her supplication of the gods, it helped show that her husband was generous to her and showed her support of him.

Let us further suppose, that a certain young woman named Blossom had been given to young Publius Scipio's household as a wedding gift, and that she was part of that fine procession. Keep in mind that Blossom is primarily a figment of this writer's imagination, but there is a reason for including her here – of that we will say more later.

Amelia's visits to the temples would have been an important part of her daily life. Not only did the size and quality of her retinue proclaim her place in Roman society, she might very well have believed that performing the rituals and sacrifices would help keep Publius safe when he was away with the military, or even when he was patrolling the streets of Rome. As previously mentioned, Rome was exciting, but it wasn't safe.

Amelia might have visited one of several temples to show her devotion and to perform rituals for the safety of her husband. For example, she might have visited Janus, the two-faced god who faced both the past and the future. Janus governed all change, and opened doors to all possibility. While Rome was at war, the door to Jupiter's temple would be open. She might have made offerings in memory of her father, and again for the safety of her husband. She might have visited Hera's temple – particularly if she desired a child. Certainly, she would have wanted one since a husband could divorce a wife who either bore no children or did not give birth to a son. Such devotion would have been expected of her. Wearing fine robes, having beautiful vessels for he sacrifices – these would all have been showing respect. She knew the risks that her husband faced.

For just a moment, let us imagine her robed in her finest clothing. The clothing for Roman women was strictly regulated until 195 BC, so her choices would have been limited. First, she would have had on a peplos or a chiton. These were garments made from two squares of cloth that were sewn up the sides, almost to the top. They were then – in the case of the peplos – fastened with pins to form short sleeves, or in the case of the chiton, long sleeves. Married women were entitled to wear the stola, although it was not required. Finally, there was the palla, a long cloak that respectable women wore when they went outside.

Since Aemilia was clearly a respectable young married woman, she would have been likely to wear her stola and palla over her peplos. Each of these garments would have been of fine cloth since her husband was well off financially. Perhaps her peplos would be linen or silk; her stola would be made from virgin wool as tradition demanded. The Palla might have been made of silk or wool, depending upon the season, and might have been decorated with a fringe or with fine trim along the edges.

The women and men servants in her retinue would also have been well dressed, although perhaps not in such finery as she herself wore. Accounts describing her procession include mention of fine crystal and gold trim on the sacrificial vessels. But for all her finery, one has to wonder what might have been her frame of mind. Having lost her father to the war, what were her feelings about sending her husband into that fray. Would her attitude be "with your shield or on it" or would she have been more deeply worried about his safety? Either way, it didn't really matter. When the time came he would have to go.

In 211, Scipio's Uncle Gnaeus and his father were slain in the battle at Ilourgeia, according to some accounts. It is probable that the front in Hispania had been starved of materials and manpower in favor of dealing with the Sicilian front throughout 213 and 212. But the Carthaginian forces had been steadily strengthened, and now included three able generals: Mago and Hasdrubal Barca, Hannibal's brothers, as well as Hasdrubal Gisco. Publius and Gnaeus decided to split their forces. Publius would take two thirds of their force against Mago and Hasdrubal Barca, while Gnaeus would take the remaining third and the Celtiberian allies against Hasdrubal Gisco. Perhaps they under estimated the might of the various generals, or perhaps they were just that desperate. Any modern participant of strategy or role playing games could have instructed them about the dangers of splitting your forces, and thus dividing your strength – but such commenters would have the advantage of historical perspective supplied by generations of critics.

The difficulties began almost immediately. Publius and his troops were constantly beset by Numidian cavalry under the direction of Masinissa, a Numidian prince who had been driven out of his homeland by his brother prince, Syphax. Publius had advanced as far as Urso, when he heard that the Spanish chieftain Andobales or Indibilis as he is sometimes called, was approaching with a force of 7500. Publius took a group of men on a forced night march to try to head off the added group before they could join the Carthaginians. The sally went terribly wrong, and Publius died fighting against dreadful odds, far from the force that he had left in the camp.

The Celtiberian's, meanwhile, had deserted Gnaeus, so he had begun a strategic retreat. However, he was not able to move fast enough. Hasdrubal Gisco's forces were joined by the jubilant armies of Mago and Hasdrubal Barca, who were all fired up and battle ready from their recent triumph over Publius. Gnaeus had his soldiers pile up the supply packs to make a rampart of sorts on a bare, rocky hill but they were soon overrun, and Gnaeus was killed.

The remnants of the army limped back across the Ebo under the guidance of Tiberius Fonteius, the commander Publius had left in charge at his camp, and under Lucius Marcius, a Roman knight from Gnaeus army. Although there were conflicting reports, it seems that Lucius Marcius must have been an able commander for he continued to hold the front with possibly around 8000 infantry and about a thousand cavalry.

In 210, Rome decided to send reinforcements to Spain, but none of the senior generals were willing to undertake the endeavor. Apparently, they had had quite enough of breaking their hearts and their armies in Spain, against the Barcas. Besides, the war was going full tilt on the Sicilian front, and they had their hands full with Hannibal tearing up the countryside in the northern part of Italy.

But Publius Scipio had an axe to grind with the Barcas and the Carthaginians. Since his father and uncle had both lost their lives in Spain, he was hot for revenge. So he volunteered to make the journey into Spain.

Now, Aemilia would have a real reason to visit the temple daily, for Publius would be gone a long while, into an area that would be difficult, dangerous and – in the long run – very hard on his health. Although he would have, no doubt, have left a man of business in charge of his affairs, she would have been in charge of running the house in his absence. One has to wonder whether she was glad to be left in charge of things, or if she missed her husband during his many long absences. We have examples from literature to indicate how women were supposed to behave under these circumstances, but one has to wonder if she were a true Penelope, or if she were a more strong minded and independent.

Chapter 5
Carthago Nova and
the Conquest of Spain

Have either accepted or jockeyed for the position, Scipio set out for Spain. There are conflicting accounts of the number of men and cavalry that he took with him, but the various writings indicate that his army was a mixture of Romans, levies from the provinces and – once he had arrived in Spain – the remnants of his uncle and father's armies. In any case, he was heavily outnumbered by the forces from Carthage.

As it happens, when Scipio first entered Spain, Hannibal was not there. In fact, Hannibal, having traveled over the Alps with his elephants and the rest of his army, was in Italy, making his way toward Rome. This might have been one reason that the older generals really were not interested in traveling to a foreign country to try to take more territory; they were intent in keeping the able Carthaginian commander off Rome's doorstep.

Under-manned as he was, Scipio decided to go for a soft target. Carthago Nova, or New Carthage had become the Barcas headquarters. It was situated on a peninsula that projected out into the sea, and was – the Barcas thought – only approachable from the land side. Because they believed that their fortifications were well established, Hannibal's younger brother, Hasdrubal, and brother Mago, had only left a small house-keeping force there, and had taken the rest of their army out in search of further conquests.

Considering that they had been channeling the wealth that they had been collecting from Spain through New Carthage, it was quite a plum – and ripe for the picking. Scipio must have smiled to think of the coup that he was about to pull off.

Scipio divided his forces, sending part of them with his friend and second in command, Laelius, to sail around on the seaward side and block the harbor. The rest of the troops he force-marched to the front side of the fortress, and – contrary to normal Roman custom – set up fortifications before establishing camp. Once he fortifications were up, he set up camp in the normal fashion, right out in front where the defenders could see him camped on their doorstep. Who knows how his ragtag mixed force viewed his actions, but the accounts available don't mention any rebellion or unhappiness about the target. Perhaps they appreciated the extra protection afforded by the fortifications.

At first, Scipio's army assaulted the front of the fortress – as the defenders probably expected. But he also talked with the local folk, and learned that at midday, the water was quite low on one side. Leaving part of his forces to continue the frontal assault, keeping the fighters who were manning the walls occupied, he took a small force around to the side of the keep, and scaled the undefended wall. With Laelius ready to hold off any chance of reinforcements from the sea, Scipio had New Carthage exactly where he wanted it – under his heel.

The subsequent carnage was said to be horrible. Scipio ordered his men to slay anyone in sight. They did a rampage through that fortress that would have done any barbarian horde proud, slaying, raping, pillaging. It might have partially been to strike terror to the hearts of the city's residents, but it might also have been in revenge for the deaths of the two older

Scipios. When the dust had settled, Scipio rounded up the survivors. There were many youths and wives who had been held as hostages to ensure good behavior of native Spanish tribes. There were a few men who had been in charge; Scipio sent them back to Rome as hostages. And there were the ordinary folk – the shopkeepers, and artisans who were essential to keeping a city running. Scipio set the men of this latter group to work making weapons and engines of war with the understanding that after a time they would be set free.

Since he expected the Barcas to return to take back their city, Scipio kept his army well-trained and fit. He made them run with full packs, clean their weapons and themselves, and practice arms. But Carthage customarily executed military leaders who failed; so the Barcas were in no hurry to make their way back to Northern Africa. Therefore, for a whole year Scipio held New Carthage without so much as a whimper from the other armies.

Meanwhile, back in Rome and southern Italy, Hannibal was playing cat and mouse with the Roman forces. He didn't have enough men or supplies to actually take Rome, so he harried their forces. His hope was to wear them down to the point that they would not be able to defend their capital city. Instead, the older generals who were tired of war and wanted to be done with it, drove him slowly back until he was only occupying the toe of the Italian boot.

When Laelius brought back the prisoners to Rome from New Carthage, Scipio was hailed as a hero. However, it would be several months before Hannibal would learn that he had lost the city through which he and his brothers had been funneling the wealth of Spain as they acquired it.

Scipio took full advantage of the wealth stored in New Carthage. Among the hostages that he returned was a beautiful young woman who was betrothed to one of the local chieftains, along with the money her parents had paid for her ransom. The townfolk offered her to him as part of his booty, but with scarcely any consideration her turned down the offer, giving her into the keeping of her betrothed, untouched by his hands at least. Thus, the fellow became one of Scipio's loyal followers. Other chieftains also joined him. By returning the hostages to their families, Scipio began to win the loyalty of the local folk.

In addition to swelling the ranks of his troops with locals, Scipio also upgraded his soldiers gear. One of the changes he made was to issue double edged Spanish swords to his foot soldiers in place of the traditional Roman short sword, which was only sharp on one side.

In 209, Scipio took his troops and sallied forth to look for the three Carthaginian armies. He knew, however, that his armies were still vastly outnumbered, even though he had collected reinforcements from the Hispanic population. He did not want to get caught between the three forces from Carthage, so he found a time when Hasdrubal's army was separated from the other two. Scipio did a rare thing for him – he engaged in a traditional set battle – almost. While what seemed to be his total forces charged the center of Hasdrubal's forces, Scipio sneaked his reserves behind Hasdrubal's lines and attacked from the rear. This broke the back of the forces from Carthage, and allowed Scipio to win the battle – sending Hasdrubal limping away.

He declined, however, to pursue Hasdrubal's army. He received some criticism for this because Hasdrubal eventually made his way over the Alps in an effort to reinforce Hannibal's position. It was well known that Scipio's father and uncle had sacrificed their lives to keep Hasdrubal and Hannibal's other kin from bringing their armies over the Alps to serve as reinforcements for the able commander.

However, had Scipio chosen to pursue, it is very possible that his illustrious military career would have ended right there. In very short order after Hasdrubal's retreat, Mago and Gisco, the other two generals from Carthage moved their forces in to fill the gap. It is likely that had Scipio pursued Hasdrubal, he would have been trapped between the three armies.

At the Battle of Baecula, as Hasdrubal's defeat became known, Scipio captured a number of Hasdrubal's forces – among them a young Numidian lad. It turned out that the young Numidian was nephew to Masinissa, the prince who was in charge of the Numidian cavalry. Cannily, Scipio gave the boy a Roman costume, a cavalry unit to accompany him, and sent the boy to his uncle. This would prove to be significant later on.

It would be an error to portray Scipio as being the only Roman general opposing Hannibal and the other forces from Carthage. Marcellus and Crispinus were the consuls opposing Hannibal as he tried to force his way northward in Italy. Marcellus played cat and mouse with Hannibal for several seasons before he succeeded in driving Hannibal down into the toe of the Italian boot. Perhaps age was catching up with Marcellus – he was in his early sixties – or perhaps he was getting a lot of pressure from Rome to finish up already yet with this upstart from Africa. Whatever the reason, Marcellus rode with several of his senior officers to scout an area to ascertain its suitability as a battle staging ground.

Hannibal also had scouting parties in the area. As Marcellus and his party rode up a little hill that they had their eye on, Hannibal's cavalry surrounded the veteran general and killed him along with every man in his party. However, Crispinus got wind of what had happened, and quickly sent out messenger, letting people know that Marcellus had fallen. This was an important step because Marcellus was wearing his seal ring – the ring that he would use as a stamp to prove that orders sent under that seal were authentic. It was a canny move on Crispinus' part because Hannibal did, indeed, immediately send out false messages using Marcellus' ring. However, this move failed because Roman messengers managed to arrive ahead of the false orders. Crispinus, who had himself been recently gravely wounded, put Marcellus' second-in-command, Claudius Nero, in charge of the grieving troops. Nero was able to rally the men, and they fought on, giving Hannibal a very hard time.

Crispinus died of his wounds, so at the end of the season, the Roman senate had to make haste to elect two new consuls for the area that Marcellus and Crispinus had covered. The year was now 207 BC, and one of the consuls chosen was Claudius Nero. The other consul was Livius, who would be sent to Rimini. Nero's army was intended to merge with the legions under Praetor Fulvius to strengthen the southern front.

Hasdrubal, who had managed to make it over the Alps in better order than Hannibal had enjoyed after he made the trip, immediately began marching south through Gaul. The Gallic tribesmen had no desire to tangle with the army, and no real reason to back up Rome, so Hasdrubal marched along with little opposition. He wanted to let his brother know that help was on the way and to arrange for their armies to meet. He, therefore, sent a messenger who was well guarded on ahead to find Hannibal. In the message, Hasdrubal wrote out the route that he planned to take.

Roman scouts waylaid the messenger party, and captured the detailed message. When the soldiers saw that it was in Phoenician, they immediately took it to Nero. Nero quickly translated it, and then did something that could have gotten him tried for treason. Instead of following his orders and remaining in his assigned area, he left enough of his men with Fulvius to make it appear that the army was still at full strength. He, and 7,000 men slipped out of camp late at night, and force marched their way to join Livius and his forces. This was not as irresponsible as it might seem. Thanks to the captured missive, Nero knew that Hasdrubal had managed to add to his army as he marched along. Without Nero's reinforcements, Livius was likely to be in trouble.

Livius has set up fortifications along the bank of the Metauro River, where he could reasonably expect Hasdrubal to march, but without Nero's forces his army would not have been strong enough to prevail against Hasdrubal. By the time Nero joined him, Hasdrubal had an encampment on the opposite bank. Seeing the reinforcements joining Livius, Hasdrubal chose a slightly different route from the one he had originally planned, but one that would still take him south toward Hannibal's location. What he did not realize was that the road he had chosen would soon run along the base of some very large cliffs, placing his forces at extreme disadvantage.

Nero and Livius positioned their forces in such a way as to pin Hasdrubal against the cliffs. Then they set up a great cry, which panicked the elephants in the Carthaginian forces, causing them to run amok, trampling their own forces. Hasdrubal ordered the elephants put down, which their handlers did right away, but not before they created a great deal of damage.

Although Hasdrubal's forces put up a valiant fight, the Roman forces steadily pushed them back against the cliffs, allowing them no maneuvering room. They bore down upon them until, realizing that the end was at hand, Hasdrubal put on his best dress uniform and waded into the fray to die in a manner so as to make his country proud.

His gesture came to an anticlimactic ending, however. Nero and his 7,000 men quickly marched back to Fulvius, and slipped back into camp.

Fulvius was fighting against Hannibal, who had no idea what had happened until a bundle was lobbed into his camp. When it was opened, Hasdrubal's head was revealed. Hannibal had not seen his beloved younger brother for nearly ten years.

Hannibal is portrayed as being a soldier's soldier. He labored tirelessly to find new strategies, to use his troops wisely and to not sacrifice them in hopeless engagements. But Hasdrubal's death hit him hard.

Grieving, Hannibal retreated to Calabria, and stayed there for the rest of that year and the next. It was as if the fight had been knocked out of him and he had retreated to rest and to mourn.

Meanwhile, back in Spain, Scipio continued to harry the Carthaginians and to collect allies. Gisco and Mago also continued to swell the ranks of their armies. The Barcas gathered their forces at Ilipo – around seventy thousand foot soldiers, four thousand horsemen and thirty-two elephants. They settled on a plain that was large enough to accommodate them, in an area that would have been very near what is today the city of Seville. They had nearly twice the numbers that the Romans could muster.

Scipio did not immediately move to engage the army from Carthage. Instead, he traveled northward, then approached their encampment from upriver. As he worked his way down river toward them, Scipio collected reinforcements – many of them Iberian tribesmen who were grateful for the return of their kindred. Once there, he took up his position on a little hill that faced the hill where Gisco and Mago had their fortifications. But he still did not attack.

Instead, each morning he roused his troops, had them stand in formation and wait. The Carthaginian army did the same. Day after day, they held this session of standing in formation glaring at each other. As time went on, the army from Carthage got up later and later, until one morning they did not assemble at all. On that day, Scipio directed his soldiers to rest, to rise early the following day, to eat a hearty breakfast and to assemble on the battlefield at sunrise. No doubt his troops were beginning to wonder about this ritual, but they had seen how Publius Scipio worked, and they followed his commands.

When the sun came up, there was Scipio's army, ready to march on the forces assembled by Carthage. Gisco and Mago hastily roused their troops out of bed and sent them to the field without their breakfast. Thus, they came to the battlefield already disorganized and unready.

Battle of Ilipa

Having set up this incredible feint, Scipio was ready to take the Carthaginian Army. Some historians believe that this battle, rather than the later battle at Zama was Scipio's masterpiece of strategy.

Scipio had been doing more than just baiting the Carthaginians, however. He had been observing their formation, noticing that day after day, it never varied – even though the army he was facing was slower and slower to assemble. The Libyans, who seemed well trained, were given the center. Their Spanish allies were assembled in the wings, back by the cavalry and protected from the fore by the elephants.

We are not told how Scipio arranged his troops day by day. Perhaps he varied them, perhaps he selected a standard formation. But on the day of battle he certainly used a novel organization of his troops. He placed his Spanish troops in the center. While they were getting into position, the velites or skirmishers and the cavalry harassed the Carthaginian troops as they were assembling themselves. Unfed and ill prepared, the Carthaginians must have found that alone a terrifying experience. Scipio's battle hardened legionnaires took up positions on either flank. Not only did this present the Carthaginians a soft center to attack, it kept the Spanish troops from being able to defect at the last minute. No doubt Scipio remembered the troops that had deserted his uncle.

When the troops were truly in position, Scipio signaled the skirmishers and cavalry to withdraw to a position behind the legions. The Spaniards advanced – but very slowly, because Scipio had no intention of allowing these poorly trained troops to come into contact with the Libyans. The legions quick marched, a rank of them passing the slower moving Spaniards. Legionnaires and cavalry swung around to either end of the disgruntled Carthaginians, catching them in a pincher movement. At the same time, all of the Roman contingency let out a great shout, and continued to make noise. This alarmed the elephants, causing them to run back through their own troops.

This placed the Libyans in a quandary. If they turned to face the forces coming up on their flanks they would present a vulnerable flank to the advancing Spaniards. Meanwhile the rampaging elephants were creating havoc. The Romans had the Carthaginians in an unenviable position. The situation looked grim for them.

Just then, the heavens opened up, and there was a torrential downpour. Drenched to the skin, the Roman forces retreated from the forces of mother nature. Without this natural intercession, the Carthaginians would have been in a bad way. As it was, they were able to also retreat, fleeing the scene of battle.

Thus, in 206, Scipio completely won Spain for the Roman Empire. This final battle sent the Carthaginians scurrying away for less contentious targets. In the case of Hasdrubal, the retreat took him over the Alps to attempt to join his brother, Hannibal.

Mutiny in the Ranks

However, Scipio's victory was not without cost. He fell ill after Ilipa, and had a rough time recovering. Perhaps it was the wetting they received, perhaps it was the many months in the field. Rumors of his demise ran through the ranks of the Roman army and its allies.

Many of his soldiers had grown resentful of their long, hard battles. Many of them were owed quite a lot of back pay, since Rome had not been very forthcoming with finances, replacement troops or supplies. They were tired of field rations, camping out and combat. At Sucro, they decided to mutiny. The mutineers included some of the native tribes, who felt that they had not received appropriate credit for their part in the victory at Ilipa. The mutineers pretended to honor the leaders of their cohorts, but instead replaced them with their own ringleaders. The men who refused to join the mutiny slipped away to join the troops that were located at New Carthage – which was, incidentally, the area where Scipio was convalescing.

There were 7000 loyal troops and 8000 mutineers. Rather than have a pitched battle between his own men, Scipio chose what seemed to be a diplomatic approach. He sent the seven loyal tribunes who had been driven out by the mutineers to talk with them about their grievances and to reassure them that Scipio was very much alive and in good health.

They seemed to come to an understanding. The native tribes that had participated in the mutiny withdrew to their own camps, and refrained from any additional rebellion. Scipio held a huge feast for the ringleaders of the mutineers, and when they were thoroughly drunk, he had his loyal tribunes arrest them. The mutinous troops were gathered in the square to witness the trial of these men, and then scolded for their participation in the mutiny. Most of the fight went out of them when the ringleaders were lashed, and then beheaded.

All of the troops were then given their back pay; and the mutineers had to make new vows of allegiance.

In 205, Scipio gave up the generalship in Spain, and returned to Rome. There, he held games in celebration; not for having conquered Spain, but for having put down the rebellion. It is said that he flung himself into these games with abandon, putting all of his grief, anger and frustration into the way he threw javelins and entered into competitions.

Chapter 6
Consul Scipio

After his return in 205, Publius Scipio was elected consul. With this official endorsement in hand, he planned to take his army to Africa, to bring the conflict to Carthage. However, he was only thirty years old, and the minimum age for consul was forty. Therefore, his detractors conspired to limit his troop strength by limiting his budget and saying that he could only take volunteers. However, many of the men who had fought with him in Spain were loyal, and he was able to raise additional troops, including veterans of the Battle of Cannae. More than that, many of the wealthy citizens of Rome and Italy recognized him as an able commander, and quickly began to make contributions to his campaign – ships, grain, pig iron – which helped relieve his slender purse.

As he marched his army toward Sicily, Publius Scipio was able to take Locri Epizephyrii, a city located in the very toe of Italy – one that had been traded back and forth between the Romans and their enemies for many centuries. At the time, it was an harbor that frequently welcomed Carthaginian ships. By conquering it, Scipio cut off a major source of supplies for Hannibal. Having struck a small blow against Hannibal, Scipio sailed to Sicily.

Sicily became his training ground, and the area where men and goods continued to pour in to assist Scipio with his ambitious effort to take the war to Carthage instead of waiting for it to come to him. Now, an interesting thing about his becoming the consul of Sicily: it also made him de facto governor of Sicily. For some time, the island had been a punishment station for soldiers who "failed" in other areas. Two legions were veterans of both Cannae and of Marcellus army. They were hardened veterans who were just as eager as the young commander to have done with Carthage, the Barcas and Hannibal Barca in particular.

In addition to these troops, Scipio gained troops from the Sicilians themselves. As a province of Rome, they were exempt from contributing men to the army. However, they could not own their land, and they had to pay taxes to Rome. In exchange, Rome was to provide military protection. Scipio found some sort of loophole in Roman law which allowed him to return lands to Sicilian control. In exchange, the grateful recipients provided militia at their own expense. He also gained Sicily as a loyal supply base for his troops.

Knowing very well that venturing into Africa where he had no supply base was risky business, and knowing that his new army was an amazing mixture of veterans with a variety of background and green, new troops who had never been in a battle, as well as contributions from the tribes in Spain where he had won some loyalty and respect, he began two processes. On the one hand, he began putting his men through extreme training sessions. On the other, he spent his nights visiting campfires, listening to stories and learning about the region. Since Sicily was so close to North Africa, the natives had considerable knowledge of the area.

In addition, he sent Laelius, his friend and second-in-command, with a fleet of ships to scout along the coast of North Africa. Scipio also asked Laelius to contact Syphax and Masinissa, and to sound them out on the possibility of joining with them in opposition to Carthage. Syphax and Masinissa were both rulers in Numidia, the source of the fearsome Numidian cavalry that had been such as asset to Hamilcar.

It was while he was busy gathering intelligence and training his men, it came to Scipio's ears that the port of Locri was about to defect from Carthaginian rule back to Rome. Scipio quickly lead a troop of three thousand soldiers into Locri, securing it for Rome.

Locri is located on the eastern side of the toe of the Italian boot. It is part of the Calabrian area where Hannibal had taken refuge after his brother, Hasdrubal's death. Calabria is an ideal region for an army to lose itself, and a difficult area from which to extract it once it has dug in. Even to this day, it is a rocky, mountainous region. When one thinks of Italy, sunny beaches, slopes with grape vines and warmth come to mind. But the plateau in that area is high enough to have snow and evergreens. The area is rugged, and even has some active volcanic activity. It was into this inhospitable region that Hannibal had entrenched himself.

In spite of his success in securing Locri, Scipio came under censure for his actions. He had moved his troops out of his assigned area, and encroached on territory belonging to another commander. The Senate sent out a team to investigate and to question Scipio about his motives in this move. However, their criticism was muted by the simple fact that Licinius, the consul who was supposed to be over that area, had done very little to slow or contain Hannibal. Scipio had reduced the size of the cage for the Lion of Carthage.

In the spring of 204 BC, Scipio was made proconsul over the area. He loaded his entire army onto a fleet of forty warships and four hundred transport ships. He had 26,000 soldiers, forty-five days' worth of food and water, of which fifteen days' worth were pre-cooked. It normally took a day and a night to sail from Sicily to northern Africa, but if the winds were unfavorable it might take longer.

They had intended to land on a cape west of Carthage, but instead found themselves on a cape to the east. This meant that in order to reach their intended destination, they had to sail around the Bay of Tunis. Carthage lay inside that bay!

There was no response from Carthage, however, and Scipio successfully landed his army near Utica, the second largest city in Carthage's territory.

The news upon landing was not good. Upon his father's death, Syphax had taken over Numidia, and had firmly sided with Carthage. Carthage had offered him alliance and Gisco's daughter's hand in marriage to seal the deal. She was formerly to have married Masinissa, but apparently Carthage found Syphax to be the better bet. Although Numidia had formerly been two allied kingdoms, it was now only one.

Masinissa brought a mere two hundred horsemen. But he brought something else: friendship. Apart from the loyal Laelius, Scipio had few that he could call friend. He welcomed Masinissa, against whom he had fought, and recognized in him a military strategist who could mesh with his current commanders. The three men were all in their early thirties, all career military, and all dedicated to acting honorably in battle. These were characteristics that would set them apart from Hannibal, who had only his brothers upon whom to rely.

Carthage responded oddly to Utica being under siege, leaving Scipio's army little to do beyond looting and pillaging the surrounding countryside. Part of this was because the Carthaginians were unused to war at home, and it took them a while to put together a force of mercenaries and Syphax' cavalry with which to respond. This was made more difficult for them in that the previous year, 205 BC, they had sent

Mago, Hannibal's youngest brother, to Genoa in an effort to get men and supplies around the Roman naval blockade.

As a result, Rome took little notice of Scipio's slow progress. They sent a consul and two praetors with six legions to meet Mago as he entered Italy from over the Alps. Unlike when Hannibal had created a route at Cannae, the Gauls did not join Mago's army. Apparently, they saw that Rome was prevailing against Carthage, and they had no desire to join the losing side. Consequently, even though the military men sent against Mago were of ordinary caliber, they sent Hannibal's little brother back to Genoa to lick his wounds. At the same time, although Hannibal did not retreat any farther than Calabria, neither did he manage to advance.

Battle of Utica

The older Romans had believed in battle with honor, and winning straight out, without subterfuge or trickery. But Hannibal had taught the young commanders of Scipio's generation another lesson: war is not fair, and a win by trickery is still a win.

Near Scipio's winter camp was the Carthaginian/Numidian camp. Traditionally, war was not carried out in winter. When spring would arrive, so would combat. Scipio suggested to Syphax that further combat was not in either of their best interest, and perhaps Syphax would like to be the go-between who would broker a peace agreement between Rome and Carthage. Syphax had what he wanted out of the current conflict. He was the ruler of Numidia, he had a beautiful young wife, and it seemed to him that negotiating peace between these two leading powers would be just the thing to make his reputation complete.

Scipio began sending an envoy with a retinue back and forth between the camps. The envoy seemed to be a harmless, elderly patrician who was accompanied by his slaves and servants. In actual fact, his retinue was a coterie of seasoned soldiers who took the opportunity at each negotiation to collect information about the Carthaginian/Numidian camp. It is truly amazing how much information a slave or nosy servant can glean from an area. The peace talks were a ruse designed solely to collect information. Scipio knew very well that Rome would not accept any peace treaty; they had lost too much to Hannibal's depredations, and they wanted revenge more than peace. But he was not about to tell Syphax that. Instead, he bided his time while he built up data about the enemy encampment.

When Scipio had gathered all the intelligence he felt he needed, spring was approaching. The envoy made one last trip to tell Syphax, regretfully, that Rome had decided to break off negotiations. He then gave the appearance of resuming the siege of Utica.

However, only a third of the army laid siege. The other two-thirds were prepared for a night raid on the other army's camp. This plan was so secret that even the generals in charge of the troops were not told of the plan until the night it was to take place. Scipio told only his most trusted commanders.

It was agreed that Masinissa and Laelius would attack the Numidian encampment first. Their shelters were made of wood and reeds, and would burn easily. Scipio would take the other third of their forces and attack the Carthaginians as soon as he saw the flames going up from the Numidian encampment.

The two parties left the Roman encampment around 9:00 pm, or just at the end of First Watch. For the next two watches, they marched toward their chosen destinations. Masinissa and Laelius arrived at the Numidian camp around three o'clock am – just at the end of third watch. They shot fire arrows into the reed huts of the Numidian's who rushed out, thinking that the fire had been set accidentally. When they realized that they were under attack, it was too late to dash back for their weapons that were inside the now blazing huts. In the panic, nearly as many men were crushed by their terrified comrades as were killed by the Roman soldiers. Many accounts estimate that there were sixty thousand soldiers in Syphax' camp.

The Carthaginians also believed that it must be an accidental fire. They climbed to the top of the walls in their camp to view what was going on. Now, however, fire arrows came raining into their camp, as well. Within moments, the same scenario was enacted in the Carthaginian camp.

Gisco and Syphax managed to escape the carnage, each with a handful of soldiers. Gisco returned to Carthage, and Syphax fled to Numidia. Many of the soldiers, who were mercenaries if you will recall, simply scattered into the bush to escape the swords and spears of the night raiders. Scipio did not attempt to catch any of them. He had accomplished his goal. The army was demoralized, and war had been tacitly declared.

Battle of the Plains

It did not take Carthage long to recover, however. Many of the scattered soldiers slipped back into the city to rejoin their units. Gisco's daughter, Syphax' new wife, pleaded with him and he agreed to back Carthage once again. Both armies were somewhat reduced by the night raid, so the effort was not completely wasted.

Gisco marched his Carthaginian army toward the Numidian capital city to add a little more pressure to his daughter's pleading with her husband. The Carthaginians needed that able Numidian cavalry to help prevail against Scipio. The plan was to meld the two armies outside the city, and then to march against the Roman forces. Scipio learned of their plan, and decided to send his own army to this meeting.

Masinissa and Laelius lead the fighting force that crashed Gisco and Syphax's party, so to speak. When they came to the field, they found that they were facing not only the remnants of the forces that had escaped the night raid, they were also facing 4,000 fresh mercenary troops from Iberia. In spite of the reinforcements, they won the battle, and bound Syphax in chains, preparatory to sending him to Rome. His wife, Sophonisbe, met Masinissa at the gates. She declared her undying love, and upon seeing the woman who had once been his betrothed, Masinissa did not hesitate. He married her, and thus regained his kingdom.

However, when Scipio heard about it, he was not pleased with his friend's nuptials. It is possible that he feared for the man's life; or it could have been that he feared Sophonisbe's powers of persuasion – she had already fed one man to her father's war machine, after all. Or it could simply have been that Scipio was, indeed, following the rules for dealing with the enemies of Rome. Whatever the reason, he explained that she would have to be sent to Rome as part of the spoils of war.

When he heard that, Masinissa sent to Sophonisbe a letter explaining the situation, and a vial of poison. The letter stated that it was a husband's duty to protect his wife, and if he could not do that, to spare her from unbearable suffering. Apparently, she found being sent to Rome a fate worse than death, so she took the poison. Her last words were, "I accept this wedding gift from my husband."

Needless to say, this whole thing was upsetting to Masinissa, and Scipio could see that his friend was in the depths of sorrow. In an effort to cheer him up, Scipio assembled the entire army and had them witness his congratulations to Masinissa. He then declared him to be a friend to Rome, and an ally. He presented Masinissa with a scarlet war-tent. These were usually reserved for the Roman consuls, so this was an honor, indeed.

Syphax was escorted to Rome and placed under a sort of permanent house arrest. Ironically, he remained there for the rest of his life, living quietly in a state of reasonable health, and eventually dying of natural causes. Had Sophonisbe gone with him, it is possible that she, also, might have survived. One must wonder what might have been her state of mind upon receiving a vial of poison from her newest husband. One also must wonder how sincere were Masinissa's protestations of love if a scarlet tent and military honors were sufficient to comfort him.

The Roman senate approved Scipio's actions, welcoming Masinissa as their first ally in Africa. As for Masinissa, who can say – looking through the glass of time darkly – what were his real reactions. It all seems a bit surreal and more than a little over the top.

The governing body of Carthage was in extreme disarray. This was the first time that they had lost a battle on their own soil. Various factions each had their own pet solution for the situation. In the end, they implemented four proposals. They mobilized their navy to attack Roman ships, and they set about fortifying the walls around Carthage. Envoys with official papers were immediately sent to Rome to recall Hannibal and Mago. Another envoy was sent to Scipio to suggest that they open negotiations for peace.

Scipio responded with genuine interest to the peace treaty. Just to show how earnest were his efforts to actually bring about peace, here is a list of his proposals:

- Rome would recognize Carthage as an independent nation, and it would remain autonomous

- All Carthaginian armies would withdraw from Italy and from Gaul

- Carthage would renounce all interest in Spain

- Carthage would recognize Masinissa as king of Numidia

- Carthage would surrender all but twenty of its warships to Rome

- Carthage would supply the Roman army in Africa during negotiations

- Carthage would pay five thousand talents (about fifty million dollars in today's economy) in war reparations

However, it soon became clear that those negotiations were primarily to allow Hannibal time to bring his veteran forces back from Italy in order to oppose Scipio's armies. As Hannibal was returning, he captured a Roman supply fleet that had run aground. When Rome sent envoys to protest this violation of the peace treaty, the envoys were killed. Perhaps this was a statement or retaliation to Scipio's devious plan that lead to burning the Carthaginian winter camp. Either way, it is likely that Hannibal found the supplies useful.

It is written in some accounts that Hannibal had so few ships in which he could transport his army from the toe of the Italian boot that he shoved soldiers away from the ships as he was leaving. What could have been in the hearts and minds of those men as they were left on the shores of Italy with no viable way home?

In all events, this the capture of the supply fleet reopened the conflict. It would culminate in the battle fought just outside Zama, the Numidian capital.

Chapter 7
The Battle of Zama

In 202, Publius Africanis and Hannibal Barca arrayed their armies on the plains of Zama in north Africa. It must have been an amazing sight: two great armies spread out before each other. Scipio had his infantry organized in columns, with skirmishers filling in the gaps in between. On one flank, he had his seasoned Italian cavalry; on the other, he had Masinissa's Numidian cavalry – a formidable force that had formerly fought with Hannibal in Spain, but were now, thanks to the recent victory over Syphax, allied with Rome. It is interesting that Numidia vacillated between being allied with Carthage and allied with Rome, and that each change of side influenced the course of a battle.

Hannibal had drawn up his armies in three ranks. He placed his barbarian mercenaries in the front ranks, then a row of less experienced fighters, then finally his seasoned troops at the back. This was not entirely unlike Scipio's tactics at Ilipa. Had Hannibal been studying his young rival's methods? Certainly, Scipio had been studying his, and learning the lessons taught very well.

Hannibal's elephants were near the front of the army, where they were less likely to trample their own people. The plan was to wear down the Romans with the elephants and barbarians, then the veterans would be able to mop up the remains.

As it happens, Scipio had the accounts of former battles with elephants, as well as some experience. He knew that allowing them to run amok among his foot soldiers would end the battle before it began; but he also knew that properly managed, those elephants could become a two-edge sword, a weapon that could be turned against the wielder. He planned to take advantage of their temperamental natures.

The skirmishers were instructed to specifically target the elephants and their handlers, encouraging them to run down the aisles Scipio had conveniently created between the regular foot soldiers' formations. The skirmishers would melt away into the regular formations, leaving clear aisles for the elephants to run through. As the elephants pursued their tormentors, the soldiers were instructed to blow on brass horns, to beat their spears on their shields and to yell loudly. They also threw javelins at the elephants and their handlers. The massed noise was too much even for these battle-trained beasts. Many of them simply ran down the corridors provided. A few bolted through the formations, but many of them – particularly those whose handlers had been slain -- turned around, charging into the ranks of Hannibal's massed troops, creating considerable carnage.

Faced with a ferocious foe and raging elephants, the mercenary troops in the center of Hannibal's formation turned to flee, only to be met with the spears and swords of Hannibal's regulars. Given a choice between being skewered by their own side or fighting Scipio's troops, they turned and fought.

Meanwhile, Scipio's cavalry had routed Hannibal's cavalry, and had given chase instead of sticking with the battle – something that probably irritated the able commander. However, they returned in the nick of time, swooping down on the flanks of the carnage occurring on the battlefield. Hannibal's veterans were brave – and were probably very much aware of the Carthaginian practice of executing failed soldiery – but they were unable to win out against Scipio's tactics.

Had not the Numidian cavalry and Scipio's regular cavalry rejoined Scipio's army, the outcome might have been very different. But the added veteran horse soldiers, along with Scipio's tactics, won the day.

There is some speculation that the Battle of Zama is a fiction created by the Romans to counter-balance their horrific defeat at Canae. There is no marker for the battle field, no dig has turned up weapons or bones. But it should be remembered that the plains of Africa are vast – even near Carthage. And local people have a way of picking up the remains of war and using them for themselves. Perhaps the battle was exaggerated – finding exact numbers for troops is difficult from this end of time's telescope. But it is probable that some such battle took place. It is known for certain that it was within this time frame that Rome broke Phoenician dominance of the Mediterranean.

The carnage at Zama was devastating, and it was nearly the last straw for Carthaginian rule. Hannibal managed to escape, leading a small force back to Hadrumetum. From there, he recommended that Carthage accept Rome's terms for peace. Hannibal would then become the acting ruler of Carthage, and would conduct an investigation into the handling of accounts while Hamilcar, his brother, and his sons were in Spain and in Italy, and generally point fingers at the nobles of that city. They would then turn the tables on him, and accuse him of treason, forcing Hannibal to flee. But that is an account for a different chapter.

Chapter 8
Triumphus Scipio Africanus

In 201, Publius Scipio, now Africanus, returned a hero. As he and his troops marched back into Rome, they were showered with flowers. Publius received official honors, and a statue that was robed in fine clothing and crowned with laurel leaves. But more than the victory earned in Africa, the Roman people were celebrating a return to peace. They were tired of war – which had been going on for more than 16 years. Far too much of the fighting had taken place in Italy. They were truly ready for peace, and they hailed Publius Scipio Africanis as the instrument of having ended all of the fighting.

Scipio would have some time to spend with his wife and his children. In 199, he was censor and become Princeps Senatus, or the head of the senate. But he was not without detractors. While Scipio had been in Spain, garnering victories and pushing back the Barcas, other generals had been battling directly against Hannibal on Italian soil. It is likely that they were jealous of his honors and more than a little bit tired of the upstart young commander.

Scipio's high-handed and individualistic ways of achieving his victories had caused a certain amount of rancor among the other military commanders – particularly those who territories had been encroached. More than that, Scipio, whose health had never been stellar, was not a well man. His health, after all, had been part of the mutiny that had occurred in Spain because the troops had feared that they were losing their able commander.

Greece was now the nation where unrest was rearing its head. During the conflict with Carthage – what the Romans of the day called "Hannibal's War" and history would term the second Punic War – most of Greece had lent its support to Rome. The exception was Macedonia, which had allied itself with Hannibal.

It should be understood that the princeps senatus was not a ruler or the head of the senate in the way that a king might have ruled or even the way the President of the United States or the way the Prime Minister of Great Britain might function. In fact, the closest modern equivalent might be the Speaker of the House in the United States modern government. The princeps had some power, but it was mostly manifested by the privilege to speak first in meetings.

After the reign of Alexander the Great, which had ended in 323 BC, skirmishes among the city states and the three regions given to Alexander's generals had been common.

One of the first moves by the Roman senate after Scipio's triumphant return was to dispatch diplomatic messengers to these regions in an effort to maintain diplomatic peace. One of these went to Egypt, where sending thanks for Egypt's continued neutrality in the recent conflict. Another went to Philip of Macedonia, deploring recent aggression against Athens, and suing for a peaceful resolution to differences.

The messenger to Macedonia was a little late, however. Macedonian troops were already on the march, headed toward Athens. The Senate agreed that the Macedonians needed to be stopped, and that they should be taught a lesson. But the Citizens' Assembly voted against sending any military against Macedonia. They had only recently been able to enjoy the benefits of peace and they had no desire to send more young men into battle.

Galba, who had been recently elected consul, appealed to the Roman people. He noted that if assistance had been sent to Publius Scipio – the one who was killed in Spain, along with his brother Gnaeus – that the recent war would have been fought in Spain rather than in Rome. He argued that the recent conflict with Hannibal had started in much the same way as the moves that Phillip of Macedonia was making – taking one or two little towns that are not much noticed, then one or two more, until those little military victories became large victories. And when those victories became large enough, they had resulted in Hannibal crossing the Alps, a direction from which Rome had not expected any problems, and bringing the fight to Italy through the Gallish states. Galba pointed out that diplomacy had not worked at Sagunto. He also pointed out that if Philip took Athens, then next was probably Corinth, and that Corinth was only five days away from Rome when traveling by sea.

After Galba's speech, the Citizens' Assembly endorsed a declaration of war against Macedonia. However, the army that was sent, they said, must be made up of volunteers.

Knowledge of the chance of intervention was enough to cause Philip to pull his army back from Athens. Instead, he focused on Pergamon and Rhodes. However, this did not in any major way reduce the threat. Alliances and non-alliances were constantly being forged and broken. Some of these were made through marriages – particularly between Syria, Pergamon and Egypt. Still, in spite of the occasional domestic spat, relations between these regions had remained relatively calm. Furthermore, Rome tended to honor her agreements with those within her circle of influence, her hegemony, by extending the protection of her armies.

This might be a good time to talk about the word hegemony. It is a relatively modern word which refers to the influence of power. It is nothing so crass as colonization, but it certainly implies influence. By creating diplomatic connections with surrounding nations, Rome extended her hegemony. This buffer of positive influence protected the central core region of Italy from external invasion. It did not exclude Rome from the general turbulence that resulted from local political and military maneuvering.

In Macedonia Greeks were under uneasy rule by outsiders. Sparta and Athens, both major players in political ebb and flow between city states rarely presented a unified front. They saw the rising national star, Rome, as being a way to teach the Macedonians a lesson and to get out from under their rule.

Rome, however, had no desire to confront Macedonia to such extent. Bloody their collective noses and keep them off the Roman doorstep, to be sure, but they had no real need to conquer territory in that direction. Furthermore, Rome had a deep admiration of all things Greek, particularly art works and literature. This admiration somewhat hampered their ability to see Greece in the same light as other nations that existed to be conquered. Scipio and Flaminius, both of whom were highly influential in the conflict against Macedonia, Flaminius, in particular, saw himself as a liberator destined to free the Greek city-states from the tyrannical Macedonians.

Even with a declaration of war, it was three years before an army made up of Roman volunteers and Greeks confronted the Macedonian forces at Cynoscephalae in Thessaly.

Approximately 10,000 of the troops were Roman, and the other 10,000 Greek. Macedonia had 26,000 men. Flaminius, who was in charge of this force, had made extensive study of Scipio's methods – which had, in turn, been learned by studying Hannibal's exceptionally effective strategies.

In spite of having superior forces, the Macedonian's lost the battle. The Romans lost only 700 men, while 5,000 of the Macedonians were taken prisoner. King Philip requested time to bury his dead and to sue for peace.

The Greek city states of the Aetolian League objected to this leniency. They argued that if they invaded now, they could defeat Philip V once and for all. However, Rome had no particular desire to conquer Macedonia – merely to stop Philip V from potential invasion. They explained gently to the Greeks that it was Roman policy to be magnanimous to their opponents. They also pointed out that Macedonia provided a buffer between Greece and the Celts and Thracians to the north. Flaminius went on to suggest that the Greeks find a way to peacefully coexist with Macedonia to their mutual benefit.

Subsequently a peace treaty was signed with Macedonia that limited the size of its army, returned all the Greek cities within its control to their own recognizance, and remanded other territories not originally part of Macedonia to Roman rule, and required Macedonia to pay one thousand talents to Rome by way of reparation – 500 of which were to be paid immediately, and the remainder to be paid in installments over the next ten years.

The Grecian communities were now safe. The Macedonians had ceased their aggression; but the Greeks were still worried. What if Rome decided to take them over? At the Corinthian games that year, the commander Titus Quinctius

Flaminius made an announcement that set their minds at rest. He decreed that Greece was completely free of Roman rule, owing no taxes or tribute to Rome. Greece would be entirely self-governing, subject only to its own rule. Flaminius even asked the Greeks to track down the Roman soldiers that Hannibal had captured twenty years before, at the battle of Cannae, and return those veterans to Rome.

However, even though Scipio maintained a vigorously pro-Hellenic policy, he argued against withdrawing all troops from Greece. While he heartily endorsed the idea of Roman hegemony, and he had great admiration for anything Greek, he was also a realist. He knew that peace was only likely to be upheld if all members of treaties and agreements endorsed it. Although Syria and Egypt had not joined the general fray, that did not mean that they were completely acquiescent.

When he was again elected consul again in 194, he continued to argue against military withdrawal, fearing that Antiochus, the king of Syria, would invade. In 193, his fears proved to be correct.

Meanwhile, Hannibal had chosen to tighten the belts of the Carthaginian nobles rather than raise taxes in order to defray Carthage's war expenses. Consequently, some of those unhappy nobles complained to Rome, and Rome sent someone to inspect the conquered city. Hannibal, anticipating that this was unlikely to mean anything good for him, boarded a ship before the inspecting party could arrive, and sailed away to join Antiochus in Syria.

In 190, Scipio served as legate for his brother Lucius. Together, they sailed to Asia. At Magnesia, Lucius won a victory over Antiochus, gaining the name Asiagenus. Publius, however, was too ill to take part in the battle. Yet, it was thanks to this battle that Hannibal, who had fled to the court of Antiochus, drank poison rather than fall into the hands of the Romans.

Scipio and his brother Lucius had not risen to power without making a certain number of enemies. Scipio had a reputation for being an exceptional orator, able to sway troops to follow him into impossible battles and to gain their trust and loyalty. However, sometimes in the course of persuading people, Scipio could depart from strictest truth.

When he was gaining the loyalty of troops in Spain, he made some fairly outrageous claims – just by way of example. He stated that Poseidon was his real father, and that his strength and abilities were beyond those of mortal man. Apparently, even though his father was dead and beyond disputing his claims, Scipio had no problem at all suggesting that his mother had sexual congress with a god. After all, it at least put her in good company, although those ladies from mythology who dallied with deities rarely came to a good end.

Could it possibly be that the golden-tongued orator told one too many whoppers in his efforts to sway the masses? Or had he simply stepped on too many toes in headlong rush to various positions of authority, gaining them in spite of the senate, completely ignoring their protests. Perhaps his easy way with his soldiers, gaining their loyalty and admiration, made certain others nervous.

Whatever the reason, by the time of Lucius's Asian campaign, Scipio Africanis the Elder had no few detractors in the Senate. More than that, it is entirely possible that his own children were a source of disappointment to him. Scipio Africanis the younger was frail of health and could not hold office, two of his youngsters were girls, and his other son seems to have been a fairly ordinary sort of fellow.

Still, his twilight years were not without their bright spots. Scipio Africanis the Younger became an augur – one of the priest class who were responsible for reading the signs and portents that would indicate the likelihood of success or failure of a venture. Augury was important to the Romans of that time, and scarcely any venture could be undertaken without reading the signs of the times. Furthermore, unlike appointments to more secular offices, an appointment as augur was for life. This younger Scipio would eventually adopt Scipio Amelius, a young man who would play a significant role in the third Punic war. But more of that later.

Chapter 9
Ungrateful Fatherland,
You Shall not have my bones

In Scipio's later years, all did not go well for the Cornelii brothers. Lucius was accused of not reporting or accounting for 500 talents received from Antiochus, this was in 187. In 184, Africanis was also accused. Whether the brothers had been victims of fraud and false accusations or whether Lucius – as some accounts speculate – had used the funds to support the army, the repercussions were upsetting and devastating to both brothers.

Angry, upset, accused of bribery and treason, Scipio withdrew to a villa he owned near Liturnum in Campania. There, he tilled the land with his own hands, living very quietly and simply. A friend remarked upon how straitened were his circumstance – for example, he commented on how small and cold was the bathroom when compared to the more spacious chamber that had been in Scipio's house in Rome. Accounts do not say what Aemilia thought of the move. It is unlikely that she was given any say in the matter. However, it was suggested in some accounts that Scipio's withdrawal was not entirely without comfort, and that he made use of the companionship of one of the household's women. The point was made that thanks to Papiria's divorce, and having seen first hand what happens to divorced women, that Aemilia simply looked the other way while Scipio carried out his affair.

It is also said that Scipio was so angry with Rome for the perfidy of the other senators that he directed that he should be buried in Liturnum rather than in the ancestral Cornelii tomb in Rome. He is believed to have requested the following inscription on his grave marker, "Ungrateful fatherland, you shall not have my bones." However, the location and the marker have long since been lost.

At age fifty-three, he passed away on his small estate. And he was, indeed, buried there rather than in Rome. A contemporary, describing the grave marker, said that it was very like an altar, and that Scipio's comment on his homeland was engraved on its side.

Some historians are of the opinion that it was about this time that the flavor of Rome began to change. As a society, Rome was always a "work in progress." During the course of its history (up until that time) it had moved from a primarily agrarian society that was patriarchally governed to a Republic that offered opportunity to freedmen and common folk as well as to the nobility. It even offered a slender hope for slaves to free themselves and to even become citizens.

The Senate had, these folk say, become corrupt. Many of the ruling class were, once again, more focused on what they could gain than what they could give. They felt that it was no wonder that Scipio had withdrawn from Roman society in disgust.

Yet his influence was not completely lacking, for he left several descendants who continued to carry out the Cornelius name and who had felt the old man's influence. While most of them were fairly ordinary, his adopted grandson grew to be remarkably similar in his battle prowess and his tendency to innovate. Even the descendants who were children of his daughters had their time and their influence. The old man's adherence to principle and his ability to step on influential toes continued to come out in the younger generations.

As the Roman Empire continued to spread itself wide around the Mediterranean and beyond, as it developed Emperors, alliances and enemies, the seed of Scipio Africanus continued to have influence for about four generations before the line seemed to quietly dwindle away.

Modern architects have speculated that there might have been several reasons for some of the older patrician families to have slowly died out. Cities in that time were notoriously unclean, and without adequate sanitation they would have been hotbeds of disease. In addition to that, the Roman love of indoor plumbing might have also had an influence. Lead, which was malleable and easy to form was often used to make the pipes that carried water. It has been suggested that this lead to such aberrations as the Nero who is said to have played a musical instrument while Rome burned around him. Although, in all fairness to the water of the time, it has also been suggested that calcification from the water would soon have coated the inside of the pipes, mitigating the effects of the lead that was used to make the pipes.

Lead was also used in such things as the seals for bottles of wine. Wine was considered to be a refined drink – and with all of its rocky hillsides, Rome was an excellent location for vineyards.

Chapter 10
Descendants of Publius Scipio Africanus the Elder

Sometime around 216, Publius Scipio Cornelius Africanis had married Aemilia, the third daughter of Amelius Paulus – as previously mentioned. Amelius Paulus had been one of the consuls who fell at Cannae. Scipio and Aemilia Tertia had four children: Publius Scipio Africanis the younger, who was barred from public service because of ill health, and so became an augur; Cornelia Scipio Major (daughter); Lucius Cornelius Scipio (second son); and (?); Cornelia Africana Scipio Minor b. 190.

Publius Scipio Africanis the younger was elected augur, thus becoming a priest of sorts – even though he did not campaign for office. He adopted the second son of Lucius Amelius Paulus Macedonicus, as he did not have any children of his own in an effort to maintain the Corneli line. Now, here is where we prove that the modern world is not alone is following the lives of the rich and famous. Lucius Aemilius Paulus Macedonicus divorced his wife, Papiria Madonis. Lucius was son to the same Aemilius who was the consul who died at Cannae, and was also brother to Scipio Africanus' wife. Lucius and Papiria had four children at the time, two boys and two girls. As was the custom of the times, the children remained with their father. He remarried, and had two more boys. Since it was expensive to foster boys through the cursus honorium or the succession of offices expected of patrician sons, he adopted out the older two boys when they were ages 14 and 9. The elder was adopted by Quintus Fabius Maximus, thus becoming Quintus Fabius Maximus Aemillius; the younger was adopted by his cousin Scipio Africanus the

Younger, becoming Publius Cornelius Scipio Aemillius – a young man whose military genius somewhat resembled that of his adoptive grandfather. Scipio Aemillius would make his mark in the third Punic war, and would earn the name of Scipio Africanus the Younger.

Without a husband, and having been divorced, Papiria's fate was pitiable. She spent the several years living in poverty. Perhaps it was her fate, in part, that influenced Scipio Africanis the Younger to adopt his cousin. In addition, it might very well have influenced his mother to look the other way when Scipio Africanis the Elder was rumored to have an affair with one of the household females. Clearly, Aemilia, wife of Scipio Africanis the Elder, enjoyed the wealth and influence brought to her by her marriage. She also had four children to consider; and she, in all probability, did not wish to suffer Papiria's fate. Even the straitened circumstance to which the family was reduced when living at the country villa would have been preferable.

However, Papiria survived to get the last laugh on the second wife. When her ex-husband died, his estate went to his older two sons. Scipio divided his portion between his sisters, and Papiria was able to return to her former home – where she lived out her final days in a state of reasonable security.

Cornelia Scipio, the older girl, married a cousin, once removed: Publius Scipio Nasio Corculum, whose father was a consul in 190. The two of them had several children, including Publius Scipio Nasica Serapio, who married Caecillia Metella; Publius Scipio Nasica, who married Licinia Crassa, and had a daughter Prima. Cornelia and Nasio also had Cornelia Scipionis, a daughter who married Cornelius Publius Lentulus.

346

If, looking at this family tree you are thinking, "Lot of marrying of cousins here," you would be right. The customs were different then, and the results of inbreeding not so very well known. In addition, these youngsters probably had a limited number of people from whom they were allowed to select a spouse – or their spouse might have been selected for them. Arranged marriages were not unusual for the times.

Scipio's youngest daughter, Cornelia Africana Minor, married Tiberius Sempronius Gracchus. They had twelve children, only three of whom lived to maturity: Tiberius Sempronius Gracchus, Gaius Sempronius Gracchus, and Sempronia, the only surviving daughter.

Tiberius Gracchi was killed by a "senatorial mob." Tiberius was often opposed to the Scipio line's point of view. He was somewhat conservative, and had begun to notice that there were problems at home. He advocated a return to the practice of dividing up newly conquered land among those who were without lands, while binding those men to existing estates – as had been the practice in earlier times in the empire. However, his suggestion was voted down in the senate – repeatedly. At that time, the lands were being divided among already landed houses, creating a situation where those who had power continued to accrue rather than raising up new plebeians. Eventually, his insistence and his policies, and his approach to getting them passed so angered the senators, that he was beaten to death by the rest of the senate. It signaled the end of the Republic and ushered in an age of rule by murder, intrigue, and violence.

His younger brother, Gaius, who was nine years his junior defended his brother at every turn, investing himself in reforms of Roman law and custom. He fell into conflict with Publius Scipio the Younger, who was married to Sempronia.

Scipio the Younger disliked his wife, describing her as ugly and barren. Apparently the dislike was mutual, as Sempronia and her mother were suspected of being responsible for Scipio the Younger's untimely death.

Only Scipio Aemillianus approached Scipio Africanus the Elder's ability as a military strategist and diplomat. His management of the final razing of Carthage was a masterpiece of military engineering – which seems to have been his forte.

As the family dwindled, they became increasingly conservative in their views and in their abilities, until at last they dropped out of public notice. Or perhaps the latter was more the case than the former. Given the attitudes developed by Scipio Africanus the Elder, and the possibility that the men who were dissatisfied with the wives chosen for them by their parents, it is entirely possible that their tendency toward innovation and independence lived on in decedents who did not carry the name.

Chapter 11
Speculation, Surmise and
a Little Fantasy

As mentioned in chapter 9 and chapter 10, Publius Scipio Africanis was a bitter man when he withdrew to his country villa. There were rumors and speculation about the lives of some of his contemporaries. We have scrutinized some of the real history; now we shall build just a little upon rumor, speculation and surmise to create a fantasy of might-have-been.

Let us set the scene. The year is 183 BC. Lucius and Publius Scipio are under suspicion of misappropriating funds that were collected from Antiochus. It is unlikely that this event would not have had impact on Aemilia, or that is would not have disturbed her marital life. But she has been visited by a friend – a woman whose life has been uprooted to the very core: Papiria, wife of Lucius Aemilius Paulus Macedonicus.

"I've lost it all," Papiria sobs, "He's divorced me. I've lost my children, my home, I don't even have enough money put by to rent a room. Aemilia, I don't know what to do."

"Did he say why?" Aemilia asked, gently wiping the tears away from her friend's face.

Papiria sighed, choked back another sob, and smiled sadly, "He didn't say, but I can guess. After four children, I am no longer so young and attractive as I once was. Oh, Aem, I have no idea how I shall go on – how I shall live. I have no desire to sell myself."

"Nonsense," Aemilia said briskly, "While it is distasteful, you have many skills. My needle work is by no means as fine as yours, nor are my skills in the dairy nearly as good. I have need of a new table runner to go with the new goblets Scipio allowed me to purchase. I will advance you some coin. I believe that there is a modest house for hire near where my cook lives – we will ask her. I will spread the word, and soon you will have enough work to keep you."

As so it was that Papiria was able to remain an independent woman, even though she was reduced to straitened circumstance. Aemilia told Scipio of the incident, of course, and he encouraged her to continue to hire Papiria for needle work and such assistance as they could afford. He, himself, was under some constraint as he struggled with censure. Publius Scipio knew that he had not misappropriated any funds, and he did not think that his brother had done so either. There was a rumor that some of the money that had been collected had been siphoned off to throw a party for troops – but there was no evidence to show that it was so, or that the money that was used came from an inappropriate source.

Indeed, it was money, politics and living space that created a temporary rift between Publius and Aemilia. Late one afternoon, Publius came home. His face was red with wrath. "Pack!" he commanded. "I'll not spend one more day in this town. I've had enough. We are leaving the city, just as quickly as we can throw our possessions in containers and load them into a cart. "But Publius!" Aemilia cried, "Our friends . . ."

"I have no friends in this gods deserted city!" Publius declared. With that, he retired to the family still room, where he gloomily settled himself in a favorite chair while he drowned his sorrows in one of the cheaper wines stored there. He was in too bad a mood to indulge in something that was expensive that would taste good. He had upheld Rome all his life, and now She had turned against him. He had walked her streets as Aedile, had fought her wars, and had in every way been a model citizen and soldier. He did not weep. He was too angry for that.

Seeing how upset he was, Aemilia went to do his bidding. Servants scuttled this way and that, collecting packing boxes and crates, along with straw and other things that would be needed to cushion the breakables. It was during this time of turmoil that Blossom found Publius lounging in the deserted room – all of the other servants were busy elsewhere, and Aemilia had gone to the temple for the daily ritual – his tunic askew and his face flushed with wine. She knelt before him, and offered him words of comfort. Before they knew it, she was offering him a more substantial sort of comfort than words. In the days that followed, it became almost a custom. Blossom would find an excuse not to attend the daily pilgrimage to the houses of the gods, and would worship in a most substantial way the one true god of her childhood – she had always liked and admired Publius, although Lucius sometimes teased in ways that were unkind.

However, before a fortnight had passed their belongings were loaded into wagons and they were on their way to their country villa. The brief affair between Blossom and Scipio ended for simple lack of opportunity.

Before they left the city, however, Aemilia found time to visit briefly with Papiria. "I'll be fine," Papiria said. "You've sent enough trade my way that I can manage – even though I am losing my best customer. But take my advice: if your husband looks to another for his pleasure, pretend you know nothing about it. This world is not made for women to be able to easily earn their own bread."

"Thank you for your advice," Aemilia said, "But I know my husband, and I am sure that he would never do that to me."

"You think you know him," Papiria sniffed delicately, "But men can surprise you – even the best of them – and not always in a good way. It is better to endure the situation in many cases rather than find yourself in such straitened circumstances as I now find myself."

Aemilia watched her friend leave, then returned to her packing. Publius arrived just in time to give the rooms a last check and to place a small casket behind the seat of the lead wagon. She then took her place in the seat behind the driver, and Publius rode alongside the lead wagon on his fine horse. The movement of the beast seemed to give him no pleasure, however, for he scowled at the road ahead. There were no flowers or well-wishers for this parade – only a few curious looks from passers-by.

Soon Aemilia realized that they were not going to the Scipio family farm. The miles passed by slowly, and at length they stopped at a small inn for the night. Most of the party made camp outside, while Aemilia had a room in the inn. Publius stayed with her for a while, but soon went back out to check the camp and their household. Perhaps he slipped into a certain tent or room and took some comfort there, or perhaps he protected his childhood friend by keeping a respectful distance in those times when he would not have been able to keep their meetings secret.

This set the pattern for the first three or four days. Then they moved beyond the areas where they could count on there being an inn. Publius unpacked his red war tent for the Aemilia and himself – it was his, after all. In some ways, it was more comfortable than the inns. For one thing, there were no bedbugs or fleas. For another, the linens were their own and had been laundered under the scrutiny of a slave who found it her business to make sure they were fresh.

As they continued southward, the air at night would swarm with mosquitos. The servants hung drapes of gauzy linen from Egypt around their beds to keep the humming insects away. Even so, the members of the party with fair skins woke each morning with welts from bites from the creatures.

It was almost a relief when they again began to come to small villages along the way. Publius explained to her that they were now in Compania, and would soon come to Liturnum, where he had purchased a small farm.

"But it is so far away from everything," Aemilia protested.

"We will not be far from Pompeii," Publius replied. "It is a bustling port town, so I am sure that we will find everything we need there. I know we have left your friends behind," he said gently, "but I am sure you will make new ones here."

Aemilia was quiet, remembering Papiria's words. How could she explain to her husband that while new friends were nice, they were not her old friends – the ones she might never see again.

Publius was different from the way he had been before the upsetting times with the Senate. Sometimes she hardly knew him. He seemed colder, more distant – and he had never been a demonstrative man. But in times past, he would joke or tell stories for her amusement. Now, all of that seemed to have departed. Often, he was somber or looked angry although he never raised either his hand or his voice to her.

When they reached their new villa, she found it to be a far cry from their comfortable town house. The rooms, including the solar were smaller; the bath was dank and cold, and frequently infested with crickets in addition to the ever-present mosquitos. Aemilia felt tired and listless. Scipio Africanus the younger, their oldest son, was frequently ill. Even with the help of her experienced staff, Aemilia felt the added work of living in the country. They did their own laundry, baked their own bread; there were no shops to send out to for a bit of something special or different.

Publius worked in the fields all day, and was moody and silent at table at night. Aemilia didn't notice at first, then she put it down to his being dissatisfied with her and with Rome. She was unhappy, lonely and miserable.

One day she noticed that Blossom, a serving maid – a slave, who had been inherited from the Scipio family estate, was moving more carefully than was usual. Blossom was a beautiful woman, lithe and strong. But on that particularly day she looked pale and sick. It took only a few minutes to learn that Blossom was in the family way, and only a few more sharp questions to discover that Publius was the father. The whole story came out – the days when Blossom had pleaded a headache to be excused from the daily rituals, the stillroom, and more recently since the move, the dairy.

"He is the master," Blossom said. "And he seemed so distraught. How could I refuse him? Oh, please, mistress, don't make me expose my baby – let me keep it."

"It will be from Publius, I'll not make you do that," Aemilia said, thinking furiously. She was angry – angry with Publius, angry with the woman for not telling her after the first time. But her own travails had been difficult, and she loved all four of her children, and it was likely she would have no more. She would not squander even one so misbegotten that came from Publius' seed. Furthermore, she thought, it could be possible that she should be grateful to Blossom. Publius was certainly changed from the brash, boasting, supremely confident young man she had married. It could even be that she owed Blossom his life and sanity after the way the Senators had treated Publius.

She sighed. Were she to adopt the child, it would cause talk. There would be talk, and probably already had been. But she could organize security for mother and child.

"The smith is unwed," she commented. "Would you find him objectionable?"

"Not objectionable, mistress, but it is well known that he prefers boys to women. I doubt . . ."

"He will lack an heir, then. I think we can make this right. You will not lose your place here, the smith will gain a housekeeper and an heir. You will be secure, and so will your child." Aemilia immediately sent for the smith.

Blossom twisted the folds of the apron nervously in her hands. "The master . . . you'll not be angry with him?"

Aemilia gave a short bark of laughter. "Of course I'm angry with him. But fear not, he'll take no harm from me. Even this cheerless place is better than should be my lot if I divorced him." She thought of Papiria, living in one tiny room, scraping out a living by taking in fine sewing. Then her face softened, "More than that, Blossom, I am fond of him. We were wed at the direction of our fathers, but he is usually a kind man and a wise one. I'd be a poor wife to begrudge him such comfort as he has been able to find in your arms – and I'll be grateful that he looked no farther afield than our own household. But it must come to a stop. I am sorry that you will pay the price for this, but I am afraid that I do not intend to share my husband. So...no slipping out and cheating on the smith – even if he has his own amusements."

Aemilia and Publius were closeted in their private rooms for a long time that afternoon, but they emerged arm in arm in time to attend the wedding of Blossom to the local smith. If Blossom's first and only child was birthed a little earlier than was seemly, it was not an unusual thing for first babies. If she and the smith seemed more like friends and business partners than husband and wife, that was not unusual enough to excite comment.

Amazingly enough, after that the Scipio home became more cheerful. Writers, generals and other famous people came to visit from time to time. Fires burned on the formerly cold hearths, and the master and mistress were often seen strolling around the fields together or sitting with their heads over lists of items and numbers. The mistress learned about preserving foods, just as she had once learned where to find the best shops for bargains in order to stretch the family resources.

Peace was restored, but it was soon clear that Publius was truly not a well man. His breath came short, and sometimes his chest pained him. He took to drinking mulled wine with herbs in it of an evening in an effort to still the pains. One evening, when the pain was worse than usual, and his bones ached in ways they had never ached on the battlefield he spoke with Aemilia, the Grammaticus – his old teacher, who was now a freedman who managed the farms accounts, and his friend, Laelius. "Don't take my body back to Rome," he said.

Aemilia made a sound, but he put his hand on hers, and said, "Hush now, I know what this body is telling me. I have been too ill, too long of late. I have put it to hard usage, now I must pay the cost." He clasped her fingers tenderly for a moment. "But I'll not give my bones back to the city that spurned my final efforts and tried to accuse my brother and I of treason. Lucius did not steal those 500 talents, and although I think I know who did, I honestly cannot dispute the use to which they were put. I fought long with men who were loyal because they felt the cause for which they fought was just – and they did it on short rations, and minimal gear. They had back pay owed; I'll not mourn that the money they helped earn went to their pleasure."

"But I'll not have my final resting place be in a city that has forgotten honor, forgotten the men that fight for her. Let my bones lie here, where my labor has been honest and the returns – although often small – are won through the skills of my household. Don't worry, Aemilia, you are provided for and so are the children – although they could scarcely be called children now." Laelius related this conversation to a famed writer of the time at a later date.

Although that week had been one of debilitating illness for Publius, he was up and around soon after. But his prediction was not wrong. He had used his body hard during the years in Spain, and he had never been as robust as his brother. At length, he died, and was buried quietly, attended by his widow, his one-time lover, his children and the other members of his household.

And if, in that far-away place, a certain blacksmith's son looked nothing like his legal father, and if he had a knack for making things work, for creating plans, then one could say that the seed did not fall on stony ground and that the genius of the Cornelius line lived on – even if the name dwindled away.

Of course, this tale is almost pure fiction. It is based on a few chance lines in other accounts and is fabricated from likelihood. Given the nature of the stories recorded in mythology, we could have ascribed a completely different response to Aemilia. No one knows the name of the household woman who was the recipient of Scipio's attentions, or whether she was willing or not. Slaves and servants alike had little choice in those days. In keeping with the evidence given that Aemilia engaged in daily rituals, that she loved her fine clothes and ritual vessels, I have extrapolated that she would have preferred to quietly find a way to deal with the fallout. As for implying that the blacksmith was not one for women, men who preferred boys or other men were well known in that region.

There are references to the possibility that Scipio did stray from his marriage bed – even if he did return the chieftain's daughter to her parents and to her betrothed, without touching her. Soldiers did, in those days, often avail themselves of the camp followers. It is written in some accounts that Hannibal had a lover in Spain, and that he fathered a son. But no further mention is made of either the woman or the child in any of the accounts. Possibly, that was because after Hannibal made his trip over the Alps, he never returned to Spain and no arrangements had been made for the woman or the child to follow him into Rome or back to Carthage.

As has been mentioned, one of the big differences between Scipio and Hannibal was Scipio's easy way with words and his ability to make friends. Even toward the end, when Scipio had turned away from Rome, he was visited by friends at his farm in Liturnum. Hannibal, on the other hand, allowed only his brothers to get close to him. He was a soldier's soldier, working long hours into the night, inspiring loyalty from his troops by his actions rather than by harsh rules or punishments.

After his trip over the Alps, Hannibal fell ill. One of his eyes became infected – an account that mentioned this suggested that he might have had conjunctivas, that common school room malady sometimes referred to as "pink eye." In the field, in a setting that did not encourage or provide opportunity for personal care, it is not impossible that such an illness could become severe. On the rare occasions when the commander cold sleep, his men took great care not to disturb him. This speaks of a man who inspired loyalty beyond that garnered through a mercenary's pay.

In many ways, Hannibal and Scipio are an interesting study in contrasts. Scipio was the son of a patrician household – even though it seems likely that they were richer in reputation than in cash. Hannibal Barca was in the field with his father Hamilcar by the age of ten. It could be said that he learned how to wage war at his father's knee and he gave little care to honor or honorability. His affections were primarily reserved for his brothers and uncles who were also doing their best to take over Iberia, or Spain as it would later be known. Hannibal was the elder by nearly ten years, and it was the records of his battles that served as Scipio's instruction in the school of espionage and dirty deeds, as it were. Scipio also proved to be Hannibal's greatest challenge. Whereas the other Roman generals adhered to the same old formations and methods, Scipio observed how Hannibal was able to use smart tactics, even dishonorable tactics, to win encounters. He could certainly see how Hannibal had managed to survive for twelve years in the Italian peninsula with minimal support from Carthage. Scipio copied those tactics, turning them against Hannibal, and adding his own version of dirty deeds for good measure.

Both were able commanders, and both were betrayed by their home city. Whereas Scipio was able to settle down in the country and run an estate, however, Hannibal was forced to run to other courts. Winding up in Antiochus III's court did little to assist him, however. His military genius was worth very little when he was given undisciplined men who were unaccustomed to precision moves. In the end, Antiochus was prepared to give him up to the Romans. Hannibal took poison rather than end up in the hands of the Romans.

Would that actually have been such a terrible fate? Or did Hannibal, like Scipio, have a body that was worn out with years in the field, eating bad food, sleeping in discomfort and always, always on the move lest an enemy catch up with you. Carthage had a very direct way of dealing with those perceived as failures. Perhaps he expected similar treatment from the Romans, and was taking steps to deal with it ahead of time. Perhaps his loyalty was such that he had secrets that he preferred to take to the grave. Or perhaps he was already dying, and the poison only shortened the time before his death.

Whatever the reason, the result was that these two able commanders died within two years of each other. It was something of the closing of an era.

Rome would go on to become an empire. Carthage would rise from the ignominy of the Second Punic war to once again become a bustling trading nation, but would be struck down by Scipio Aemilius and laid waste in the Third Punic War. Much of that would be because Rome had developed an obsession with Carthage and the Big Bad Enemy that must be destroyed. There were senators who called for it daily in the senate and promoted the idea that Carthage was a Bad Seed that should not be allowed to grow.

Some accounts of the destruction of Carthage say that the land was salted so that nothing would grow there. Other historians say that the salting was a later embellishment and that it never happened. However, the location was ritually cursed. The substance of the curse was that nothing would again grow there – neither crops or buildings. This proved to be a bit of a problem when Rome wanted to build its own city on that spot. The Romans were, in many ways, a superstitious lot. A curse would have had real meaning to them. Perhaps that should be a lesson to subsequent generations – be careful of the legends you create because they can become a weapon that will turn in your hand and bite you. One of the old legends of the region is the story of the dragon's teeth, which when sown in a plowed field would become an invincible army. The method for defeating them was to throw a rock at one, convince the guy next to him that he was being attacked, and then stand back and watch them battle it out amongst themselves until they were all slain.

One has to wonder about some things. The area around the Mediterranean has been the scene of so many epic historical battles, it is almost as if someone had sown the whole region with dragons teeth, then thrown the rock and stood back. Perhaps this is a skewed perception, an incorrect historical view. But it does cause one to speculate as to why that particular region is constantly contended. Some of it is location, some of it is resources. But perhaps some of it has to do with the temperament of the people who live there. This is only speculation. Or perhaps someone goes through that region nightly, sowing dragons teeth.

Chapter 12
Some Thoughts on Written Records

Tracing the lives of the rich and famous centuries later presents a variety of challenges. As has been previously mentioned, Scipio Publius Africanis is a classic case. On the one hand, he is sufficiently famous as a military genius that accounts of his battles have survived as military lore, or even legend.

The problem with this is that military legends – even ones that are carefully crafted and recorded – tend to be like fisherman's stories. The numbers get a little exaggerated, episodes get blown up larger than life, various accounts fail to match. In fact, in some cases, historians can even begin to doubt that an event truly happened. The Fall of Troy is a good example of this syndrome.

The Battle of Zama is an example of an event which is well-recorded, but is doubted in some circles. As discussed in an earlier chapter, historians note that we aren't sure of the exact location of the battle. Archeologists have not found evidence of a battle on Zama plain.

Yet this battle is one that has a plethora of records about it. Was it a propaganda event manufactured by Rome to counterbalance Cannae? Was it an ordinary maneuver blown up into epic proportions? Did it actually occur? Some account question the veracity of the records, contending that it was a hoax intended to make Rome looks good. It is well known, after all, that the victors write history. It is only later generations that look through the records, trying to ascertain the veracity of the accounts in order to develop a better idea of what actually occurred. A desire to look great, to sway the home population to see an event as essential for national security, and to dissuade enemies from thinking that a nation is a soft target. That last can be an important point for deterring unnecessary or unwanted wars.

Accounts of personal events – how Publius and Aemilia met, whether or not he was faithful, how she felt about the move to Compania – are even more hazy. Chapter 11 is built entirely on one or two sentences of an account that mentions that Publius might have had an affair, and that Aemilia, not wishing to share Papiria's fate, chose to publicly ignore the incident. I have made my fictional Aemilia a little warmer and more understanding than perhaps is likely. Aemilia was fond of her public displays of devotion to the gods, her fine retinue and her fine ritual vessels. It is unlikely that she happily acquiesced to moving out of the city onto a farm.

It is known that Publius was angry with Rome over the lawsuits and accusations that marred Lucius's triumphant return from Asia. He was also tired of the vacillations of the Senate and the mercurial shifting of the popular vote of the people. Of this much we can be fairly sure. It is mentioned by both Livy and Polybius, and it makes sense. But many of the things that we would really like to know, such as Publius date of birth, the exact birth order of he and his sibling, and whether or not he was really born of a Cesarean – or whether that was simply propaganda, is lost in the sifting sands of time. Was his mother still alive when he proclaimed to the world that she had been unfaithful to his father with a god? Or was that a subtle reflection of a real event? In all probability, that particular claim falls under the same heading as some of the tall tales about Daniel Boone and Davy Crockett, when they are out claiming relationships with wild creatures an their ability to whip alligators and wild cats. Publius Scipio Africanus was, after all, reputed to be a golden-tongued orator, capable of swaying crowds, influencing hardened military veterans – and doubtless persuading virgins to his bed if he should so desire. His was, in his day, the hero of the hour, the quick fix for unsolvable problems and even the blazing sword of revenge. Small wonder that the quieter side of his life should have been obscured by lack of attention or accounts smudged by bombastic prevarication.

Battles, on the other hand, are covered in loving and precise detail by a variety of different sources. Apparently, these events were the things that the Romans found important. Social sentiment was reserved for graphitti and gravestones. Perhaps that reflects something of the Roman mind. Even their legends and stories tend to focus on the combative side of things. Can we say that our modern tales are so very different? A few hours viewing of that modern orator, broadcast media, brings to the viewer explosions, combat, plots, vengeance, and more. Only a scant few minutes of an episode or cinematic story are devoted to ordinary events or even to more tender relationships. Perhaps this says something more about the human race in general than it does about the Romans specifically.

According to some accounts, there were other historical records. Publius is said to have kept a journal – but that is long lost. It is said that there was a chapter in Plutarch's lives about him, but that is also lost. The ages are not kind to written material – not even that which is engraved in stone or marked on clay tablets. Papyrus, sheep skin parchment, and other organic matter is subject to decay and to burning. Generations of editing the past by flame, destruction of libraries by zealots, and simply the ravages of time tend to obscure the past.

This makes these histories fertile ground for fictionalizing. Unlike the Adamses, who were the first political family in the United States to have filled the presidency twice with different members, very little that is personal remains of this famous Roman general.

Even going back and reading translations of the primary sources is of little assistance. The historians of the time fill in their pages with ranting at the gods or long flowery speeches to other political figures. It should be equally noted that while historical figures such as Cleopatra or Helen of Troy are credited with a degree of influence, they are mentioned more in passing than in any other way. Gods and Goddesses figure large in speeches that the heroes are supposed to have made. One suspects that this speaks more to the tastes of the theatre audiences of the day having loved a good spectacle than to veracity. In any case, home life and family are given short shrift in the annals that record the deeds of Publius Scipio Cornelius Africanus the Elder.

Again, we can look to other accounts to gain some idea of how people behaved in those days. We can, again, look at the climate, and real distances between locations and how it might have been to move a household. We can look at statues, paintings and mosaics to discover how people dressed. We can even turn to regulations, which dictated what was worn by each class – particularly for the men. Human emotions are pretty consistent, even if human customs change. Some people are tolerant, some are not. Fear, affection, sorrow, and anger hold true across the board as responses that a person might have. Child mortality might have led to customs such as not naming a child until after his or her first birthday, but parental affection for a child usually still existed, and most frequently begins with first contact with a warm, wiggling baby body. As in many societies, boy children were valued more than girls in ancient Rome – an odd state of affairs, biologically speaking. But humans are the animals that rationalize – rather than being rational.

So what can we gain from these histories? Perhaps, as Shakespeare wrote, "The good that men do is oft interred with their bones," right along with their personal histories, the very real things that they felt and thought, their fears, challenges and anxieties. Writing was not a universal skill, although the Romans were not an illiterate society. Classes were held in the open square of a city, and the boys taught there were disciplined with a rod. Girls, if they were fortunate enough to be taught to read, write and figure, were taught at home. However, learning was a privilege ofte reserved for the upper class and for scribes and priests. It was used to record tithes, taxes, and numbers of soldiers. Small wonder that the primary places we find the emotional responses of individuals are tombstones and on the walls of their houses.

Looking at the coins that remain displaying the balding head of Publius Scipio Africanus, he was a man of strong feelings off the battlefield as well as on. But his deepest feelings, or the things that he felt sufficiently important to record in a journal, are lost to us. We don't even know what sort of medium he used as the pages in his journal. Was it papyrus from Egypt? Was it parchment? We can be certain that its leaves were not clay, for clay tablets would have been too difficult to carry in a soldier's kit. The deeds of Publius the soldier and commander remain for us to read and speculate over; the thoughts and feelings of Publius the man are more difficult to obtain. Even after cross-referencing many sources, including accounts of his supposed rants to the gods, although his military might is plainly displayed, getting a handle on the man himself – his feelings, his ideas, his dreams and aspirations – is much more difficult.

Therefore, we extrapolate, we fictionalize, and we fantasize. Who was this man who defeated one of the most creative and able commanders of his day? Who was this man who was sufficiently canny to study the moves of his opponent? Like two great chess players using live playing pieces, Hannibal and Scipio's war spanned nearly twenty years of conflict. These two great generals studied each other's tactics. They spied upon each other, they each tried to out-guess their opponent.

More than that, it was the opening for the third Punic war. In fact, one of Scipio's grandson was instrumental in the final demise of Carthage. It seems that in addition to being an able strategist, like his grandfather, Scipio Aemilius, who also earned the title Africanus, was a talented engineer. With that in mind, one must then consider the influence these two generals, these fighting men, had upon their world and the world that was to follow. Indeed, we can still see conflict in the areas where they once battled. If we could resolve their wars, would we be able to resolve our own?

Who can say? Perhaps our children or our children's children will look over this account or similar ones, shake their heads and say, "Why did they choose to record these things? Why did they not tell us more about that?" They might even say, "Why was so much of it electronically recorded? Why was so much of it on impermanent materials such as paper? The only things we have left are words chiseled on monuments." Or will digital media become more permanent, and will they instead shake their heads over the multitudinous accounts of cute kittens, crazy pratfalls and semi-spontaneous instances of flash dance and ask, "Why didn't someone show us how to extrude wire? Or plant vegetables? Where are the plans for various field tactics? Why can't we find those?"

We who can speak with friends or family who are half the world away, and have access to news, books and documents of all sorts, are, in some ways, no better informed than many of the plebeians who lived in Rome. We read for pleasure, we read to learn about the latest Hollywood or Bollywood scandal, but we avoid dealing with the more serious topics in our world. Perhaps that is a natural thing. Goodness knows, it those weren't serious messages that were scratched on the outsides of the houses in Pompeii. Even some of the messages inscribed on tombstones show a sense of humor or the foibles of humanity. It is only the scholars, such as Plutarch, Polybius or Livy who has worked their way through serious accounts of the various battles that occurred so long ago.

The records that we find left by the common people, through such media as the well-preserved ruins at Pompeii indicate that the Roman people were probably not so greatly different from us. Most of them were concerned with the ordinary day to day details of their lives. They were focused on their sweethearts or their business rivals. Were Scipio and Hannibal greatly different? Or were their concerns simply a little larger than those around them? The scholars leave us little to go on in this regard. They were more concerned with the major political issues of the day than they were with such things as birthdates, wedding dates, or whether the great commander of a particular army preferred beef or pork. Yet it is these small things that flesh out the character of a historical figure. Lacking such information, we must become as the novelist or playwright, ascribing motivation to certain actions as we peer darkly through the telescope of time into a world that could have had completely different motivations from the ones that govern our world today.

Perhaps that is the answer. Perhaps we should look at the things that these ancients emphasized, the things that they recorded, as a means of understanding the things that they valued: prowess in battle, excellent oration, integrity in the face of difficulty, and the ability to leave wife and child behind and go make a barrier against the enemy using only their bodies, a shield made of wood and hide, and such weapons as could be held in their hands. Could it be that this is the message that these elders from a past and a culture that is long ago would truly wish for us to understand? We can but speculate and wonder.

Afterword

Some say that the passing of Publius Scipio Cornelius Africanus marked the beginning of the great age of the Roman Empire. Or perhaps it only marked a different sort of beginning. History is more like a great stream that runs in a circle rather than a river that has a head water and a delta where it exits into the sea. Perhaps it is even more accurate to say that reasoning by analogy is flawed and presents only single way to provide understanding to those who are not familiar with an event or process.

Certainly, Publius saw the beginnings of the Third Punic War. His adoptive grandson, Scipio Aemillius Africanus the younger, fostered and cared for by his oldest son, the augur, was a central figure in the third Punic war and the actions that finished Carthage for good and all.

Readers might recall that at the end of the Second Punic War, Carthage had been forbidden to declare war on any other nation without permission from Rome. Numidia, having become something of an ally of Rome under Masinissa, grew increasingly aggressive toward Carthage, attacking and taking over small towns and lands that had traditionally belonged to Carthage. At last, Carthage had had enough. They retaliated to an attack, thus tacitly declaring war on Numidia.

This action was all the excuse that Rome needed to come down hard on their erstwhile enemy. Hannibal, who had proved to be an able governor had fled the city when her nobility had grown restive under his policy of tightening belts rather than imposing more taxes in order to balance budgets. Perhaps it was after his governing hand was removed that Numidia grew bold, and the aristocrats irritated that Rome was handed this ready-made excuse to come down hard on their former enemy.

Rome sent notice to Carthage that because of its violation of treaty, that they intended to raze the city, and burn it to the ground. Carthage did not respond as directed – which was to move 16 kilometers inland and rebuild. Instead, they released all their slaves, and began to prepare for battle.

Carthage had amazing defenses. They had 34 kilometers of defensive wall – in triple layers in some areas. The harbor was also well defended. The initial attack on the city, led by Manius Manilius and Marcius Censorinus did not go well. For one thing, they were unable to successfully block the harbor, and Carthage continued to receive supplies by sea. For another, in the hot summer of 148 BC, the besiegers were hit by a plague.

The city of Utica had defected to Rome, but Hippacra, another city, remained stubborn in its defense of Carthage, successfully resisting the forces led by Consul Piso. The Numidians were under a new king, Bithyas, and had also swapped sides as it were – sending 800 cavalry to swell the defense of Hippacra. Things did not look good for Rome.

Then a new player came on the scene. You will recall that Publius Scipio, son of Scipio Africanus, was unable to serve Rome due to health problems; but that apparently did not deter his ability to train up a new Scipio – his adopted son Scipio Amelius. This young Scipio was like his grandfather in ability. He not only had studied the maneuvers made by his grandfather and by Hannibal, he had a knack for engineering.

Under his guidance, the Romans built a better siege wall around Carthage – one that enabled them to attack the Carthaginian defenses. He also built a siege mole – a contraption similar to a tower, that contained a catapult of sorts. This mole prevented ships from being able to sail into the harbor without running the risk of being holed by one of the projectiles from the tower. With their supplies cut off, the Carthaginians were in a desperate way.

Meanwhile, the rest of the Carthaginian army is being held at Nepheris. With a firm chokehold on the harbor, Scipio Amelius felt sufficiently confident to send forces to help deal with it.

In the spring of 146, using the mole, the Romans force their way into the harbor. Then begins the hand to hand fighting in the streets, with the Romans forcing the defenders back and back through the streets and the Carthaginians resisting with all of their strength.

Commander Hasdrubal and 900 Roman deserters resisted nearly to the last in the central citadel. He gave himself up, but his wife threw herself and her two children onto the funeral pyre for the Carthaginian fighters. Such was the depth of her shame and outrage that he should have surrendered.

The city burned for seventeen days. A population of over 150,000 had been reduced to less than 50,000. The land where Carthage stood was ritually cursed so that no one would rebuild on that location.

The Punic culture, however, did not disappear, but continued in small villages in the countryside. It was not until the reign of Julius Caesar that Carthage would be rebuilt.

Publius Scipio's descendants would be part of the continued saga of the Roman Empire, with its dramas, its betrayals, its alliances and foreign wars. But it was almost as if with the destruction of Carthage, so also began the slow downfall of Rome.

It was a slow process – a slave uprising in Rome, a defection of allies, a marriage between a Roman Emperor and an Egyptian princess, complicated with the princess having an affair with a Roman senator. The leader of a new religion is born, stirring up the Hebrews, and the Druids revolted in Great Britain. Steadily, inexorably, the world changed.

Or is that merely a perception? Perhaps the more the world changes, the more it stays the same. Therein lies the real value of studying history. When we read of the wild emotions of these long-ago people, they seem almost unreal. Wives who drink poison or throw themselves on funeral pyres? Ingesting poison carried about in a ring, as Hannibal was said to have done rather than be turned over to Rome?

Yet is that any more strange than a woman who has her ribs surgically removed so that she can resemble a cartoon character?

These are questions that perhaps will be answered by another generation – one that might find our customs, mores and responses just as strange as we might find those recorded about those old Romans or Carthaginians.

Bibliography

Scullard, Howard Hays.(20150 Scipio Africanus the Elder. Encyclopedia Britannica, online. https://www.britannica.com/biography/Scipio-Africanus-the-Elder

Scullard, Howard Hayes Publius Scipio Cornelius Africanus (236-184/3 BC) Latin Library, http://www.thelatinlibrary.com/imperialism/notes/scipio.html

Locri Epzephryii https://www.britannica.com/place/Locri-Epizephyrii

Clare, John. (?) Livy on the Battle of Zama, 202 BC http://www.johndclare.net/AncientHistory/Hannibal_Sources8.html

Polybius, Histories. http://www.perseus.tufts.edu/hopper/text?doc=Perseus%3Atext%3A1999.01.0234%3Abook%3D15%3Achapter%3D12

Calabria https://en.wikipedia.org/wiki/Calabria

Locris https://en.wikipedia.org/wiki/Locris

Augur https://en.wikipedia.org/wiki/Augur

Publius Cornelius Scipio Nasica Corculu https://en.wikipedia.org/wiki/Publius_Cornelius_Scipio_Nasica_Corculum

Scipio Africanus https://en.wikipedia.org/wiki/Scipio_Africanus

Publius Cornelius Scipio Africanus
https://www.geni.com/people/Publius-Cornelius-Scipio-Africanus/6000000005944438076

Mark, Joshua J. Scipio Africanus the Elder, Ancient History
http://www.ancient.eu/Scipio_Africanus_the_Elder/

Publius Cornelius Scipio Africanus (236 – 184/3 B.C.)
http://www.thelatinlibrary.com/imperialism/notes/scipio.html

Carthage, Roman Empire
http://www.roman-empire.net/republic/carthage.html

Battle of Zama
http://www.unrv.com/empire/battle-of-zama.php

Mark, Joshua J. *Hannibal, Ancient History*
http://www.ancient.eu/hannibal/

Hannibal
http://www.biography.com/people/hannibal-9327767

Tiberius Semphronius Gracchus, Biography, Encyclopedia Brittanica
https://www.britannica.com/biography/Tiberius-Sempronius-Gracchus#ref87735

http://sites.psu.edu/cams101groupi2014/carthage/siege-of-saguntum/

ex.oup.com/view/10.1093/oi/authority.20110803095639712

Battle of Ilipa http://www.roman-empire.net/army/ilipa.html

Trebia and Trasimere https://sites.psu.edu/hannibal/battles-of-trebia-and-trasimene/

Siege of Tyre Map (Examples of Siege Moles)
http://sillysoft.net/lux/maps/SIEGE%20OF%20TYRE

Third Punic War http://www.ancient.eu/Third_Punic_War/

Roman Time Line
http://courses.wcupa.edu/jones/his101/web/t-roman.htm

The Punic Wars
http://www.historyworld.net/wrldhis/plaintexthistories.asp?historyid=ac53

The Punic Wars: The History of the Conflict that Destroyed Carthage and Made Rome A Global Power, by Charles River Editors. July 13, 2015

Made in the USA
Middletown, DE
29 September 2020